NATIVE'S RETURN

Previous Books by Herbert Kubly

American in Italy
Easter in Sicily
Varieties of Love
The Whistling Zone
At Large
Gods and Heroes
The Duchess of Glover
Italy (Life World Library)
Switzerland (Life World Library)

Plays

Men to the Sea
The Virus
Perpetual Care

NATIVE'S RETURN

HERBERT KUBLY

STEIN AND DAY/*Publishers*/New York

First published in 1981
Copyright © 1981 by Herbert Kubly
All rights reserved
Designed by Louis A. Ditizio
Printed in the United States of America
STEIN AND DAY/ *Publishers*
Scarborough House
Briarcliff Manor, N.Y. 10510

Library of Congress Cataloging in Publication Data

Kubly, Herbert.
  Native's return.
  1. National characteristics, Swiss. 2. Switzerland—Description and travel—1945- 3. Elm (Switzerland)—Description. 4. Zurich (Switzerland)—Description. 5. Kubly, Herbert.
I. Title.
DQ36.K8   949.4   80-5894
ISBN 0-8128-2768-6   AACR2

For Kap Rhyner
and my grandsons Nicholas, John, and Kristopher

Jesus said man cannot live by God and mammon both.
But we Swiss have proved him wrong.

—Karl Barth

CONTENTS

FOREWORD

"Good family portraits," said Swiss historian Herbert Luethy, "are never painted by members of a family. It would take a non-Swiss to produce a really good portrait of Switzerland."

If Dr. Luethy's point is valid—and I would not deny that it is—I should be both qualified and unqualified to attempt a portrait. I am a fourth-generation American. I am also a hereditary citizen of Elm, a village in the mountains of the Swiss canton of Glarus from which my eight great-grandparents emigrated in the mid-nineteenth century to New Glarus in Wisconsin. My position, then, is the ambivalent one of a foreigner who is also a family member, an outsider-insider whose role in Switzerland is curiously like Switzerland's in the world.

This equivocal role has had both advantages and disadvantages. Certainly, an advantage has been my ability to speak *Schweizer-deutsch,* a language that is nearly incomprehensible to a non-Swiss. Another has been intuitive perceptions and insights, not accessible to an outsider, into the enigmatic and complex Swiss character.

But a portrait is a suspension of time, a truce with history. It would be difficult to pinpoint a period in the modern history of Switzerland with more revolutionary changes than the two decades just passed. In once pristine landscapes there are now nuclear power plants and suburban sprawls of supermarkets, crowded housing and fast food. The majestic mountains are riddled with hidden military redoubts, weapon depots, and survival bunkers. Industrial valleys are blanketed with smog.

The revolution is moving too swiftly to stop time, especially the time required to produce a book. During the course of my writing, espionage and monetary scandals shook public confidence in Switzerland's army and banks. In the summer of 1980 Swiss complacency was shattered when thousands of rioting young people battled police for three days over the closing of a youth center which police considered a location for drug activities. In succeeding months young dissidents rocked other cities in the land. The youths' message rang clear: The image of Switzerland as a model of orderly democracy, an island of peaceful sanity in an explosive world, had become a visionary myth. It was time to come to terms with the twentieth century.

Though some of the beginnings of the revolution are evident in these pages, my report is not a history. Being American, I have measured my insights against an American point of view. The result is a chronicle of confrontation, a confrontation of myself with the Swiss and, in a more immediate sense, a confrontation of my insider's self with my outsider's self.

I have drawn from visits and residences in Switzerland extending over a quarter-century. The longest of these was a sabbatical year extending from September 1968 to July 1969, the most recent in the summer of 1977; in each visit changes were apparent. But the Swiss psyche and character are slow in changing and my attention has been focused on an introverted and troubled people that many in the world have known but few have understood.

Though most of Switzerland is present in these pages, the two principle settings are the city of Zurich and the village of Elm (population 900), two theaters of my experience that typify the urban commercial-industrial and the rural agricultural societies and cultures which make up the dichotomy of Switzerland.

I am indebted to Kaspar Rhyner of Elm, my cicerone on journeys and my guide in understanding. To Max and Midi Schuler of Zurich, and to Alphonse Kubly of Netstal, Switzerland, and Sarasota, Florida, I am beholden for a careful checking of the manuscript, for correcting errors in fact and sometimes in judgment, and especially for steering me through the mazes of spelling in the Swiss language. To the University of Wisconsin-Parkside, I am grateful for a research travel grant.

Herbert Kubly,
Wilhelm Tell Farm
New Glarus, Wisconsin

NATIVE'S RETURN

THE RED CARPET

"You may feel assured," the letter from Zurich said, "that a rousing welcome will be given you at the airport. Everyone is dying to roll out the red carpet."

The unrolling commenced on a September day at O'Hare Field. The Swissair plane had hardly levitated from the runway and I had barely settled in a roomy lounge before stewards were plying me with frosty martinis and lissome stewardesses brought Russian caviar and Strasbourg pâté de foie gras and placed soft slippers on my feet. The princely blandishments were no glorious dream; they were quite real. I had a dossier of documents to reassure me.

I was embarking on an academic sabbatical as a guest of the country which was my ancestral home, a study sojourn which had been more than a year in the planning. In the final months before my departure the correspondence from my sponsors had accelerated to a high pitch. Memos bearing the code title "Operation Herbert Kubly" contained lists of prominent persons waiting to meet me, details of levees planned for my pleasure, and descriptions of available accommodations. While I deliberated whether I would prefer to live in "a little villa" or a Zurich apartment in a private park where, a memo said, "You will be as rustically happy as on your Wisconsin farm," the uniformed youths and maidens brought me lobster and a bottle of ten-year-old Heidsieck

Brut. I slept and did not awaken until we were descending toward Zurich.

Three men rushed out to the plane to fetch me and rush me through customs. One of them, Hans Meister,* from the Confederation Information Bureau, had written most of the letters. The second was a secretary from the government-supported cultural office called Pour Une Renaissance Suisse, known by the acronym PURS. The third was a banker who was an officer of the Association of Swiss-American Societies.

My escorts led me to Meister's Mercedes and we began the drive into town. Meister asked if I might wish to activate my hereditary Swiss citizenship. He had, he said, spent the evening before with Gore Vidal, who was in Zurich investigating his Canton Graubünden ancestry with the possibility of becoming a Swiss citizen. I said I did not, and Meister went on, saying that Vidal was staying at the Hotel Bauer-au-Lac, where his room was costing $100 a day. For a moment I had the uneasy feeling that a literary comparison was being made between my role as a *pensionnaire* and the price of Gore's hotel room. Meister told me about receptions and parties being arranged for me, running down lists of journalists, bankers, parliamentarians, and educators who were waiting to meet me, and I assured myself that my sensitivity was no more than a flash of writer's paranoia. He spoke of a press conference after which, "you will be as famous in Switzerland as Gore Vidal." A new apprehension swept over me: Was I to be hostage in a choking web of press agentry? I wondered how I would be able to cope with my celebrity role.

It was after twelve when we arrived in the city and I assumed my welcome included lunch. Approaching the offices of PURS, the secretary, looking at his watch, murmured that he had to return to his desk. As we were crossing the Limmat the banker said he also had urgent matters awaiting him in his office. He departed. When we were alone, Meister said that the "little villa," would not be available until January so it could not be considered for my domicile. Instead he was

---

*The names of Hans Meister and Fritz Vogt and their offices are fictitious.

taking me to the "very first class" Hotel Im Garten, where I was to live until November 1, when the apartment with a private park would be vacated. The hotel, he said, was known for its distinguished artist, writer and theatre clientele; Mussolini had rendezvoused there with his mistress, Clara Petacci. But the "Mussolini suite," he added, was in great demand and he had been unable to get it for me.

The hotel, a multilevel complex, was spread over a hillside garden rampant with flowers and an almost soporific scent of jasmine. I imagined a room facing the garden in a fairyland milieu. The one to which Meister led me was large and had a satisfactory bath, but it was dark, with a stone wall outside French doors, which gave me an immediate feeling of claustrophobia. "Now you will have a rest," said Meister, and he departed.

Slowly I realized I'd been abandoned. I had known Hans Meister for five years and I liked him. He was a short, dark, dynamic man who had worked and trained in America. There he had turned himself into a Swiss version of what he believed an American press agent to be. To him the word was important, its intent of secondary significance, and he was frequently carried away by enthusiasm for projects beyond his reach. I remembered an occasion when Meister arranged a visit for me and two other journalists to the Pestalozzi Village, a colony for refugee children in Trogen, in the mountains of Canton Appenzell. Arrangements for the trip continued through a week of telephone calls and memorandums. On the appointed day, bearing a letter to the director of the Village, we left Zurich by train for St. Gall where we were greeted by a Chamber of Commerce official who bought us drinks and put us on another train. When we arrived at the Pestalozzi Village we found it deserted; the staff and children were on a fortnight's holiday on Lake Constance.

With an uneasy foreboding I began to wonder if the letters to Wisconsin had been another fantasy, if the red carpet did not exist, if there was no immediate prospect of an apartment, if no one was palpitating to see me, if, corralled finally in Switzerland, I was on my own.

Through the next frustrating days I tried to suppress my apprehensions. The idea for my Swiss year had come from the Swiss themselves after the publication of a book I'd written about Switzerland for *Life* magazine's World Library series. The conditions outlined for my sabbatical were attractive: I was to receive a subsidy, sufficient to live on, which would be deposited in a bank for my withdrawal. The offices of my two sponsoring organizations, the Confederation Information Bureau and PURS, would take care of the logistics of my stay and provide introductions. I would give lectures, including some on American studies, at the University of Zurich. The result of my "study sojourn" was to be a book, a human evocation of a country and a people I knew well; a book that I considered myself qualified to write. Because of hereditary citizenship I was myself Swiss.

I telephoned friends. Jim and Sandra McCracken who lived in Dübendorf, near Zurich, were in London where Jim was singing *Otello* at Covent Garden. Kap Rhyner, a friend in my ancestral village of Elm, was making his annual two-weeks military service. Hugo Brenner, a publisher, and his wife, Jenny, a fashion designer, were delighted I was in Switzerland but were leaving for a week in Florence. An architect I had met in America was busy and said he would call.

To assuage the melancholia into which my loneliness was plunging me, I took long walks along the lake and went to the opera. I called on Hans Meister to inquire about my money. He told me that the "Kubly fund" would be administered from his office, that whenever I was in need of cash I should come to get it from him. I replied that I found such an arrangement intolerable and reminded him of the promised bank account which I would control myself. He said that the papers could not be prepared until Fritz Vogt, the Cultural Extension Officer of PURS, returned from a trip to Greece. I asked if he could arrange bank credit so I might cash dollar checks and he replied he did not want me to spend my own money, that I was a guest of Switzerland. "Why can't you be patient?" he asked. "I can see you are a real Swiss, very impatient." Changing the subject, he said, "People are standing in line, waiting to talk to the famous Professor Kubly."

"Where is the line forming?" I asked.

"They are waiting for you to call them."

"For me to call them!"

"Swiss are shy," he said. "And very considerate. They think, poor Professor Kubly, he must be tired; we must let him rest. We will wait for him to call us."

I realized that although we shared two languages, we were not communicating at all and were wearing each other out in the attempt.

I telephoned a friend from years past, a playwright and scenarist to whom I shall give the name Carlo Minori, and he was delighted to know I was in Switzerland. The next day, a Sunday, he came to take me to his home in the village of Rüti for dinner. The house, a remodeled 150-year-old stone barn, was furnished with antiques and filled with paintings and theater memorabilia. Carlo is a gaunt, loquacious man, an Italian-Swiss with a keenly comic view of the *Alemanni,* his word for German-Swiss. I told him of my frustrations with bureaucracy and he laughed. "*Ja, ja,*" he said, speaking Schweizerdeutsch. "I see it all very clearly."

"These office holders who have brought you here," he said, "are controlled from above. Someone is always asking them, 'What are we getting for our money?' They had an idea to bring you here to write a book, favorable, of course, about Switzerland. No one stopped to think what would be involved and now that you're here they're not sure what to do with you. This is going to be your problem. But the joke is on them. They do not realize, nor could it have occurred to you, what an opportunity they're offering you to observe Swiss bureaucracy as it is.

"You will need your humor. And don't forget two things. The first is that we are a very small country with a village mentality. We call it *Dörfligeist,* a small-village spirit. Because no Swiss is more than one or two generations removed from a village, the rural attitudes and habits have not changed, even in our cities.

"The second thing to remember is the Protestant ethic. (Minori is Catholic.) Life is a vale of sorrow through which one must ceaselessly work to earn the ultimate reward. Not many Swiss go to church and few accept this archaic code in any rational way. But its force flows in our blood. Perhaps the ultimate reward has really become the large bank account one leaves at one's death. It is an irony that the only group to have risen above the village parochialism are the bankers and businessmen who, in traveling and meeting foreigners, have acquired the sophistication necessary to enjoy life. The Swiss economy controls the government and not, as we like to believe, the reverse."

As Minori was talking the bells in the church next door began to peal, ringing out Sunday vespers. Though the Swiss are not church-goers, bells still ring out several times on Saturdays and Sundays to remind them the Sabbath must be observed. "A man in the village was admonished when a neighbor reported him pulling weeds in his garden on a Sunday," Minori said. We laughed. The bells rang and Minori's dog barked.

The next week it rained. Trees and flowers in the hotel garden dripped moisture and my walled-in room became a gloomy prison. I thought of packing and returning home. But returning to the University would have been a defeat. The inability to accept defeat, a quality I had always considered to be part of my Swiss heritage, was strong in me. I wondered if some of the difficulties of communication might be my fault. My critical attitude toward the Swiss was based, after all, on a recognition of qualities present also in myself. I was not known for patience and I had a considerable capacity for querulousness. I would, I vowed, try to bring more tolerance and understanding to the situation. I would make an effort to be amiable.

So I went to see Meister and accepted his temporary arrangement of handouts "from the fund." Now that I was rested, he said, people would begin to call me. He introduced me to Max Schuler, the education director of Swissair, and his wife, Midi, who invited me to dinner. The Schulers were warm-hearted cosmopolites who traveled frequently in and out of Europe and sensed my alienation at once. Midi, who had an American grandfather, said, "We Swiss want to be friends but we don't know how. The idea of socializing terrifies us. I suppose it has something to do with a guilt in spending time frivolously. We feel we must be working all the time." Though she was using the first person "we," the explanation in no way applied to Max or herself. They became good friends almost immediately.

From Meister I was receiving daily memorandums urging my attendance at art gallery receptions, the anniversary of a hotel school, and a *Schweizer Mode-Woche,* Swiss fashion week. On one memorandum he had written, "You see, all of Switzerland awaits you." One invitation interested me. It said, "Jack Zweifel will take you to Glarus by train for a luncheon in your honor." Jakob Zweifel was the architect I had met in Wisconsin where he had come to design the Hall of History, a library-museum building in my hometown of New Glarus.

My relatives had been struck by his and my physical resemblance. He was a man of enthusiasm and intellect who during the train ride described his American pilgrimage to buildings designed by Louis Sullivan and Frank Lloyd Wright.

The gathering in Glarus had nothing to do with me. It was a meeting of archeologists and historians to examine the excavation of an ancient basilica discovered under the Glarus courthouse. After a lunch of chamois ragout in Glarus's best restaurant we were conducted on a lecture tour of the ruins, which dated to the seventh century, a period coinciding with the conversion of Glarus by Zurich's trio of patron saints, Felix, Regula, and Exuperantius. A Basel archeologist was in charge of the digs which, because they were beneath the courthouse, would be studied, sketched and photographed, and then reburied.

After the inspection I walked alone up a street to call on two spinster sisters, Anna and Martha Ott, who were my mother's cousins. I rang the bell on the street door of their patrician house. When there was no response I rang again and after a moment I started back. Then I heard a voice calling and, looking up, I saw one of the sisters leaning from an open window. I explained who I was and she said, "Please excuse us. We thought you were a Mormon." A minute later both sisters were at the door, urging me inside. They were handsome, rather corpulent ladies in their sixties. "You must forgive us," Martha said. "We did not wish to be rude. You see there are so many Mormon missionaries ringing the bell one doesn't know what to do." They led me up two flights of stairs into a beautiful room lined with old walnut cabinets. "People are always wanting to buy them," said Anna. "Can you imagine selling a whole room? What would we do without it?" The sisters were the sole survivors of their father, a venerated patriarch who had died at ninety-two, three years before. Longevity was an Ott trait; in New Glarus my great-grandfather and his brother both lived to be ninety.

"The house is too large for us," Martha said. "We cannot even begin to use it all."

I asked if they had thought of renting part of it, of letting rooms.

"Oh, yes, we think of it," Anna replied. "But it's impossible. You see, only Italians rent. So you understand how one can't?"

I understood very well. I was quite aware of the Swiss attitude toward an Italian labor force of more than 700,000 factory and hotel workers without whom the country's industry and economy would collapse, but who were considered an inferior people. Except for a few African students, there are no blacks in Switzerland, but the Swiss are always expressing shock at the subservient role of blacks in America, forgetting that they themselves assign Italians to an even more humiliating subservience. Only after ten years of residence in Switzerland could a foreigner become a voting citizen and even then subtle social and economic discriminations against him continued.

The sisters served me vermouth and cakes, and brought out a charted Ott family tree on which my grandfather was a branch on which I was a leaf. The tree included Austrian and Norwegian Otts whose ancestors had emigrated from Glarus at the same time mine had left for America. The Norwegian Otts were wealthy shipbuilders, Anna boasted, and one of them had the unforgettable name of Olaf Ott.

It was time to go and the sisters escorted me to the courthouse, walking proudly with me between them, aware that neighbors were watching. Zweifel was waiting to take me on an architectural tour of Glarus. We began with his own designs: a modern office building, a hospital and nurses' home built into the mountainside like cliff dwellings and, most astonishing, a modern 200-bed underground hospital, covered with gardens and trees, a medical redoubt to be used in case of a war.

We walked through the *Wiese*—the word means meadow—an old quarter of steep-roofed mansions built by eighteenth-century textile mill owners, and by governors in the centuries of mercenary soldiering. The aristocratic patricians of Glarus have maintained a tightly elitist society through the centuries and, marrying only within their own class, a near-incestuous clanship. The result in some families, not surprisingly, has been a degeneracy of bloodlines and some biological abnormalities which are accepted as a condition in the preserving of family fortunes.

The grandest of the mansions was known as *Das Haus auf der Wiese*. It had five stories built in 1744 by Joshua Streiff, a founder of Glarus's textile industry, and had come by inheritance to Dr. Aegidius Tschudi, a retired chemist whose healthy family was the most distinguished in Glarus history. The frail, scholarly old man led us through beautiful high rooms lined with carved walnut, and others in which elegant

Parisian wallpaper applied in 1810 was in perfect condition. Floors were inlaid maple and oak, and stuccoed baroque ceilings appeared as fresh as when they were frescoed in 1770. Windows looked down on topiary gardens unchanged for two hundred years. In the library the red, orange, and gold leathers in which the books were bound gave the chilly room a warm glow. On the top floor there was a family museum filled with pewter, china, silver, and weapons used by Tschudi ancestors in foreign wars. The heavy, dark rooms were strangely dispiriting. Though it was still midafternoon, the autumn sun had already disappeared behind near-vertical mountain walls. I remembered a theory of Dr. Jung's that the imprisoning claustrophobia of mountains was a cause of Swiss melancholia.

I spent the night in the Hotel Glarnerhof. In the morning I would take a train out of the valley up to the mountain village of Elm, of which I was a citizen.

2

A NATIVE RETURNS

I remembered an earlier season, the summer of my first visit to Switzerland. It was 1951, a century after my great-grandparents left their mountain village to go to America, and I was returning like a time-dislocated Rip Van Winkle to a home in which I had never been.

"You must be a Glarner," a taxi driver in Zurich had said.

"How can you tell?"

"That peculiar dialect I would recognize anywhere."

I was speaking the tongue of my childhood, the language brought to Wisconsin from Canton Glarus, and I was on my way to Elm, the village from which my ancestors had emigrated—the Elmers in 1847 and the Kublis in 1853—the village in which, after my Wisconsin birth, I was registered as a citizen.

An express train from Zurich took me to Ziegelbrücke where I transferred to the Glarus local, a slow-moving provincial train with slat seats. In changing trains I seemed to have changed countries, to have entered a land in which I was immediately at home. Country folk with lined faces and gnarled hands were speaking the earthy, elemental patois familiar to me. The men were short, strong troglodytes with thick legs and muscular shoulders bent like Atlas's from carrying the world on their backs. Everyone seemed to know everyone else. Passengers lowered windows to converse with friends on station platforms. A woman at a window sneezed and a pale object flew from her mouth through the window. The train began to move and the woman screamed for someone to retrieve her teeth. A man picked them up and, running along the side of the car, handed them up to her and she popped them into her mouth. The men roared and made crude jokes, suggesting to the woman that she mortar the teeth in place, or wire shut her jaw. A girl with large breasts entered the car and some youths jeered her with ribald innuendos.

The train rolled deeper into the walled valley, past factories producing textiles, furniture, dyes, and electrical appliances. Glarus, in east-central Switzerland, one of the smallest and most rugged of cantons, is both industrial and agricultural. Its 35,000 people live in three narrow valleys forming the shape of a Y and covering an area approximately twenty miles long.

We stopped first in the capital town of Glarus and five minutes later in Schwanden, a village at the fork of the Y, where I transferred into a bright red electric trolley for a nine-mile journey up the Sernftal, also known as Chlital or small valley, to Elm, the second-highest village in the canton.

The trolley clattered up through an abyss so narrow that the same passage served as track, auto road, and footpath. At a spreading of the tracks we waited for a descending trolley and when it passed we strained upward until we arrived at an opening in the canyon into a sunny valley of gardens and small fields clustered around dark brown buildings. It was a bright Sunday in July and the air was brisk and biting, the light blinding. The valley thundered with a crescendo of waterfalls, scores of shimmering cascades, emptying a thousand feet from the snowfields above. Ahead, recognizable from pictures, rose the snow-covered Zwölfihorn, or "Noon Peak," so-called because the sun shines over it at midday. To its left I found the vent known as Martinsloch through which, for a brief moment each spring and autumn, the sun shines on the cheese-wedge spire of the seven-hundred-year-old church in which my ancestors worshipped.

The trolley arrived at its terminus, a small station from which Elm stretched upward along a single road for a half-mile. I began to climb, moving through a place I'd never been, yet which was hauntingly familiar. The village was empty as a ghost town and some of the chalets were shuttered. Through the open church door I heard singing and I walked into the churchyard through rows of begonia-covered graves on which I read the same names with which I had grown up in New Glarus—Elmer, Rhyner, Zentner, Disch, Freitag—and the same familiar Christian names—Kaspar, Niklaus, Oswald, Werner. The mixed black slate and white marble stones had an eerie effect and I felt a chill of terror when I saw my own name on three of the stones. On the wall of the church was a large plaque commemorating a landslide that wiped out half of the village and killed 115 persons in the year 1881. Among the names of the victims were forty-one Elmers—my grandmother's family—and a single Kubli named Peter. The Kublis were farmers who lived on higher land, and I thought with a shudder that if my ancestors had not left Elm before the catastrophe, I might never have been born.

A man with a great bundle of hay on his back passed by the cemetery and stopped. Shifting the weight of his load he turned his grizzled, beard-stubbled face to me.

"You carry the hay lightly," I said.

"There was a day when it was lighter."

"Does the preacher approve of your working on Sunday?"

"The preacher does not have a hayfield. If the Lord God sends two weeks of rain and then sunshine on a Sunday, He cannot be too surprised to find people making hay." He turned and continued down the road. Following him, I met a girl and asked her if she knew any Kublis.

"An old grandmother Kubli lives there," she said, pointing to a house across the road. I went to the door and knocked. As I waited, a man appeared from between some buildings and stood in the road watching me. He was thin, middle-aged, and his skin was burned brown. I was thinking how much he resembled an uncle back in Wisconsin.

"No one seems to be home," I said.

"Everyone's making hay," the man replied.

He started down the road and I walked beside him.

"Can you take me to the old woman?"

"I can," he said as we walked. "You are a stranger?"

"I'm American. My name is Kubly."

He stopped and looked thoughtfully at me. "My name is also Kubli," he said. "Jakob Kubli."

"Are you related to the old woman?" I asked.

"Yes, we are related," he replied in a dry voice. We walked another hundred feet or so in silence and he said, "The old woman is my mother." He stopped to stare at me. "What are you called?" he asked.

"Herbert Oswald."

"Oswald, naturally. My father and grandfather were named Oswald. So is my first son an Oswald."

"We are many in America too," I said. "An uncle, my grandfather, and my great-grandfather were all Oswalds and so are two first cousins."

We climbed up into a meadow where two women, a pale youth, and two children—an earnest blue-eyed boy and a flaxen-haired, freckled girl—were making hay. The women, who were wearing the Glarner black skirts, embroidered girdles, and white stockings, were Jakob's wife and mother. The sad young man who walked with a limp was my cousin Oswald; the shy, pink-cheeked boy was named Hansueli, and the merry little girl wearing a pink apron was his sister, Anna.

"Someone has come to see us," said Jakob slowly. "Oswald from America."

His wife dropped her rake. "Is it possible?" she exclaimed. The old woman leaned on the handle of her fork and studied me intensely. "Yes, I can see you are my nephew. You are the picture of my husband!" I tried to tell her that while we were certainly kin, the relationship was not as close as that. But she did not hear me. "Your eyes, your hair are just like his. You speak in his voice." Her eyes filled and she embraced me. "And you have come all the way from America to see an eighty-three-year-old woman before she dies."

The child, Anna, began to jump up and down on a cock of hay.

"Stop!" her father ordered. "Have peace."

"I can't," Anna cried, leaping like a dervish. "Oswald from America is here and I feel just like a wild goat."

I took the grandmother's fork and began to gather hay.

"Is it possible?" she exclaimed. "You know how to make hay?" The younger woman asked what I did in America and I said I was a professor.

"*Herrgott!*" cried Grandmother. "A professor from America and we let him make hay!"

We cocked the hay and I was invited to Grandmother's house for a supper of cheese, cold veal sausage, bread, and strawberry jam; the same Sunday night supper I might have had in New Glarus. Afterward Grandmother and I sat on a grassy slope behind the house, watching the shadows spread over the valley. She told me there were three more in the family, a grandson working in Winterthur and two granddaughters who were waitresses in Zurich. "Once when I was a girl, I went to Zurich," she said. "*Ach,* such a noisy place! I did not like it at all." She was one of the last survivors of the great landslide, and she told how she escaped death on that dark night. "I was visiting a school friend in a house outside the village," she said. "We were playing our zithers and suddenly there came a thunder so loud we could no longer hear the music our fingers were making. Those who did not die lived in sorrow and no one thought laughter would ever again be heard in Elm." Years ago she had broken her leg and was taken to the hospital down in Glarus. "I rode in an automobile; it was the only time." She sighed. "Today many automobiles come into Elm. It used to be restful but now it has grown dangerous. Sometimes on Sundays an automobile goes by almost every half-hour."

When it was time for the last departing trolley, the family walked with me to the station and the little goat girl, Anna, danced around me like a wood sprite. Sucking on his pipe, Jakob bid me goodbye. "Life in Elm is very heavy, very hard," he said. "You are lucky your people went to America."

Three summers later, in 1954 and on another Sunday, I drove up to Elm. It had rained for a week and the waterfalls were spraying the valley with mists. Farmers were trying desperately to cure their soaked hay on drying racks. Young girls under bright plastic umbrellas reminded me of strolling geishas. I saw Jakob Kubli on the road and I stopped.

"Home once again?" he greeted me. He had aged shockingly; his face was gaunt; his shoulders stooped. "With me everything has gone badly," he said. "I lost my wife and my mother." He took me to the cemetery to view the new graves, which were covered with glistening rain-washed begonias. His wife had died two years before of cancer, his mother a year later of old age. "Life is heavy," he sighed. He invited me to the house to meet his daughter, Gertrude, a buoyantly handsome girl of twenty-two who had come home to care for the family. I took some photographs of her and the two younger children, Hansueli, eleven and no longer shy, smiling radiantly, and nine-year-old Anna, less playful and more thoughtful than I remembered her, and strikingly pretty. "Life grows always harder," Jakob lamented. To earn money he traveled on the trolley to a factory job down in Schwanden. His land and animals he cared for mornings, evenings, and Sundays. "It always rains; the hay rots," he said. "*Ja, ja.* Be glad you don't live here."

I did not return again until nine years later when, upon arriving in the little red train, an intuition sent me directly to the cemetery where I found more new graves and was not surprised. "Jakob Kubli, 1904-1959," I read from a stone and on another I saw the name of Jakob's brother, Kaspar Kubli.

I went to the church to ask the minister what had become of the family. He told me that the children, with one exception, had vanished. The one who remained was Hansueli, who was working as a truck driver for the local soft-drink factory and living in the *Bürgerheim,* a municipal shelter for the poor and homeless.

I walked up through the village to the ramshackle Victorian building which in better times had been a spa. Wandering through its depressing, dark and sour-smelling halls I had the dour thought that if ever I became indigent my Elm citizenship would qualify me for residence in this place. An old man told me that Hansueli was most probably in the *Sonne* and I returned down through the village and found him alone at a table in the crowded cafe. He recognized me and stood up. He was short, sturdily built, and good-looking, but the boyish warmth was gone, replaced by an introspective, melancholic earnestness. We had a drink and I asked about his family. "It is a complex story," he said. "When my father died of a heart attack the house was sold for debts. Oswald, the eldest, was so dissatisfied with his life, he began to drink and was sent to a sanitarium in Berne." An older sister, Berta, whom I had not met, was married to an Indian lawyer and lived in Calcutta with her husband and three children. Trudi, the warm-hearted daughter who had come home to care for the family after the mother's death, had returned to waitressing in Zurich. Another brother, Jakob, was working as a machinist in Schaffhausen. Anna, the happy little goat-girl, had grown up with Hansueli in an orphanage and now, at seventeen, was working as a domestic in Neuchatel.

The extent of the family's dissolution affected me like a chronicle of catastrophes in a Greek play. Though there were other relatives in Elm, this stricken family was the only one I had come to know and identify as kin. I wondered if Hansueli was accepted by other Kublis, and I asked if he knew a farmer, also named Jakob Kubli, who was a cousin.

"He is not at this moment in Elm," Hansueli replied. "He is with his cows up in the summer pasture and will not return until September." The young man was silent a moment and then added, "I do not know him well." While we were talking some young Italian workers had entered the cafe and were dancing to a jukebox with Swiss girls. I asked Hansueli if he had a girl friend.

"No, and that's a problem," he answered sadly. I wished I had not asked and said no more for I understood how an orphan living in a poor house would not likely be an acceptable suitor, nor be recognized as kin by relatives.

"One takes life as it comes, there is no other way," he said, and it might have been his father's voice that was speaking. "I came back to Elm and here I will stay."

Now, on a September afternoon, the sun is dazzlingly bright in the high valley and early snows cover the slopes almost down to the village. I arrive in the midst of a pastoral festival: the return of cattle and herdsmen from summer alpine pastures. The single street is filled with bawling cows wearing clanging bells and crowns of golden marigolds, pink asters, and blue gentians bobbing on their horns. Herdsmen's hats are covered with flowers. Villagers shout and wave from porches and open windows and wives rush out to embrace their homecoming husbands and sons. I had seen a theatrical representation of this event many times in the opening scene of Schiller's *Wilhelm Tell,* performed each year by the people of New Glarus. Garlanded cows appear from every direction. Church bells ring; children are dismissed from school. Men puffing on long, curved pipes fill cafes to drink wine and beer.

In my pocket there is a package of American tobacco which I am to deliver from a New Glarus friend to Mathias Elmer, the village archivist, the keeper of historical records. I ask a woman where he lives and she directs me to a house in a narrow lane behind the church. A soft-voiced woman invites me into a low-ceilinged, dark-paneled room where an old man is seated at a wooden table in a shaft of light falling through a window. He looks strikingly like a painting of a prophet. With the help of a cane he rises and scrutinizes me, creating with his silence a dramatic tension. He stands tall and straight and has a handsome, heroic face.

"I have waited for you," he says, taking my hand, speaking slowly in a deep, sonorous voice. "I hoped one day you would come to visit me. We are related, you and I. Your mother was an Elmer."

I reply that my mother was an Ott, that he is thinking of the mother of my father, my grandmother, who was an Elmer.

"Yes, of course," he says. "You must excuse me. You are a younger man."

I give him the tobacco and he thanks me gravely. He urges me into a chair near the table. The sun is sliding behind the mountain, the room darkens and he lights a lamp. "It is a pleasure to my ears to hear you speak our language," he says. "Do they still speak it in New Glarus; do they continue to teach it?" I reply that only old people spoke the old tongue, that my generation was the last to whom it was taught. He sighs. "Ah, yes, it is to be expected. One could not hope for it to continue forever." The woman brings a bottle of wine and he pours from it slowly into two glasses. "To your good health," he toasts. "And to the health of your people." We drink, and he asks, "Do you live there, in New Glarus?"

"On the land of my great-grandfather," I reply. "I am the fourth generation."

"That is good to hear. It is *our* way." He tells me he is also a farmer, an owner of land. But his engrossing preoccupation is the custodianship of the genealogical records of Elm. He calls for his daughter-in-law to "bring the books."

She appears in a moment bearing three great brown volumes and places them before him on the table. Mathias selects one and opens it, and the old leather flakes to dust in his hands. He turns yellow pages and then he stops and says, "Here it is, the time of emigration when each year ten or more families left for the new colony in America." He moves a slow finger down the columns of a page on which the ink, faded to pale brown, is barely legible. His finger halts and he says, "Nicholas and Verena Elmer departed in 1847, taking with them four children. Two more children were born in America, and the youngest, Anna Marie, born in 1851, was your grandmother." Turning to a cross-reference on another page he shows how he and I are related through this grandmother, his cousin. "I have heard she was a proud woman," he says.

I reply that she was indeed, a patrician who, though she never saw her ancestral homeland, would not let it be forgotten that she was born Anna Marie Elmer-Elmer von Elm, a name indicating that not only her father but also her mother had been an Elmer. "Yes, in those days Elmers were the first family of Elm," says Mathias. "Now we are in second place, the Rhyners outnumber us."

"Let us look at your other side," he says, turning to another page. "In 1853 Oswald and Barbara Kubli emigrated to New Glarus, taking with them four sons, Hans Ulrich, Paulus, Jakob, and Oswald. It was Oswald who became your grandfather. In the first year in Wisconsin, Paulus and Jakob died of cholera, but Oswald and Barbara had three more children, Susana and two sons, also named Paulus and Jakob. It is recorded here, 'Through hard work and love of God they prospered in the new world.'" Mathias pauses. "Of no other immigrants is it so written," he says.

It was true, I say, their Protestant piety included a dedication to work. My grandfather continued to work on the farm that was later passed on to my father. My grandfather's older brother, Hans Ulrich, lost a leg in the Civil War and afterward lived on his pension. But the brothers Paulus and Jakob were stonemasons who laid the foundations for most of the houses built in New Glarus before 1930; the builder of the houses was Oswald Altman, the son of their sister, Susana.

Mathias reads on, of the marriage in Wisconsin of Maria Elmer-

Elmer and Oswald Kubli in 1874 and of the birth in 1882 of their son Nicholas, who was my father. As he reads I try to comprehend the measure of the books, the woof and warp of five generations woven into a single tapestry and I marvel how the skein of threads has found its way back here to Elm. The collaborator, says Mathias, was his own cousin, Verena Elmer Ott, a New Glarus immigrant who kept the New Glarus family records and sent them to Elm. I remember her, a tiny old lady who was married to Jakob Ott, the brother of my mother's grandfather, which made her my great-great-aunt. Mathias shows me a packet of her letters, yellow pages on which the faded lines are a ghostly shadow, and each letter is the chronicle of a New Glarus season. "Thanks to her the books will remain forever a bridge between the two worlds," Mathias says. "After her death in 1927 it was a problem to continue the records."

His finger traces more columns and comes to rest at the marriage of my parents and on a notation, two years later, of my birth: "Herbert Oswald Nicholas Kubli von Elm."

Seeing my name there in the company of the ancestors, recording my place in their history and affirming my filiation to the village in which I am a stranger, fills me with an extraordinary exhilaration. Something is resolved; an important bridge is being crossed. The frustrations of Zurich are forgotten; my sense of alienation vanishes. The moment in the small dark room becomes a rite of welcome, a gathering together with my own people, an affirmation of the man who I am. To hide my emotion I drink some wine, but the old man is not deceived. He places his arm on my shoulder and says, "The 'von Elm' of your name is important. It establishes you as a citizen of Elm, as a son."

3

The Little Canton Spirit

For a Swiss a new idea is something like an unknown dangerous animal which is to be avoided if possible or at least only approached with caution.

—Carl Jung

I was showing an American journalist through Switzerland's capitol building in Bern. He asked me who was president of Switzerland and I did not know.

In the rotunda, among huge vases of gladioli and dahlias, I saw a guard, a small Chaplinesque old man wearing baggy pants, a seedy unbuttoned jacket, and an official cap. I asked him the name of the president. He thought for a moment and said he did not know but would find out. He shuffled through a door and disappeared. He returned in a moment and said, "It's Willy Spühler. He is president now."

Though the year was 1963, the guard's innocence would be just as possible today. In a test of Swiss army recruits, more than ninety percent could name the president of the United States and fewer than fifteen percent knew who was president of Switzerland. Few Swiss know the name of the president or recognize him as he goes to work from his rented apartment on a streetcar. The cult of personality is not tolerated in Switzerland; no Swiss is permitted to rise above the crowd. "We don't like leaders; we don't trust people who put themselves out in front," said Hans Baer, director of a wealthy private bank. "If they move too far up, we chop them off."

A Swiss is not a citizen of the Federation. He is born a citizen of his commune, of Basel or Lucerne or, as in my case, of Elm, a village of nine hundred persons. Patriotism is local and no matter where in Switzerland a man may live, he boasts of being a Glarner, or an Emmentaler, or a St. Galler. The cherished parochialism is known as *Kantönli-Geist,* "the little canton spirit." Jealousy is one of its strongest emotions and the citizens of each community delight in gossip and jokes about rival communities and cantons. There is a vast lexicon of ribald humor based on humiliating characteristics assigned to the citizens of other cantons. A popular Zurich joke about Appenzell, whose people are known for their short stature, tells of an Appenzell "Watergate," in which the postmaster was discovered renting mail boxes for duplex apartments. A Basel joke about Fribourg, where according to popular belief bathing is not popular, tells of a load of manure preceding a wedding procession to keep the flies off the bride. In a Lucerne joke, a man of Uri who, keeping a goat in his parlor, is asked how he solves the problem of the smell replies, "After a while the goat gets used to it."

Such crude humor helps to expiate a chronic hostility which the crowdedness of a small country with population growth and urban expansion increases rather than diminishes. The primal alpine emotions of suspicion and mistrust continue to prevail. Mountains, said Dr. Jung, are not only geographical barriers, they limit also the horizons of the human spirit.

Until the middle of this century a mistrust of modernism, the progressive and avant-garde, made Switzerland the most archaic democracy in the world. Though contemporary in outward appearance and technical and monetary proficiency, Switzerland seemed to have long ago stepped off from the restless, troubled world and prospered despite puzzling contradictions.

In natural resources the poorest country in Europe, Switzerland is now the richest country per capita income in the world.

A historically conservative people who fear liberal political ideologies, the Swiss enjoy a structure of welfare paternalism in which poverty does not exist.

In an area just over half the size of Maine, with boundaries that can be crossed in four hours by train and twenty minutes by jet, a federation of twenty-six sovereign states made up of three ethnic, two religious, and four linguistic groups, govern themselves with clockwork precision and, until recently, few outward indications of disharmony.

A belligerent people who squabbled among themselves through a stormy history, the Swiss have lived for more than a century in uninterrupted peace with the rest of the world.

Though its tourist offices continue to perpetuate an image of an Alpine Arcadia of frolicking goats and yodeling peasants, Switzerland is, next to Belgium, the most industrialized country in Europe and has fewer of its people engaged in agriculture than any other country in Europe.

A country which prides itself in its social enlightenment, Switzerland did not until 1971, after a long and bitter political battle, grant suffrage to women. In one canton—Appenzell—and in isolated rural communities in Canton Graubunden women in the present time are still not permitted to vote on cantonal and local issues.

For clues to an understanding of the enigmatic contradictions it is necessary to look briefly into geography and history.

In prehistoric times the mountain valleys were settled by tribes of Celts. Conquered by Caesar, the area became about 58 B.C. a Roman colony named Helvetia, and continued so for three centuries. Alemanic tribes invaded the country in A.D. 260 and, by the middle of the fifth century Helvetia was completely under Alemanic control. The impregnable mountains served the Germanic tribes as ramparts not only against the outside world but against each other. The battle for survival in a hostile natural environment fostered an alpine character that was suspicious, independent, frugal, and contentious.

The federation of regional units that was to become Switzerland began in 1291 when three central forest cantons, Uri, Unterwalden, and Schwyz, formed an alliance to liberate themselves from the feudal suzerainty of the Holy Roman Empire, an event immortalized by Schiller's *Wilhelm Tell,* and later by Rossini's opera. In the fourteenth century the pugnacious mountaineers fought and defeated Austrian armies in three violent battles and were joined by five new states, or cantons. Another five were added in the next two centuries.

In the sixteenth century Switzerland was turned into a battlefield for the Reformation when Ulrich Zwingli, a Zurich priest, joined Martin Luther in resisting the Roman Church's sale of indulgences. In Geneva, which was not to become a Swiss state until 1815, John Calvin set up a Protestant Vatican that he ruled more imperiously than any pope ever ruled Rome. Geneva became a seminary from which a new school of zealous apostles carried Calvin's harsh doctrine of predestination abroad. When the Reformation subsided it left Switzerland three-fifths Protestant and two-fifths Catholic, a ratio that continued more or less to the present century when an influx of Italian and Spanish workers increased the number of Catholics. In 1648, by the Treaty of Westphalia, the Swiss Federation was recognized for the first time by the power nations of Europe.

For three centuries after Zwingli and Calvin, Switzerland continued to be a battlefield of religious crusades. One canton, Appenzell, split into halves and, for a time, it appeared that a similar division would be made of all of Switzerland. Before this civil infighting could be resolved Switzerland was convulsed by a greater crisis, the French Revolution and its Napoleonic aftermath. In 1798 the French army defeated the Swiss, the ancient confederation was dissolved and Switzerland was turned into a French-controlled republic. Anarchy followed and Napoleon, recognizing that the belligerent Swiss could never be turned into French subjects, dictated in 1802 an Act of Mediation which established a new Swiss Confederation and added six more cantons to the original thirteen. When Napoleon was finally defeated, the three small states of Valais, Geneva, and Neuchatel, which had been incorporated into France, asked to join Switzerland and were welcomed into the Confederation. Switzerland's religious wars finally were concluded in 1847 when seven Catholic cantons formed a separate league called the *Sonderbund* and were defeated in a civil war which lasted twenty-five days and took a total of 128 lives. The next year a new Federal Constitution, modeled after the Constitution of the United States, was drawn up. Echoing the language and spirit of the charter of 1291, it established an alliance of small autonomous states of free men governing themselves without the restrictive controls of a powerful central government. Four of the twenty-two cantons have split politically. The last split occurred in 1978, when a popular vote throughout all of Switzerland permitted three French-speaking and Catholic districts to separate from Protestant Berne and become a twenty-sixth canton, named Jura.

A federal bicameral parliament consisting of the *Ständerat,* with two representatives from each canton, and the *Nationalrat,* with members proportioned according to population, has limited powers and any legislation it passes can be rescinded by popular referendum and frequently is. The alliance is not, says historian Herbert Luethy, "a rationally evolved entity" but a medieval concept on which centuries of trial have been superimposed with no present ever abrogating the past. By maintaining its cherished medieval structure, by zealously avoiding either monarchical sovereignty or a powerful central government, Switzerland passed through the turbulent European wars swimming against the stream of history, an archaic island unaffected by the rise and fall of powerful nationalist states.

Switzerland's most striking achievement is its awesome prosperity. In a small land abundant only in stones and water this is earned by conscientious hard work, by frugality, by a mechanical ingenuity which has produced an abundance of international industrial patents and by a genius for financial management.

Because of its prosperity, Switzerland is in trouble. Its people are too rich; its money is too strong in the monetary market; its banks are too powerful. The all-powerful Swiss franc, inflated by foreign money seeking safe haven in the famous secret accounts, threatens the crucial export and tourist industries by making Swiss goods and travel too expensive for foreigners. The controversial Banking Secrecy Law, which attracts foreign funds, assumed an important purpose during the

Nazi era by protecting the resources which German Jews managed to smuggle abroad. Its advantages were quickly recognized by deposed foreign politicians, by criminals, and by the international rich seeking tax evasions or fearing the instability of banks in their own countries. Now that the Swiss have become rich enough to themselves enjoy the advantages of secrecy it is not likely that they will vote to abolish the law. Tax evasion is a civil offense in Switzerland so criminality is not involved.

Another worrisome monetary imbalance is created by labor. A Swiss tradition, during several poor centuries, of sending sons abroad as mercenary soldiers, has in this century been ironically reversed by the importation of a massive foreign labor army of almost one million workers (thirty percent of the total labor force) who send much of their earnings to Italy, Spain, Yugoslavia, Portugal, and Turkey. Though the Swiss have defeated three national referenda, the last in 1977, to expel foreign workers, 300,000 have been sent home since the oil crisis; about 700,000 remain.

While it is true that Switzerland's direct democracy has dealt successfully with matters of domestic housekeeping, there is increasing evidence that in external policies the real power is concentrated not in government but in the powerful banks and in huge Swiss-based multinational corporations. It is certainly true that involvement in international banking and commerce has, in economic matters, turned Switzerland's cherished neutrality into a meaningless ambiguity.

But neutrality is based on *Kantönli-Geist,* which in some cases means a narrow preoccupation with regional issues and an exaggerated pride in one's particular community. The collapse of the League of Nations, which the Swiss joined, fortified the neutralist spirit that kept the country out of the United Nations and the Common Market. To protect this cherished neutrality Switzerland has had to become one of the most militarized of Western nations.

Today the disharmony between economic expedience and political philosophy is Switzerland's most perplexing contradition. It has become increasingly clear to the country's movers that Switzerland may be in trouble, that in order to endure it must cease running against history; that it must modify, if not relinquish, its "little canton spirit" to the realities of the modern world.

4

A STUDENT CRIB
IN A LOW VILLAGE

After a month and a half I was still living in my gloomy hotel room, checking out newspaper advertisements and tips from friends in my search for an apartment. I was insisting on some minimal requirements—in addition to a sleeping room and bath I wanted a room in which to work and entertain. Since Zurich was a marvelous walking town, I had decided against an automobile. This eliminated consideration of districts outside the center. The area in which I had chosen to live centered about the medieval section, called the Niederdorf, on the right side of the Limmat River.

The Niederdorf, which translates into "low village," is Zurich's Montmartre, a lively Bohemian artists' and students' quarter of narrow winding streets between the Limmat and the university. It is an area that had enchanted me ever since my first visit to Zurich twenty years before and I had always wanted to live in it. But apartments in the area were scarce and those I looked at were claustrophobically small.

Early in November a friend who was an art historian heard of a vacancy in the Wellenberg Apartments in Hirschenplatz, a small square in the heart of the Niederdorf. The first floor of the building housed shops and a cinema. The apartment was small—two rooms plus a combination kitchen and bath. But it was clean and tastefully

27

decorated and it had dormer windows that looked down on the square and across a *La Bohème* panorama of red-tiled roofs and chimney stacks. The sky and clouds and some snowflakes wafting by the windows elevated my spirit; I felt immediately at home. The rent was 550 francs, less than $150 a month.

On the day of my moving in, Fräulein Guler, the manager, filled the apartment with bouquets of fresh flowers. The first evening I heard music and, looking down on the square, I saw a procession of merry children carrying poles on which bobbed strange lanterns with merry faces. It was the *Räbeliechtli Umzug,* a turnip-lantern parade, an annual harvest tradition of Zurich children. The lanterns were hollowed-out turnips carved with roguish faces and lit with candles like Halloween jack-o'-lanterns.

The Swiss have a Germanic concept of academic dignity and, when word spread that I was living in the Niederdorf, there were some shocked reactions. "A professor in the Niederdorf," said a lady at a party. "That is very comical. Will you be studying the milieu?" My friend Jenny Brenner was appalled. "But only Bohemians and *petit bourgeois* live there." I replied that I was a bit of both and expected to be quite happy. "The nightlife is of a very vulgar quality," she went on, "it appeals to country people." A professor who came to call said the apartment was a *Studente Bude,* or "student crib." A banker, noting my address, said, "If you leave town from Friday until Monday you may find it quite pleasant." And Peter Studer, editor of the newspaper *Tages Anzeiger* said, "You are going to have an experience. You will meet many easy girls . . ."

I was aware of this. The Niederdorf was the center for Zurich's thriving commerce in prostitution. Girls wearing miniskirts, leather pants suits, or see-through blouses wandered through the maze of streets along the Limmat, argued under plane trees over claims to stations, and negotiated softly with dark-suited businessmen, foreign laborers, and country rustics. Estimates of the number of girls went as high as ten thousand and were of three categories: "standing girls," who established and fought over *Standplätze*; "moving girls," who frequented the Niederdorf's cafes and cabarets; and "auto girls," who cruised the area in Mercedes cars. Switzerland's sex code legalized all sexual contact between consenting adults, including homosexuals, who made the Niederdorf their center of revelries. Newspapers described the area as a "sexual ghetto."

Though I was happy in my student "crib," certain annoyances existed. For one thing the apartment telephones were shut off from Saturday evening to Monday morning, a time when I seemed to need mine most. Then there were bells. Most of Zurich's churches were either in the area or just across the Limmat and their bells pealed out early each morning like holy alarm clocks to arouse people from sleep and rang again at dusk to let the city know that night was falling.

An 11 A.M. ringing was a tradition held over from villages where men were summoned from fields for their midday meal. For the Swiss, the bells were a necessary cuing of their daily lives. A friend told me of a relative who emigrated to Nebraska and so desperately missed the daily pealings that after eight years he repatriated back to his homeland so he could hear them again. Most of the churches also had great clocks that tolled each half-hour.

There were times in those first weeks when I feared the bells and clocks would destroy my sanity. In the morning I would awaken before they began and wait in a kind of panic, listening in the meantime to the clatter of garbage cans in the street. I attempted to shut out the bells by closing windows and once I turned on the radio and found that the ringing bells were being broadcast. On weekends the tyranny of the bells was increased by special pealings to indicate worship and prayer hours. As the hour approached for the Saturday evening curfew bell I would find myself growing tense and nervous. Watching the clock I would bolt some whiskey to fortify myself against the dreaded clamor. One Saturday, unable to endure the suspense of waiting in my room, I ran into the street and down alongside the river and waited at the foot of the dour statue of Zwingli behind the Wasserkirche. When the din broke around me, from the Grossmünster and the Frauemünster, and from Peter's and Augustine's churches, I threw back my head and shouted as loudly as I could, "You blustering son-of-a-bitch!" By mocking the din with my laughter, I was able to exorcise some of my terror. A friend told me I would become accustomed to the bells and it turned out he was right. After a month I was hardly aware of the pealing and tolling.

Though my rooms were quiet during the day, the night's stillness was frequently shattered, especially on weekends, by midnight revelers. A Swiss man's best friends are frequently the colleagues with whom he works and it is a custom to celebrate weekends together, bachelor fashion, with a night on the town, usually in the Niederdorf. Evicted from bars and cabarets by a midnight curfew, too stimulated and frustrated to end their conviviality, bands of drunken workers, military recruits, and farmers would stagger in their group security through dark streets, supporting each other morally and physically by an interlocking of arms. Filling the night with raucous fellowship, they shouted bad jokes and defiant curses, yodeled and sang and stopped sometimes to piss, with roars of laughter, into the fountain below my windows. Awakened, I would listen to the night singers and sense a dark motif in their desperate merriment: the fear of loneliness in solitary men who were striving, with the exuberance of drink, to cross an unbridged human gap; and I knew the silent, remorseful solitude into which each would be withdrawn in the morning.

There were also the very intricate problems of housekeeping. In my imagination I would compose an article, perhaps for *Woman's Day,* entitled, "Cooking in the Can." The entire bath-kitchen measured about two and a half by one and a half yards. This included the bathtub, so small it required Yoga positions to use it. There was a "shower" on the end of a hose that sprayed the entire complex and I had to give it up. The "kitchen" was a drop shelf with two hot plates and a cupboard facing the toilet from a distance of about twenty inches. I could sit on the toilet and cook; it was in fact the most comfortable position, except that caution was required in standing up as the refrigerator was suspended from the ceiling just above the toilet and I was always bumping my head. Since the refrigerator was too high to see inside it with any ease, I had to reach for perishables with the result that they frequently dropped into the toilet. I established a protocol about retrieval: tomatoes, no; oranges, yes; and eggs if they did not break. There was a tiny hand sink in which I could rinse a few dishes but to wash a batch it was necessary to use the tub, which had a board fitted over part of it to serve as a washing and drain shelf. With the board in place I could not get into the bathtub so it was impossible to take a bath when there were dishes to be washed. Washing dishes on my knees was awkwardly uncomfortable so I tried washing them and myself simultaneously by getting into the tub with the dishes. But the detergent gave me a rash and I was never quite free of a fear that I might accidentally end up a eunuch. Washed dishes were stacked on the closed toilet seat, and this also required prudent timing. There was only one place where the drain board could be fitted when I wanted to use the tub and that was against the wall under the refrigerator, where it covered the paper roll and the waste basket that served as a garbage receptacle. It was a problem I was never able to solve.

Flailing about in my Lilliputian quarters, I would recall the Marx Brothers' famous ship stateroom scene. The narrow bathroom-kitchen door opened inwardly and I gave up trying to close it. When Jenny Brenner came one day to examine the apartment, the location of which she had so strongly disapproved, she asked, "Why is it Americans always keep water-closet doors open?"

Hans Meister also came for an inspection. Ever mindful of his trusteeship of "the fund," he said, "Now that you are in the center of the action you will no longer need your street-car pass."

He was right. Everything that I required for a rich life was within walking distance. Two blocks away, on Zähringerplatz, was the great municipal library and the university was a brisk climb up the hill behind it. The art museum and the Schauspielhaus, one of the most famous German-language theaters in Europe, were five minutes away. An easy ten minutes took me to the Stadtheater, the intimate rococo and acoustically excellent opera house where that season my friend Sandra Warfield was a resident star. The Tonhalle, where the symphony played, was across the river and so was the Fraumünster—the Cathedral of Our Lady—with windows designed by Chagall. In the immediate area were a dozen medieval guildhalls, once trade- and craft-union headquarters and now exclusive social clubs with excellent restaurants. One of my favorites was the 500-year-old Schmiden—blacksmiths— which Napoleon, during a Zurich occupation, filled with young ladies and operated as a bordello for the entertainment of his officers. Excellent smaller restaurants were everywhere. On Rindermarkt—cattle market—was the four-hundred-year-old Öpfelchammer—the apple chamber—favorite of the nineteenth-century novelist Gottfried Keller.

On Spiegelgasse, in the house where Lenin lived, there was Jakob's Ladder. Jim McCracken, Sandra, and I went there for the best cheese fondue in Zurich.

Niederdorfstrasse began at the Station Bridge and, changing its name midway to Münstergasse, followed the curve of the Limmat to the thirteenth-century Romanesque Grossmünster Cathedral, the twin spires of which dominate the skyline of Zurich. Across the bridge was the National Museum with its great collections of German gothic and Swiss primitive art, and the railroad station that looked out on Bahn-hofstrasse, Zurich's elegant combination of Wall Street and Fifth Avenue. The Niederdorf's network of quaintly winding streets and lanes was a casbah of book, art, and porno shops, cinemas and night-clubs, antiquarians, publishers' offices, and student cafes. Music was everywhere. The square beneath my windows was popular with ren-dezvousing street musicians and at night a tumult of Dixieland, rock, yodeling, Spanish guitars, and Italian and German ballads pealed out of the cafes.

Such a hyperkinetic atmosphere had its effect on Niederdorf resi-dents. A survey revealed that children of the area were the most nervous, prematurely sophisticated, and violent in the city. Parents from the neighboring upperclass Zurichberg area were alarmed by the bad influence on their well-bred children who attended the same schools.

Sometimes on a clear day I would walk down through the Hogarth-ian turbulence to the river and gaze up and across the lake to the majestic and serene snow-covered Glarner alps, the home of my ances-tors, sixty miles away.

After I had been a week in the apartment a summons came from the *Kreisbüro* to apply for a resident permit. From the office in City Hall I was sent several blocks to the *Fremdenpolizei* where, after standing in line for an hour with Italian and Spanish workers, I was told I would need an official letter explaining my purpose in Switzerland. Next stop: the PURS office where I was promised a letter within a day. The letter never came and when I phoned a week later I was told it had been sent to the Kreisbüro. So I trudged back to City Hall where the clerk, to whom I paid a 24-franc fee, was struck by the fact that I was from New Glarus and waived the required physical examination and other details and gave me the permit at once. If I wished to activate my Swiss citizenship, he said, he would see to it. On examining my passport he discovered that, but for one week's difference, we were exactly the same age. This so exhilarated him that he embraced me like a brother and begged me to come with him to his vacation house in the Toggenburg for the weekend.

My first visitor was the Irish poet James Liddy, who was on a pilgrimage to the city where James Joyce lived, worked on *Ulysses,* and died. By trolley we went to the cemetery where Joyce is buried and asked some workmen to direct us to the gravesite. An Italian pointed to a bronze statue of a young foppish dandy seated on a chair with knees flexed, ringed fingers holding a swishily poised cigarette, and spectacles covering the eyes which gazed down on a book in the left hand. "A bottle and a glass would be more appropriate," Jim said. The realistic statue, which seemed so absurdly Swiss, yet was the work of an American sculptor, stood over the isolated graves of Joyce and his wife in a wooded glen.

While we were photographing the graves we heard a lion roar in the zoo nearby. "A salutation from the king of beasts," Jim said. "How appropriate!"

We decided to visit the lion and found that his ululations had been subdued by a chunk of red meat. A mynah bird was shrieking to us saying "*Grüss Gott! Verstehen Sie mich?*" (Greetings! Do you understand me?). In front of the bird's cage a fat woman was convulsed with laughter. Holding her stomach, she addressed us, saying, "He's talking to us. He's talking to us just like a real person." Jim, also overcome, cried, "Dear James! Your spirit lives."

A drink seemed the appropriate commemoration of Joyce and the place for it had to be the cafe that he had frequented, the Odeon. Its seventy-five-year-old Edwardian parlor, with marble tables, potted rubber plants and crystal chandeliers, was the traditional male redoubt for a distinguished clientele that had included Thomas Mann, Hermann Hesse, and Thornton Wilder, as well as Nikolai Lenin. The price of coffee or a Cinzano entitled a guest to spend the morning reading from the Odeon's large library of current newspapers and magazines.

We found a corner table at which Joyce used to sit and ordered Irish whiskey. As a young man I had felt out of place in the sedate company of distinguished men quietly conversing or sitting alone, reading. Now I felt displaced for another reason. In recent years the old salon had been invaded by students who had turned it into a crowded, noisy youth emporium. The high-spirited international fraternity included Orientals and Americans, and loud conversations in a mélange of languages covered politics, rock music, and local gossip as well as literature. Some of the foreigners were exotically garbed and a few Swiss wore suits and ties but most of the patrons, in casual Levi's, were nationally indistinguishable from one another.

In another aspect the Odeon had not changed. As long as I can remember there has been a cabaret on the upper floor, where exotic girls perform disrobing dances for well-heeled businessmen. On this visit, posters proclaimed a current extravagance, "*Wunderland bei Nacht*" and in the evening Jim and I climbed the stairs to the promised wonderland.

A dozen dark-suited men, most of them sitting alone at tables, were listening to a peroxided doxie shouting "I love Delilah" against a combo of piano, saxophone, electric mandolin, and drums. The ear-splitting cacophony continued while waiters hustled drinks at ten francs each. A few more men arrived and finally, forty-five minutes late, the lights dimmed and the entertainment commenced. A large blonde, introduced as "Babs," wearing silver metallic pajamas, strutted out to "A Pretty Girl is Like a Melody," amplified to ear-bursting intensity, and began to shimmy. Within three minutes she had wiggled out of her costume and slouched offstage while a waiter picked up her garments and carried them away. A man at his solitary table applauded drunkenly; the others waited silently. The orchestra played the opening measures of "Scheherazade" for "Farida of the Casbah," a dark-skinned and black-haired girl, wearing a white skirt and metal cups over her breasts and clicking castanets. She swooped about for three minutes during which she divested herself of everything but the castanets. The waiter gathered up her accoutrements and the drunk applauded. The next performer, named Laura Lee, appeared wrapped in a black cape. Accompanied by a scratchy Sinatra recording of "That's Why the Lady is a Tramp," she whirled the cape, placed a leg on the table of the applauding drunk and when the record finished she dropped the cape and trudged off. The orchestra leader announced the "Abschluss," the climactic finale, and revved the musicians into a fanfare of "Tea for Two" for the entrance of Michelle, a pink pudgy blonde covered from neck to feet by a fuschia gown of Grecian pleats. The music changed into "A Man Without Love" during which Michelle whirled and fluttered like an addled butterfly, causing her dress to billow into an inverted morning glory. In four minutes she had unzipped to her pink flesh and her dress lay like a crushed blossom on the floor. I checked my watch. The entire *Wunderland bei Nacht* had taken fourteen minutes.

In no time at all the girls in fresh dresses reappeared with a half-dozen others, and several men got up to join them at the bar. Other girls lingered at tables, awaiting invitations to sit down. Laura Lee took custody of the drunk and Farida sat at our table and we bought her a drink. Speaking French and then faulty English, she asked, "You like show?"

"It passed very quickly," I said.

She shrugged. "You like some more?" she asked. "For two I make not so expensive. Only two hundred francs."

We excused ourselves and as we prepared to leave she flipped the ash from her cigarette into my glass and moved to the bar.

Walking in the night mists along the Limmat, following the flow of the dark river to our left and the gray profile of the Niederdorf on our right, Jim observed how in that moment Zurich seemed like Dublin and that Joyce must have sensed the similarity when he chose the city for his exile home. "It reminds me," Jim said, "of Stephen Dedalus, his own somber thought: 'Darkness is in our souls, do you not think?'" We passed young men in hushed negotiations with prostitutes and I told Jim how I sensed a distrust and hostility between the sexes in Switzerland, that genders meeting as adversaries seemed always on the edge of war and Jim replied that in this the Swiss were like the Irish and that it was something Joyce would also have recognized.

We climbed up into the Niederdorf and entered the Pigalle, a crowded windowless cave of black walls covered with gaudy frescoes. A whore I remembered from earlier seasons accosted me, saying, "I never can resist Americans." I told her that her words were precisely the ones she had addressed me five years before. With chilling disdain she said, "With a different man every night how would I remember you?"

"Ah," said Jim. "The dear dead days beyond recall, love's old sweet song." I recognized the voice of Mrs. Breen in the bordello in *Ulysses.*

Behind me I heard a male voice, speaking English, say, "The Grand Inquisitor arrives at midnight." I turned and faced a grubby little man about thirty years old with bad teeth and tattooed arms and a boyishly elfin smile. "I'm a businessman," he said. "If you're looking for something I may be able to help you." I asked where he'd learned his excellent English and he replied, "Two and one-half years in Regensdorf."

"A school?" I asked.

"No, a prison," he replied. I was not sure how to continue.

"My crime was living from the earnings of women," he went on, solving my dilemma. While prostitution was not a crime in Switzerland, pimping was. "I still do," he said.

His name was Stefan. We bought him a drink and he reimbursed us with the story of his life, which he seemed to have a penitent's need to share. "My father was a schoolteacher in Thun. I was his best pupil, a real scholar. My mother was proud; she was sure I would be a famous man, a professor or a doctor. I came to Zurich and met a girl who said she loved me and was happy to have me live with her. I became her manager and some enemies reported me to the police. In prison I made friends and I studied. I read Dostoievski, Thomas Mann, Hemingway, and Steinbeck. Dostoievski was my favorite. When I got out I met another girl and I married her so I could not be arrested. There she is."

He pointed across the bar to a heavily made-up, worn-looking woman, older than he and surrounded by a covey of men. "We were married four years and then I divorced her. I'm living with another now and I've taken up the profession of stonemason at which I work now and then to fool the police. My father died and my mother makes a great sorrow over me. I would like to tell her I'm sorry I've caused her so much pain. But how can I tell her that '*Zwei Seelen wohnen ach in meiner Brust.*' How could she understand that?"

Two souls live in my breast. It was a line from Goethe's *Faust.* "A good soul and a bad soul," Stefan said. "And the bad makes a warmer fire." Jim was back in Monto, Dublin's night town, quoting from Jorge

Luis Borges's *Invocation to Joyce,* saying, "In the streets of night, your splendid hells survive."

"What a literary parallel!" he said. "It applies to Zurich as well as to Dublin. But there are no longer many pimps in Dublin; their era was Leopold Bloom's, when British soldiers were garrisoned there. In any case, a Dublin pimp would not be quoting Goethe; he'd be singing 'Sweet Molly Malone.'"

In the morning a gull landed on my windowsill and tarried there. It was the kind of low-clouded, chilly day when Zurich's inland gulls appeared frequently on rooftops and in the squares below. Quite certainly, said Jim, they were Protestant gulls, converts to Zwinglianism.

5

RED PAINT

In November Fritz Vogt, the Cultural Extension Officer of PURS, returned from his vacation in Greece. He called to look over my apartment and to take me to lunch.

I had met Vogt five years before and I understood that the idea for my sabbatical year in Switzerland had originated with him. The invitation for my sojourn was issued jointly by him and Hans Meister and the stipend to make it possible was to be provided by their two offices, both government funded.

After my discord with Meister I had resolved to conceal my irritation and be as cooperative as possible with my two "coordinators." There were striking differences between them and each had a low tolerance for the other. Meister, who was fifty years of age, was an enthusiastic extrovert who was given to speak in hyperbolisms. Engrossed by people, he enjoyed gossiping about them. Vogt, ten years younger, lean and blond, with a low-keyed subdued voice, had a confiding manner with which he always seemed to be assuring me that my welfare was his deepest concern. During our lunch he told me, confidentially, that Meister was irresponsible and warned me to be careful of what I said to him because "Switzerland is really a village in which everyone tells everyone everything."

The morning after our lunch Meister telephoned. "I hear you lunched with Fritz Vogt. You must be careful with him. He thinks he is much too important and he is not very popular in his office. He is always making a lot of red paint."

"Red paint," by which he really meant "red tape," was one of Meister's favorite expressions. When there was a problem each gentleman blamed the other for causing it. Vogt suggested that I might find a television set in my apartment useful and I agreed. The next week he told me he was trying to arrange for one but that Meister was obstructing the idea. Since the television shop was a block from my apartment I suggested I would arrange for one myself and Vogt said this would be impossible. "It is impossible because he is making red paint," Meister said. The battle of the television continued for a month before a set was finally delivered.

As this was going on something became increasingly clear. My two dragomen were engaged in a power battle and I was its object. Each was fighting jealously for control over my affairs, which appeared to have become a matter of upmanship between them. When a banker with whom I lunched arranged for me to meet the editor of the *Neue Zürcher Zeitung,* I received an angry call from Vogt. The editor, he said, was a member of PURS's board of directors and no one had the right to arrange for me to meet him except Vogt himself.

The two men competed in programming my time, in suggesting things for me to do and people to meet. But many of the suggestions failed to materialize. Meister had a short attention span and was often unable to project ideas into reality. Vogt, on the other hand, found it difficult both to make decisions and to follow through on them. His response to crises was to make himself inaccessible. He would not answer his phone or return calls and was often reported out of his office.

The major contention between the two men concerned the matter of my stipend funds. Vogt and Meister each blamed the other for the delay in the opening of the bank account that had been promised me. On a December Friday, Vogt said dourly, "If Meister doesn't arrange this by Monday I'll find out why." Meister kept reassuring me, saying, "Don't be so impatient. You're going to get your money. As soon as we take care of some red paint it will be in the bank." In January, when I expressed dismay over the continued delay, he said, "You're a real Swiss, always worrying about money. A regular mountain type, you don't trust anyone." When I expressed discontent over his humiliating arrangement for a weekly cash handout and said I would prefer drawing on my own funds, he said, "That's what people are saying, 'Kubly's a rich man, what does he need our money for?'" I recognized this idea as his own for I had become aware of his habit of assigning his own thoughts to anonymous voices.*

My strategy for coping with the frenzy of intrigue and accusation was to keep a soft voice. I knew it was not in language that communication had broken down—all of us spoke both English and *Schweizerdeutsch*—the problem was a difference in mentality. With all the finesse I could muster, I tried to maintain an air of soothing calm so as not to further ruffle the turbulent waters. But the chaos was having its effect. My sense of alienation was increasing. Because I had no one to talk to I commenced talking to myself. Sometimes on the streets I would become aware that talking to oneself was not unusual in Switzerland, that others were doing the same, and I would break into laughter.

Finally a seemingly trifling incident brought matters to a climax. I had written a play that I wished to have typed and when I mentioned this to Vogt he replied that there were many English-language typists in Zurich and he would arrange for one. Our conversation was on a Friday and he said he would have a typist by Monday.

When I had not heard from him by the following Wednesday I phoned and he said a certain Frau Held was to have called me about the typing. He gave me the lady's number and told me to call her. The lady's husband answered and gruffly demanded to know who I was and what I wished of his wife. I explained, with what I believed to be heroic patience, the purpose of my call. He refused to call his wife to the phone. "My wife does not work for strange men," he said. I thanked him and said goodbye, thinking how astonishingly rude the man had been.

I telephoned Vogt and told him that Frau Held had decided she

---

*As a result of pressures exerted by banker friends, a drawing account of 4,000 francs was opened for me in the Bank Leu on April 16, seven months after my arrival in Switzerland and two months before my departure for home.

would not type for me. He said he would call a lady who frequently typed for him. Five minutes later he called again to ask that I come to his office in an hour to meet the lady. I trotted over to the dark, gloomy PURS offices on Munsterplatz and found the typist waiting in Vogt's office. Her name was Fräulein Stoller* and she was a tiny, nervous creature of middle years. She wore a black dress and her hair was in a tight knot. Casting her eyes toward the floor to avoid looking into mine, the little Fräulein said she thought she *might* be able to type for me if I would answer to her satisfaction some questions.

"Does the play have shooting and killing?" she asked in a small whimpering voice.

I replied that it had neither and she seemed relieved. "I do not type those things," she said. I was thinking how the play, which was about an interracial marriage, had some raunchy dialogue and I sensed trouble ahead.

"Does it have a happy ending?" Fräulein asked anxiously.

"No, it does not."

"Well, if it's not happy I will cry and then I'll not be able to type."

I suggested that she read the play first and have her cry before beginning to type. The little lady began to think of reasons why she would not be able to type my manuscript, one of which was that her typewriter did not have a tabulator which was necessary for typing a play. Vogt said she could use an office machine. No, she said, that wouldn't do at all. "You see I have to work at home because I cannot leave my mother alone. In any case, with Christmas coming I would not be able to begin until after the fifteenth of January."

It went on and I had the feeling that always seemed to descend on me in the PURS offices: I was trapped in Dr. Cagliari's cabinet. With as much patience as I could summon, I said, "I am sorry you will not be able to do it, Fräulein Stoller."

"Well, goodbye then," she said, getting up and leaving. She was hardly out of the room before Vogt, his face red, turned to me and commenced raging over what he said was my rudeness to Fräulein Stoller. I could hardly believe what I was hearing. Holding his voice

---

*The name, like others in this account, is fictitious.

low, he went on to say, "Your rudeness is becoming well known. Everyone speaks of it. You were rude to Mr. Held on the phone, which is why he could not permit his wife to type for you. The girls in our office are all upset by your rudeness. You are very much an American, an American-Swiss. They always seem to be angry when they are in Switzerland. In Switzerland we do not show anger."

"And that's a pity. A little expressed anger would serve you better than polite suppression," I said, trying to control my temper.

I stopped. Perhaps I was wrong. In a country so small, one angry voice was an earth tremor radiating out to the borders and beyond. I would need to make a still greater effort to understand the bedlam of miscomprehension in which I had become embroiled. Rather than anger, I should feel sorrow for those I was confronting with their own desperate shadows.

At this moment a secretary entered from an outer office and said she would type the manuscript during her off hours. She was young and fair and her name was Gertrud. Vogt seemed relieved. His composure restored, he said that Gertrud had once been married to a Korean. She would understand the theme of the play and would do a good job. We came to an agreement—the fee would be 200 francs and Gertrud would finish before Christmas. I left the script.

A week later I telephoned Gertrud to inquire if she were encountering any difficulties and she said she was not. Two days later Vogt's assistant, a very tense dark woman named Fräulein Nussbaum—Miss Nuttree—telephoned to ask when the script needed to be finished. I replied that everything was in order, that Gertrud had promised to finish it by Christmas.

"Impossible," said Miss Nuttree. "It is very slow work and Gertrud cannot possibly finish it so soon."

"All right, then," I said. "New Year's."

"New Year's!" The voice on the phone was shrill. The thought occurred to me that Gertrud had not begun to type and that I was being caught up in a wave of hysteria sweeping through the PURS offices and that, in characteristic Swiss rationale, the responsibility for it was being assigned to me. I said that Gertrud could type the script when it was convenient to her and that I would wait.

"It may be February," said Miss Nuttree.

That was longer than I expected and I said, "In that case I would prefer to make other arrangements and I will call for the script."

"You'll have to take it up with Mr. Vogt and he is not here."

"Well then, couldn't I take it up with you?"

"I'm afraid that is quite impossible since you have the arrangement with Gertrud."

My self-control was wavering. "Considering the problems involved," I said, "wouldn't it be better for all of us to bring this to an end . . ."

"I think you are very nervous, Professor, and I am sorry for you," said Miss Nuttree and she hung up. The next day Hans Meister telephoned. "I hear you are rather nervous," he said. "That you have been having a tantrum. You must try to relax . . ."

Early in January I received a call from a male clerk at PURS who said that the typing of my manuscript would be finished the following Monday. When I went to the office on Monday the young man who had phoned said Vogt was out of town and that Gertrud was not yet back from lunch. He described how difficult the typing was for Gertrud, how incomprehensible the American slang. "She spent twenty minutes looking up just one word," he said.

"But she didn't have to understand the word," I said. "She needed only to type it."

At that moment we were joined by Miss Nuttree who said, "Your handwriting is very difficult for Gertrud to read."

As gently as I could, I said that my original script was not handwritten but typed. Miss Nuttree looked as if she were about to break into tears. "How far has Gertrud progressed?" I asked.

A girl I had never seen before appeared and replied, "I think she is halfway through the first act."

"Halfway through . . ." I stopped and I lowered my voice. The three persons forming a triangle around me were all talking at once, saying, "It has been very hard for Gertrud . . ."

"So many strange words . . ."

"She has been ill with the flu . . ."

"She is working as hard as she can . . ."

"We are not accustomed . . ."

The fugued skirling was like a parody of a Mozart opera trio and I began to laugh.

"What is the matter?" Miss Nuttree asked in alarm.

"Nothing! Nothing at all." I stopped laughing, aware of the danger, how my laughter was tilting us toward the abyss. "Please tell Gertrud not to upset herself and when she is finished to call me."

"Gertrud is not upset," said Miss Nuttree. "You are upset. You are shaking, Professor. Why, you must be sick." As I walked out of the office I saw Gertrud peering from behind an almost-closed door.

A fortnight later Vogt phoned to say that the script was typed. I went to fetch it and he gave me a bill for 400 francs, exactly double the price we had agreed upon. When I reminded him of this he said, "There were so many problems. The play was very upsetting to Gertrud, whose Korean husband used to beat her. But of course you are right. It is high. I will speak to Gertrud. Perhaps it can be reduced."

I wanted only to extricate myself from the situation. I left 400 francs with Vogt, who said he would take it up with Gertrud and if she agreed to modify the fee he would return the difference to me. I went to my apartment and checked out the new script. There were sixty-five errors, some of which could be repaired with a pen. While I was working Vogt phoned to say he had discussed the matter of the fee with Gertrud and she had agreed to reduce it by fifty francs. I asked him if I might myself retype two pages containing errors on the typewriter Gertrud had used and I said I would bring them in the next day and at the same time pick up the fifty francs.

When I arrived the following afternoon Vogt reported that Gertrud, having brooded over her decision through a sleepless night, had come to work in the morning in tears, insisting she must have the full 400 francs. By noon she had apologized for her outburst but had not returned any francs. All I could feel was relief to have the matter concluded.

Something in my expression must have betrayed my thoughts for the color rose like a storm signal into Vogt's cheeks and he said, "You may not know it but your bad manners have been very upsetting to everyone. I think you are either going to have to calm down or get out of the situation."

His suggestion, clearly implying that I leave Switzerland, was one with which I was close to agreement. The charged atmosphere was making it increasingly difficult to maintain any degree of objectivity.

Paranoia was a Swiss affliction which, I had learned during a period of analysis, was at least mildly latent in myself. I was beginning to think of my presence in Switzerland as analogous to a patient with a lung spot moving into a tuberculosis ghetto. For the second time since my arrival I was becoming depressed and thinking seriously of going home.

As usual Mesiter had the last word. "I hear you are getting more nervous all the time," he said. "Maybe we should send you to a headshrinker."

6

ON THE ALP

It was a dream I had cherished since childhood, to make a "Heidi" journey into an Alpine pasture where herdsmen lived with cows and children frolicked with goats. The opportunity to realize the dream came with a magazine assignment for an uplands summer story. I was to work with a photographer I shall call Doyle, a high-strung fellow whose temperament was sometimes incomprehensible to the Swiss.

Because it would be difficult to manage my own research and act as liaison between my excitable colleague and the easily ruffled Swiss, I invited an engaging young cousin, Andreas Luchsinger, a student who spoke both English and Glaronese, to accompany us and look after Doyle. Our expedition was arranged by the Glarus Tourist Office from which I received a memorandum of logistics.

> 14:00 hours, arrive in Elm. Three hours walk to the Mühlibach Alp. Your leader will be an English-speaking guide from Elm. Staying of night on alp. It is absolutely necessary to be well-equipped with good boots and a raincoat. A pullover is advisable.

Doyle and I spent a day in Zurich searching for boots. Both of us had large feet—mine were Swiss size 46—and we were not successful. When we met our guide, to whom I shall give the name Hans Hosli, he was

47

shocked to see us wearing light tennis sneakers. He was a short, round man with a toothy grin, who explained that he spoke English "only a little much," which as it turned out was a hyperbolism. Since I spoke the local dialect and Andreas could interpret for Doyle, I anticipated no problems.

Herr Hosli expressed dismay also at Doyle's three bags of photography equipment. Carrying those, he said, would lengthen the steep ascent by two hours. In a hurried conference it was decided we would engage a jeep to take us as far as it could travel, about two-thirds of the way, and finish the rest on foot. After several phone calls a jeep and driver were engaged in the village of Engi, about five miles down the valley. Herr Hosli warned, somewhat ominously, that "on the alp there are no hotels" and he suggested we might wish to make both the ascent and descent on the same day. This would hardly be the experience I was anticipating and I insisted we spend one night on the alp sleeping with herdsmen in the hay. Herr Hosli looked at Doyle and his face was troubled.

We agreed to meet at four that afternoon, the earliest hour the jeep was available. Andreas and I went shopping for provisions, some dried meats, bread, pastries, and fruit. I bought a bottle of Scotch.

When we met, Herr Hosli had changed to corduroy knickers, boots, and a huge rucksack stuffed with food. With him was his son, a plump ten-year old edition of himself who, the father explained, was making his first trip into an alp. We met our driver, Samuel Marti, an uncommunicative youth of eighteen who was the son of the jeep's owner. He surveyed his cargo—six men and considerable gear—with apprehension. The jeep was old, he said, a World War II veteran.

We began our ascent through pine forests against a stream tumbling down a series of waterfalls. The crawl up a 35 degree incline at three miles an hour was at the same speed a man might walk. The jeep exhaled smoke and became uncomfortably hot. After an hour we passed the first *Staffel,* a name given a cluster of huts and sheds at which cattle are grazed for a fortnight in the spring ascent and again in the September descent. The trail disappeared completely and we continued to chug precariously over rocks and tree roots. The forest loam was slippery and several times we skidded. The calves of my legs ached from bracing against the jeep floor.

At an altitude of 5,000 feet we arrived at a flat spot where the jeep was able to turn around. We arranged with the driver to fetch us there the next afternoon and we continued on foot up into an open meadow carpeted with gentians. Although it was dark in the valleys below, the sun still shone on the heights. I had difficulty keeping to the measured slow pace of our Swiss companions and moved ahead. Soon I tired and felt dizzy. Doyle and Andreas were panting under their loads of equipment. No one had breath to talk. We followed a multicurved footpath, trudging over one summit after another and after an hour we were relieved to see a barn ahead. A herd of cows was waiting to be milked and there were people about. Women were sitting on benches in the evening sun, gossiping, showing ill-fitting pink dentures. A horse stood among the cows. Neither beasts nor people seemed to be aware of our arrival; there were no greetings. Doyle began scurrying about making photographs and no one paid attention. Herr Hosli appeared at a loss as to what to do. We had been assured by the officials below that it was a tradition in the alps to offer visitors hospitality. There was only one building, half of which was filled with cattle stalls and the other half by a cheese factory in which kettles of milk were cooking. In the shadows I saw a boy on a stool turning a wooden butter churn. Mud and muck were knee deep and the smells of manure and the cooking milk sickened me. We sat on the ground a short distance away and watched three shirtless young men milking cows. Two appeared to be brothers; they had the same short legs, brawny brown shoulders and chests, the same curly brown hair and beards. The third, whose black hair was sleeked, looked like a Spaniard. All three had a one-legged milk stool strapped to their rumps and when they carried the buckets of milk to the kettles, obscenely waggling the wooden legs behind them, they looked like lewd actors in a Greek comedy with grotesquely misplaced phalluses. All smoked long curved pipes with filigreed metal caps.

A herd of goats arrived, filling the evening with braying and the tinkling of bells. In their anxiety to be milked they almost climbed into our laps. Finally Herr Hosli mustered courage to speak to one of the milkers, to ask him for room to sleep. The man replied that all the space was filled, that the women on the benches were sojourners like ourselves and there was no more room in the stable.

My heart sank. The sun was setting, the air was turning cold and the gnats were ravenous. In desperation I began a conversation with a stout woman I judged to be the matriarch of the establishment. She told me she was Frau Landolt, a widow, and that the two look-alike milkers were her sons, Willie, twenty nine, and Fritz, twenty six. Neither was married; they were, she said, still too young for that. The third milkman was a hired hand, Hans Hofer. The Landolts had 47 cows and ten goats that produced 400 liters of milk each day all of which was made into cheeses. The residue whey was fed to a herd of pigs behind the barn and the ripened cheeses were pulled down the mountain by the horse on a self-braking sled.

I returned the conversation to the urgency of our dilemma. The widow said there was another *Staffel,* a quarter-hour farther on the path, where we might find room. The farmer who managed it, she said, was Jakob Kubli of Elm. I could hardly believe what she was saying, for the man of whom she spoke was a cousin I had never met.

As we were leaving I passed Hans Hofer laving himself with soap in a tank and asked him how a young man adjusted to the summer solitude in the alps. "No problem at all," he replied. "It's a prime life." He spoke English which he had learned during three years traveling about Europe as a horseman in a circus. "It's never lonely," he said, interrupting his washing to let a heifer suck on his hand. "Animals are more trusting friends than men."

We set out, single file, behind Herr Hosli. Trudging through the dark and deepening chill, I thought of the curious group behind us, the sturdy women, probably spinsters, climbing the mountains for a pastoral weekend in the company of men who, nearly thirty, were too young to marry and preferred the society of animals. The men in their isolation seemed linked to another romantic myth of my childhood, the American cowboy, the solitary male in mystical fellowship with nature. Without horses to ride the Swiss were in a very real sense "cowboys."

We saw the flicker of a light ahead and walking toward it arrived, after a quarter hour, at two connected low-roofed buildings. It was ten o'clock. We looked through a door into a barn where a man and a boy were milking. In an adjoining room another boy was building a fire under a kettle of milk. The man, small with graying hair and a beard, got up from a stool and poured milk into a large metal container, which he then shifted to his back. Staggering under the weight of the bucket, which was curved to fit his body, he carried it to the kettle where, twisting from side to side without removing the container from his back, he emptied the steaming milk into the kettle. When he finished Herr Hosli spoke to him, explaining that I was a writer from America and that I was a cousin, also named Kubli.

"*Vo Amerika?*" Jakob Kubli looked at me from under the bucket as if he did not believe us. Without stopping work the two boys turned to listen. "*Herrgott!*" Jakob said. "For a relative from America we must make room." Then he apologized for not shaking my hand with his soiled one, and for not having time to talk and he returned to his milking.

Like silent gnomes the two boys never stopped working. They were dressed in muck-covered high-waisted breeches supported by suspenders, blue shirts, and rubber boots. I asked their names and their ages and the larger replied that he was Jakob, aged fifteen, and the smaller said he was Heiri, aged thirteen. I had guessed them about twelve and ten. Slow maturation, I remembered was a characteristic of alpine people. Jakob was fair with red hair standing out in all directions over a cherubic face set in an earnestly doleful expression. Heiri was dark with a lean face, an elfin smile, and extraordinary long black lashes. They shared a single feature, large, bright blue eyes, and both were handsome. The boys' polite good breeding contrasted with the demeanor of our guide's son, who, being larger and a village boy, showed his disdain.

It had turned freezingly cold and Heiri invited us to warm ourselves by the fire under the great copper kettle in which the milk cooked. The barn was divided into the milking area and a cheese factory in which there was a hot water heater, a cheese press containing four white, freshly made cheeses, and a rough plank dining table. Joining it was a cheese cooling room where food was stored. On the door of the cheese room I saw a printed form in outdated German, a bill of fare that read:

Alp Tariffs for Kanton Glarus

Raw milk ½ liter	40	pfennig
Raw milk per liter	60	pfennig
Cooked milk per liter	90	pfennig
Buttermilk per liter	30	pfennig
Cream unwhipped	50	pfennig

Butter 100 gram	1 franc
Cheese 100 gram	50 pfennig
*Fenz one person without bread	3.50 francs
Fenz for extra person without bread	3.00 francs
Bread 100 grams	30 pfennig
Night's lodging in hay without quilt	1.20 francs
Night's lodging in hay with quilt	2.00 francs

The blended odors of steaming manure and hot milk were nauseating. To subdue my stomach I went outdoors to breathe fresh air. Doyle followed, complaining that he could not bear it and would not spend the night there. I reminded him that it was almost eleven o'clock and no alternative existed. Our dilemma, he said, was my fault. If I had told him of the conditions he would never have come. Muttering, he returned to the barn.

Above the encircling mountain peaks the sky was filled with stars but below in the valley the night was black as pitch and filled with strangely disquieting rustlings, the sighings of cows and grunting of pigs, the whinnying of a horse. Through a door in the second building, which was joined to the first by a common wall, I saw a pale lantern illuminating an operation separated from, but similar to, Jakob Kubli's.

The bitter cold drove me indoors. I found my group seated around the table, huddled in pullovers, raincoats, and caps, trying to keep warm. Andreas had suggested that perhaps if we smoked we would be less aware of the offending stench and he and Doyle were puffing wildly on cigarettes, filling the barn with smoke. Jakob and his sons, their sleeves rolled up, were washing their faces and hands in a kettle of warm whey. Under their opened shirts they were wearing long-john underwear. When they finished, Heiri began cooking a pan of milk and young Jakob whittled some sticks into kindling, preparing them to light the morning fires. I asked him about the adjoining barn and he replied that it was rented by a farmer named Weber and that each unit maintained forty cows and a herd of pigs.

Two strangers appeared suddenly out of the night and silently took

---

*Fenz, an alpine staple, is curdled milk, sweetened and cooked to a custard. A pfennig, or Swiss cent, was at that time worth approximately one-fourth of an American cent.

places at the table. One, about fifty, had a grizzly beard and walnut-colored skin and he wore a gold earring in each pierced ear. His name was Heinrich Hefti and he was a hired man who assisted with the cattle and cheese making. The second was younger, perhaps twenty-five, and had a lean weathered face and thick black curls. He was named Jakob Rhyner and he was a herdsman who spent his days on still higher slopes, tending young cattle.

I brought out my whiskey and passed it around. Rhyner took a long draught, sighed and said, "That's crazy good American whiskey." I replied that it was from Scotland and passed the bottle to Hefti who took a gulp, swished it about in his mouth and swallowed. "*Herrgott,* those Scotsmen are devils," he said. I offered it a second time to Rhyner and he said, "First I'm going to have to breathe a little." Jakob returned from feeding the pigs and I offered the bottle to him. He tasted it cautiously and said, "That's goddamned strong! Is it Indian firewater?" The two boys carried bowls of the cooked milk to the table, one for each of us. Andreas and I spooned the milk, which tasted warm and fresh. Doyle refused his and commenced a speech about the lack of sanitation. Andreas offered him some coffee cake and he asked, "Did we bring that or did they make it here?" The two boys, who could not understand what Doyle was saying, watched him curiously. The rest of us, huddled in overcoats, slurping milk in the pale lamp light, casting eerie shadows, were hardly characters from *Heidi.* We were like peasants in a Russian novel.

Since Jakob and his sons and the hired men did not eat with us I assumed they had eaten earlier. Then, when I saw the boys watching, I realized they were waiting for us to finish the milk so they could use the bowls and spoons for their own supper. Andreas and I put aside our spoons and sucked the milk from the bowls like Chinese drinking tea. Doyle, who hadn't touched his, went on about the lack of hygiene, and the Kublis and their hired men looked at him in bewilderment. Herr Hosli, on the other hand, seemed awed by Doyle and, whether from fear or respect, was nodding agreement to whatever Doyle said. Clearly our guide considered him the captain of the expedition. I guessed that the cameras had much to do with this, that Herr Hosli hoped Doyle would photograph him and his son. In comparison, my own pad and pencils were no credentials at all.

Rhyner, the herdsman, was boiling a kettle of macaroni in milk and into this he carefully sliced two large onions. We unpacked the bologna, bread, and fruit we had brought. I gave some of the meat and two pears to the Kubli boys and they thanked me politely and ran off with the food like hoarding squirrels. Herr Hosli and his son were unpacking a rucksack filled with meats, bread, and cheeses, which seemed like carrying coals to Newcastle but the guide explained that, "Some people don't like fresh cheese."

There was a muffle of voices. The door opened and the light shone on a cluster of faces, three men's and three women's. One of the men asked for sleeping accommodations and Jakob replied that his loft was filled but that the adjoining loft, the one belonging to Weber, had space. The man nodded and led his party, single file, up a ladder through the ceiling to the loft. One of the women appeared startlingly old to have climbed the mountain. I asked Heiri if he liked visitors and he shrugged and replied, "Well, some. There are different kinds." Politely he added, "Not all are as interesting as you." The two boys dipped the whey from the cheese kettle and carried it out; in a moment I could hear the pigs splashing and oinking. When the boys returned they washed and scrubbed the cheese kettle and stirrers and hung the paddles to dry.

At the table the whiskey bottle was being passed a third time, and I observed it was two-thirds empty. The whiskey was helping me forget the odors and everyone was beginning to talk. Herr Hosli was giggling merrily and his son was doing the same without whiskey. Jakob brought a transistor radio from the barn and hung it on a nail. It was loudly tuned to a waltz that filled the room with a bizarrely festive mood. Then Jakob pumped pressure into the lamp and the flame heightened, lighting the laughing faces as in a painting by LaTour. I was watching Heiri take the new cheeses from their molds and wrap them carefully in salt-soaked cloths. They were soft and sagging and shone like flat pale moons. I asked him how many hours a day he worked and he replied, "From half-past four in the morning until eleven at night.

"That doesn't leave much time for play," I said and he laughed as if I'd made a joke. "Who needs to play?" he replied.

A fat youth with a thatch of black hair and a wispy beard entered from outside, and behind him came a younger, slender boy with a soft smooth face. The fat one was Jean Pierre, nineteen, cheese maker in the Weber complex next door. The other was Weber's son Sepp who was seventeen but appeared younger. "They have never tasted whiskey," Rhyner said, passing them the bottle. The older boy took a deep gulp and began to cough. The younger swallowed hard and blinked back tears. "That will make the hair and beard grow," Rhyner said and the men roared.

Jakob ladeled milk into the same bowls that we had used; Rhyner set the kettle of macaroni on the table and the boys brought bread and cheese and then father, sons, and hired men took places around the table and commenced their meal, spooning macaroni from the common kettle. Doyle began taking photographs, moving dishes and food, creating a pandemonium during which the men and boys continued, with dignity, to eat.

When the meal was finished the boys rinsed the bowls and spoons. Everyone was talking and laughing, even the boys who had taken no whiskey seemed drunk by osmosis. Men and boys were slipping outside to prepare themselves for the night, to piss. Andreas and I went out together. The night pealed with cowbells; the heavens glittered with stars and it was bitterly cold. I told Andreas that I was curious about Hefti's earrings, and he said, "Don't ask about them. They don't want you to pry; they don't like you too close."

When we returned the men were climbing single file, behind the boys, up the ladder into the loft. I followed Andreas, and Jakob, who was waiting, came behind me with the lamp. A railing divided the lofts of the two barns, each about fifteen- by eight-feet square. The Weber area was packed with the sleeping bodies of herdsmen and the six night guests. Matted hay and some old, ragged, and very malodorous quilts covered the floor of the Kubli loft. Jakob indicated a place for our party near the railing. He and his sons settled by the outside wall and the hired men in between. The arrangement was about what I expected but Doyle was shocked. He could not, he insisted, spend the night in such a smelly sty. Then he began moving about with a camera, hurdling bodies, taking photographs. The two boys commenced to giggle. The Kubli men were putting on more clothes, bundling themselves in thicknesses of sweaters and shawls. I was wearing two pullovers, a raincoat, and a beret pulled down over my ears. Determined to sleep, I took two Nembutals with the final slug of Scotch, and squeezed between Andreas and Herr Hosli. Men and boys were as cozily curled as a box of cats—one could not move without creating a chain reaction and disturbing everyone in the loft. The hay, which smelled foul, got into my clothes. I was appalled to see that Jakob, Hefti, and Rhyner were lying in the hay still smoking their pipes. Comprehending my apprehension Jakob said, "That's why pipes have covers. There's no danger. I smoke myself to sleep and in the morning the pipe is lying beside me." I was not entirely assured. "My damned pipe won't go out," Rhyner said and the boys laughed wildly. It was the last thing I heard.

Sometime in the night I seemed to hear a voice shouting in Swiss, "Let them out! Let them out!" But I was not certain whether it was a real voice or a voice in a dream. I was awakened by the harsh skirl of an alarm. The loft was filled with sunlight and only four of us were there in the hay, the two boys curled into one another like Geminis, Rhyner, and myself. Rhyner turned off the clock beside him and groaned. "Now the whole calamity begins again," he said. The two boys threw off their wrappings and followed Rhyner down the ladder, leaving me alone in the loft. I looked at my watch and discovered it was 4:45 A.M. I heard bells and voices outside. The hay in my clothes was causing me to itch. When I descended the ladder Heiri was building a fire, and his brother was helping Jakob and Hefti carry buckets of milk from the barn to the cheese kettles. Jakob asked how I'd slept and whether I'd heard shouting. When I replied that I had, he laughed and said, "It's the older boy. He dreams of herding cows and he yells to them in his dreams."

Outside the sun was a red ball glowing through a lattice of peaks, filling the morning with dazzling pink light. Rhyner was washing at a trough. He pointed to a plateau between two peaks and said it was up there that he spent his days herding 120 young cattle. The taller mountain, called the Magerau, was the boundary between cantons Glarus and St. Gall and from it he could look across Lake Constance into Germany.

I took my toothbrush from my pocket and began brushing my teeth over the trough. Rhyner watched closely as if he thought it a curious thing to be doing. When I finished he went inside. I looked around me. The connected barns built of native gray stone followed the contour of the mountain, their upper ends disappearing into the mountain wall, so that winter avalanches might roll over them without damage. Toilets, I'd discovered the night before, were wherever on the mountain one found privacy. Wandering off I was cheered by thoughts of Heidi in the same situation.

Returning, I met Rhyner who was setting out for the heights. He pointed to the rising sun and said, "I go up there where the sun is." Softly whistling "Lili Marlene," he stalked upward, as if the boots on his long legs were seven-leaguers. He wore a large-brimmed fur hat at a rakish angle and about his lean waist a wide belt with a grand metal buckle. He carried a long curved crook and on his back was a rucksack of untanned red cowhide containing food and a pair of field glasses. Striding up the slopes into the blinding glare, he seemed turned into a silhouette of Hermes, the pastoral son of Zeus and protector of cattle, also the wearer of a broad-brimmed hat and carrier of a staff. When he reached a small plateau he turned around and waved. Then, as if leaping off the earth, he disappeared over a ledge.

I went inside the barn where the two boys were preparing breakfast. They had resumed their reserved shyness. In the cooling room Heiri showed me some day-old cheeses which were hardening. On the shelves were chunks of fresh butter, a supply of bread, salamis, and dried meats. Stashed away on one side I saw the bologna, coffee cake, and fruit that we had given him and his brother the night before. They were saving them, Heiri said, for their Sunday dinner.

At this moment Doyle appeared from the stables and ordered me to move out of range of his camera. I crossed the room but this failed to satisfy him. My conversation was distracting, he said; he was unable to work in my presence. His anger expanded; he commenced shouting his greatness as an artist, saying, "When I make a photo I am God! That moment when I click the shutter is my moment of truth." I replied that since he had already made more than two hundred pictures I could see that such a rapid succession of truth moments might be a strain. The Swiss listened to this incomprehensible exchange with consternation. Andreas followed me outside and explained that Doyle had had a bad night. Unable to sleep, Andreas and Doyle had wandered for three hours in the cold.

It was seven o'clock. The sun was warm and I shed some of my layers of clothing. Andreas and I followed a path through a meadow filled with blue Canterbury bells called *Fingerhut,* or "thimbles," and maroon and yellow gentians, from the roots of which a liqueur called Enzian is made. I heard a chirping and looked for a bird. Andreas said it was not a bird singing but a *Murmeltier,* or marmot, a small, toothy, herbacious animal. To see one was a rare event and Andreas searched the slopes with his field glasses. He found two, standing upright like woodchucks, chattering to one another.

Back at the barns a new group of visitors had arrived. Two of the men, first cousins named Fritz Blumer and Hans Hammerli, asked if I knew an uncle who had emigrated to Wisconsin in 1907. The old man, still living near New Glarus, was a friend of my father's.

Inside, Heiri was laying breakfast. We drank *Gepsa* which was coffee and hot milk in equal portions and ate bread and cheese, and a dried sausage called *Landjäger.* Two hundred liters of milk were cooking in the kettle into which Jakob was carefully measuring ten grams of rennet. He explained that the milk would cook for thirty-five minutes then it would be stirred into curds. I was growing accustomed to the coalescing odors of manure, milk, and cheese and decided it was because I was commencing to smell the same way myself.

While we were eating a boy arrived, breathless from running down the mountain, to report a sick calf in Rhyner's herd. A rescue party was organized and I volunteered. I walked with Hans Hammerli, who told me he had danced all night at a wedding down in Engi and then, without sleep, had climbed up the mountain in early dawn. He was fifty years old. We passed ruins of barns crushed by avalanches and followed a stream, walking sometimes in its bed. We heard echoed shouts and fragments of yodeling. Sunday alpinists seemed to be everywhere. We climbed for an hour, ascending 2,000 feet. The air grew thinner and breathing became strenuous. We paused frequently. Finally we came to a herd of heifers. Rhyner was nowhere in sight. After a half-hour of searching I discovered him in a crevice on the highest pinnacle, asleep in a thicket of alpine roses. The sun shone on him; his head was pillowed on his rucksack, the rakish hat covered his face. He was no longer Hermes, but young Jacob of the Bible, dreaming of a ladder into Paradise.

I had to prod him three times with his staff to awaken him. He gazed at me for a moment, muttered something, then leaped up and strode off to direct the rescuers. I was exhausted. My ankles were sore; my lungs ached. The other volunteers followed Rhyner, leaving me alone. I sat down to rest. I seemed to be in the lair of an animal. Bits of bread lay about and peels of sausages like the abandoned skins of snakes glistened in the sun. The world was far below.

The strange young man and the burrow that I had invaded were arousing in me a primal response, a mysterious recognition. How natural, I thought, in such a lofty place to imagine one's godliness, to believe oneself a changling of the ancients, the offspring of a god's coupling with mortals, the foaling of a divine heifer sired by Zeus. Of what, I longed to know, did such a one think during his long hours in his aerie, what dreams did he dream with only the tinkle of bells, the whistling wind, and insects buzzing in the flowers to distract him?

The sun was warm, the swell of bells merged into a single lullaby and before I knew it I had fallen asleep in the place where he had slept, in the bower of roses.

I was awakened by Hammerli who reported the calf rescued. It had been tethered and was being carried down to the barn. Peering over Hammerli's shoulder was the lean dark face of Rhyner. "One sleeps as well here as in heaven," he said.

"Yes, as on Olympus," I replied. I got up and Rhyner fell back into the bed I abandoned and he prepared to return to sleep. On a jagged crest of gray peaks to the north I saw the silhouette of a single file of moving cows and I remembered how Hermes stole the cows of his sleeping elder brother, Apollo, and that he was known also as a conductor of souls.

I could not put the herdsman from my mind and as we walked down the mountain I asked Hammerli about him. He was, said Hammerli, a "*Halbstarke.*" The word, translating into "half-strong," referred in Switzerland to wild and impulsive youths. "He is the youngest child of a respected family," Hammerli said. "He has had many troubles and was sent into the mountains to be away from temptations. He seems to have found something here. Perhaps he is happy." I asked how much Rhyner might be paid for his summer of solitude and Hammerli said, "Perhaps a hundred francs a month and his food—milk, bread, cheese, and occasionally some meat." One hundred francs was less than twenty-five dollars.

Suddenly Hammerli stopped and raised his binoculars toward a distant ledge. He handed me the glasses and urged me to look. Poised on a summit, brought close by the lenses so that I could see it watching us, was a chamois. With its front hooves poised on a rock it appeared exactly like the chamois on the coat of arms on the signet ring I was wearing. I felt a stirring of emotion and I heard Hammerli say that to see a chamois was a rare event, the culmination of an alpine excursion.

Down in the barns they were waiting for me. Doyle, anxious to leave, was in a temper over the delay I had caused. I reminded him that our appointment with the jeep was not until four o'clock, and added that Heidi had spent an entire summer on her alp.

"Fuck Heidi!" Doyle retorted. Andreas broke into laughter and Jakob asked what Doyle had said. I improvised a translation and added that Doyle was not feeling well. "It is not unusual," said Jakob. "Many women have headaches from the mountain air."

It was Sunday noon and for the Kublis the beginning of their week's half holiday. The cheeses were made and Heiri carried the whey to the pigs which grunted happily. The two Jakobs, father and son, were cooking the Sunday meal, preparing in our honor the alpine specialty *Fenz*. The boiled pudding of cream, flour, sugar, and salt was cooked, as usual, in a common pot from which everyone ate with a spoon. I found the *Fenz* palatable in taste but gagged on its slimy consistency and ate it with bread to give it texture. There was also boiled bologna and finally black coffee mixed with what Jakob called "our whiskey," an apple schnapps called *Trester*. The Sunday treat was ladeled with spoons like soup.

At leisure for the first time since our arrival, Jakob was eager to talk. He told me he did not own the grazing slopes and barn but rented them from the commune of Engi, that the factory was a cooperative of which he was manager. Only eight of the forty cows were his; the others were on loan from other valley farmers. The milk from each cow was measured daily and he, as caretaker, was entitled to 180 francs' worth of milk from each cow for the summer. All milk in excess of 180 francs' worth, he purchased from the cattle owners, so that actually all the milk produced on the alp became his. A season on the alp was sixteen weeks. The descent, which would take a month with two fortnight stops along the way, was scheduled to begin on the eighth of September. Heiri, the younger boy, would have to return earlier to begin school and this had him in despair.

It was time to meet the jeep. After three coffee-schnapps each, everyone was feeling slightly drunk and farewells were merry. Having accepted me as family, Jakob urged me to return and I promised I would. He pointed to a small, primitive hut in a ravine a short distance below the barn which he said belonged to a man in Engi who did not use it. He would arrange for me to live in it, Jakob said. I would eat with him and his sons and we would have a jolly summer. Winking suggestively, he added that it would be nice for me to have a *Freundin*—a female friend—in the hut. "*Da chamae guet usruobae,*" he said. One could rest well. In parting, Jakob asked me to take his greetings to his wife and mother in Elm and I agreed to it.

We descended by a different path, following a stream, walking sometimes in its bed through sunlit meadows, never separated from the tinkling of bells nor the sound of running water. In an hour we arrived at the place where the jeep was waiting.

7

Kubli Rooms

After the night on the alp my first priority was a bath. Hay chaff filled my clothes and hair and I smelled like a goat. I planned to spend a night in Elm and asked Herr Hosli if he would arrange a room with bath in one of the three hotels listed in my guidebook. He was unusually long at the telephone in Engi and when he returned he looked perplexed. There were, he reported, no baths in Elm's hotels.

How, I asked, had Queen Wilhelmina of Holland managed on a visit to Elm? Herr Hosli said he did not know but added that he had arranged a "private" bath for me in the only bathroom in the village. This was in the home of an architect whose name was Kaspar Rhyner. His house was next door to the hotel where a room was reserved for me.

An hour later I was knocking on the door of the Rhyner house, which appeared to be new, The door was opened by Herr Rhyner himself, who had arranged to be home for the unprecedented event. He was a burly, handsome young man with merry gray-flecked hazel eyes and a winning smile. He introduced his pretty wife, Pia, and a small boy named Hansjörg, and without further ceremony showed me to the bathroom where a tub of hot water was waiting. When I finished undressing the tile floor was strewn with hay. I soaked luxuriously for an hour, washing away not only chaff and odors but also the kinks from muscles and joints. When I emerged, restored in clean underwear and shirt, my host was waiting in the living room with a pitcher of iced martinis. "I thought you might also need an internal wash," he said.

"I don't believe it," I said. A martini was the one thing next to a bath I needed most, but the idea that anyone might have heard of a martini in a village without bathrooms hadn't occurred to me.

"I have lived in Zurich," Rhyner said. "There I became addicted to the more decadent luxuries, like baths and martinis." The gin was Beefeater, the vermouth sparingly measured, and the mixture wondrously soothing. Engrossed, both of us, in the exhilarating experience of making a new friend, we drank and talked for two hours, plunging pell-mell through free-association accounts of ourselves. He told me he was the eldest of a factory worker's five children; that when he was eighteen he went to Zurich to study architecture at the Federal Technology Institute. By working days as a stonemason and attending classes at night he completed his degree in six years. For another six years he had worked with a Zurich construction firm. "But I always knew I would return to Elm," he said. "I never considered anything else." The influences of his city life were everywhere about us. Fine paintings hung on the walls; there were shelves of books, bowls of flowers, a well-stocked liquor cabinet. There was also Pia, a self-effacing Swiss wife, hovering about, leaving the pleasures of conversation to the men.

He was called "Chap"—pronounced *Kop*—the Glaronese form of "Kap," a shortening of Kaspar, the most popular Christian name in the Rhyner clan. In Elm there were thirty-two Kaspar Rhyners and on New Year's Eve there had been a "Kap Rhyner party" with only bearers of the name present. They ranged from small boys to grandfathers, with as many as three from a single family. To differentiate between themselves each Kap Rhyner had his village designation, some of which were *Hinderhaus-Kap, Klepberg-Kap* and *Gerstboden-Kap,* named for regions in which they lived; *Sager-Kap,* who operated a sawmill, and *Habamine-Kap,* whose mother was a midwife. My host's village name was *Baumeister-Kap,* which translated into Building Master Kap.

"We Elmers are not especially imaginative," said Kap. "We prefer the familiar. A peculiar thing since the one condition we cannot endure is anonymity."

"I can't believe anonymity was ever a problem for you," I said.

He laughed. "In Zurich I was one of a half-million people. In Elm we are nine hundred and each is recognized for what he is. Of course there are disadvantages in that. In Zurich when you get drunk you sleep it off and that's the end of it. In Elm everyone knows; it turns into a community crisis. Perhaps even that is a good thing. We have no police, no law-enforcing officer. We handle such things our own way. We take drunks home. If someone's goat crosses a neighbor's fence we see that the argument is settled. So far as anyone can remember there has never been a crime in Elm. Perhaps that's what life here is about. We have our need to trust, our need to be trusted."

"Still a young man in his time of growth needs to leave, to evaluate the world, to explore his options," I said, justifying my own experience.

"Yes, of course," Kap said. "In my youth I heard it was better in the city. That you worked only eight hours, five days a week, and earned more. I lived in Zurich for twelve years. I worked in a firm and I married and I learned that all they said was true. You *don't* work as hard; you have the good things, like operas and concerts and the theater. I learned how to meet people, to influence them. But being a member of a firm I could not be myself; my individuality was not permitted. When I learned of an opportunity in Elm I came home."

The opportunity that brought him back was the expansion of the soft-drink factory in which his father was a laborer. The factory was built over mineral springs and produced *Elmer Citro,* Switzerland's most popular nonalcoholic beverage. Except for a local dairy and the home production of cheese it was the only industry in Elm. Some workers commuted by trolley to factories down in the highly industrialized Glarus valley. Up in Elm, a rural dairying culture was zealously preserved.

"In Elm we have two hundred families and a hundred and fifty of them work on land," Kap boasted. "Our farmers are sly foxes. They are prosperous but keep their prosperity a secret. Jakob, whom you met on the alp, is one of the richest. He owns much land and at least twenty cows. Elmer cattle are famous all over the world. A cow is worth four thousand francs, a bull six thousand. In Elm we have only ten automobiles, but there are many jeeps and tractors which the farmers buy with government subsidies."

I spoke of visiting villages in the Valais and Graubünden where only old people lived, villages which were dying because the young people were leaving.

"That is true elsewhere but not in Elm," said Kap. "To be from Elm is to never leave it. Families stay together. My brother, Hans, is in Zurich now, following my course, studying architecture. But he is homesick and cannot wait to return." I reminded Kap of the first Jakob Kubli family in which five of six children had left Elm after their parents' deaths. "Yes," he said, "that was a sad case; the circumstances were unusual. The family was very poor and when the parents died there was nothing for the children here. They had to go to the city to earn their living. Such cases are not ordinary. Less than ten percent of Elm's young people leave their homes; the rate is probably the lowest in Switzerland."

He poured the last of the martinis. "It is the way we are, like trees with roots that never quite adapt to unfamiliar soil." Drinking, laughing softly, he said, "And here *you* are! An Elmer back after a hundred and fifteen years!"

He intended a joke, and more than a joke. I was aware of truth in what he was saying. The roots of which he was speaking were also a womb to which one never ceased longing to return. To this I was a witness. After twenty years sojourning in the cities of the world, I looked forward to returning to the Wisconsin farm on which I was born.

Talking with Kap was an eerie experience, a growing recognition of something not at once clear. The ease with which we entered into an almost filial familiarity was extraordinary. Part of it was due to the language we spoke, but it was more than that, it was an easy understanding of one another, an intuitive response which I was trying to explain to myself, to which Dr. Jung had given the name "blood memory." I was feeling a kinship, a sense of arriving home, a bond not only with Elm but with my host. I wondered if we might be related.

"There's little doubt of it," Kap said. "Through a grandmother I'm related to the Elmers and I've heard of a Kubli in my father's family. In a village as incestuous as Elm it's inevitable. It will not be difficult to trace."

In the evening, after supper in the hotel, I walked up through the village to Jakob Kubli's home. It was an old two-story farmhouse set neatly in a field some distance from the road. I introduced myself to Jakob's wife, a tidy, pink-faced woman in her forties whose family name was Elmer; his sprightly seventy-seven-year-old mother; and his eldest son, Rudi, a tense, bespectacled, immature youth of sixteen. Shy and wary, they warmed when I told them I had been on the alp with Jakob and his younger sons. "How are they?" the old lady asked in a high, skirling voice. "Why didn't Heiri come back with you? Doesn't he remember school starts in a week?" The questions were those she might have asked of someone gone a long time on a distant journey. "You know why they like it up there?" she shrilled. "Because there are no women, because there's no way for us to get there and they won't come home until they have to."

We were in a low-ceilinged, dark-paneled parlor filled with portraits of dead ancestors, ticking clocks, and a variety of well-thumbed magazines. "How did you come; did you fly in a jet?" the old lady asked. I replied I had flown from Chicago to Zurich in nine hours.

"*Herrgott!*" she exclaimed, laughing merrily. "I suppose for you that is nothing at all; I suppose one day you will be going to the moon." I replied I had no such plans. "Neither do I," she cackled. "We're not accustomed to flying like birds. I went to Zurich once to visit my daughter. What a confusion! All the people in the station frightened me and I never went again. God put me here in Elm and that's where He intended me to stay." At the same time that the grandmother firmly asserted her disapproval, I sensed her considerable curiosity in what she was rejecting and even pride that I, a relative present in her house, had experienced it.

"What did you have to eat on the jet?" she asked. "Did you sleep in a bed?" I slept in a chair, I replied, and I watched a film.

"A film!" The old lady's voice rose with excitement. "Do they have theaters on a jet?" I began to explain how films were shown on planes but she did not listen. "Films are wicked; they corrupt young people," she cried. "No one in my family has ever seen one."

"Besides," said her daughter-in-law, rubbing two fingers together, "films take *Rappen!*"

"Not *Rappen,*" shrilled the grandmother. "*Francs!*"

I noticed the youth, Rudi, listening with interest and I said, "Perhaps one day you will fly in a jet."

Grandmother shook her head. "No," she said firmly. "He will not."

Rudi appeared startled by the idea. "I don't think so," he said. "I will never leave Elm." He had been as far as the town of Glarus, fourteen miles down the valley, once to be fitted for eyeglasses, and a second time when he cut his leg with a scythe and had to be taken to the hospital to have the wound stitched. "It is not a good thing to leave the cows," he said.

Dark clouds were rolling in over the mountains; a storm was gathering. I walked down to a cafe called The Sun to meet Kap and Pia Rhyner. With them was Kap's sister, Barbara, a tall, dark-haired, handsome girl who had worked as a secretary in England and America. In the ambience of Elm her perfect Oxford English seemed almost comic. Though she had enjoyed life in the United States, she told me, she had never ceased being homesick for Elm and her happiest American experience had been a visit to New Glarus where she could hear the Elm dialect.

Kap introduced another Kap Rhyner, one known as *Maurer Ueli's Kap,* indicating that he was the son of a stonemason named Ueli. I remarked on the number of Rhyners in the town; how they outnumbered by far the once dominant Elmers. "It is true," said Kap. "The Elmers and the Kublis were enterprising; they emigrated. The Rhyners were too lazy to do anything but stay home and breed like rabbits."

The cafe was filled with young people, some of whom were dancing to Louis Armstrong playing "That Old Feeling" on the jukebox. "Elm is the Broadway of the canton," said Kap, taking in the cafe with a sweep of his hand. "Young people come from down the valley because this is the jolliest place they know. In Elm we don't believe enjoying life is a sin." I wondered if he were joking and told him of the Kubli family's attitude on motion pictures. "Ah, yes," he said, rolling his eyes. "Films are tools of the devil. The minister preaches about them and he's convinced the old people it's true. Some of the young people sneak down the valley to films but I'm sure more than seventy-five percent of our people have never seen one."*

Outside it was lightning and the thunder rolled. A man came up and told Kap that a fifty-year-old Zurich spinster, who had set off by herself for a Sunday hike into the mountains, had not returned and was believed lost. Kap excused himself to join the rescue party.

The storm raged through most of the night. Haunted by thoughts of the lost woman, I slept badly. I thought of Kap seeking out familiar abysses and crags, sure-footed in the tumultous landscape, and I was certain the woman would be saved. Suddenly, in a sleepless flash of recognition, a mysterious permeation which had been haunting me became clear. The complexities of Kap's personality, the warm humanity, the bold thrusts of his mind and the mercurial shifts of mood from humor to sentiment, to compassion and indignation, were uncannily like my father's. Even physically, in the strong square face, the mood-flashing eyes, and the commanding voice, the resemblance was striking.

In the morning Kap came to tell me that the woman had been found and brought down with a tractor. I told him that I had been confident she would be rescued because my father, in whose omniscience I believed as a child, would also have found her. I spoke of my revelation in the night, how he had evoked the presence of my father.

He saw no mystery in it. "Of course," he said. "It is the Elmer character. We are a different species; we have our own demons and angels and they give us no rest."

"My father was born and died in Wisconsin. He never left America," I said.

"He stayed in the place that he knew," Kap replied. "He kept his faith with the earth that was his. It makes no difference where one goes. The Elmer blood does not change."

The people of Elm, persisting in their conviction that they are a race apart from other Swiss, believe that it was over the nearby Panixer pass that their ancestors arrived in the valley. Exactly who they were is not

---

*At the time television was not accessible in the valley. Today cable TV exists and most families have sets.

certain. One theory is that they were Roman descendants of Julius Caesar's armies. Another is that they were antipapal political refugees from northern Italy. One of the more interesting speculations is that they were a Balkan tribe, perhaps even Greek. Proponents of this theory offer as evidence such classical first names as Octavian, Appolonia, Euphemia, Balthaser, and Pancratius, popular in the valley but not in the rest of Switzerland. "There is no doubt that our blood is different," Kap said. "Our hearts are lighter; we are more life-loving than the heavy-hearted Germanic types in the valleys below." He laughed and said, "One sees it in you. You are of us. *Du bist un Elmer Loli!* You are an Elmer fool!"

So it began, one of the most inviolable, tempestuous, and enduring friendships of my life. Though Kap was fifteen years my junior the sense of my father's presence continued and it grew. Like my father he was provider and protector, custodian and guide, patron and tyrant. He was magisterial and comprehending, joyous and petulant, expansive and withdrawn, proud, and sometimes jealous. His language of spontaneous metaphors, bawdy colloquialisms, and earthy idioms was, to my unabating frustration, almost impossible to translate; a Zurich writer to whom I introduced Kap, called him an "oral poet."

One of Kap's favorite stories is about the bath that marked the beginning of our friendship. When the story was published in my book for *Life,* he wrote me that the people of Elm, shamed by the public revelation that they had no bathrooms, were moved to install them. The Jakob Kubli family was one of the first. On my last return Kap reported nine bathrooms in Elm. In another five years, he predicted, there would be more than twenty.

"The people call them 'Kubli rooms,'" he said.

8

NOTES FROM A
LOW VILLAGE

A journalist friend, Beat Hirt, offered an explanation for what I had felt to be an aloofness toward me. "It's a natural reaction to your professorship," he said. "In Switzerland it becomes more and more necessary for professional status to acquire a *Doktor* title. Bankers are doctors of *Nationaloekonomie*. But a 'professor' is something else and the Swiss intuitively place a wall between themselves and a professor. It is an attitude encouraged by Swiss academicians and few Swiss would presume familiarity with a professor."

In the Linthal, the large valley of Glarus, a factory worker, who had never slept away from his home at night, resolved during his fortnight vacation to see all of Switzerland. He bought a two-week railway pass and set out every morning in a new direction and returned home late each night. By the end of the fortnight he had seen all of his country and had slept each night in his own bed.

The clocks in church towers—the one in St. Peter's Church is said to be the largest clock in the world—are a constant Calvinist reminder of the passage of time, a warning not to waste a minute. The roosters on the steeples of Protestant churches, where Catholic churches mount a

cross, are also—roosters being morning crowers—sentinels of time.
Some say they represent the cock that crowed in Gethsemane reminding Christians not to betray Christ.

Modern scholars have assigned the national folk hero, Wilhelm Tell,
to mythology and agree that he never existed. His legend closely
resembles an ancient Danish saga about a hero named Toko who was
ordered by a tyrant king to shoot an apple off the head of his child. A
similar hero has been traced in the mythologies of several countries,
including Japan, in which shooting is popular. Sometimes it is an
orange that is shot off the child's head, and sometimes a coin.
    Belief in Tell is strongest in Uri, the canton where he is believed to
have lived, where shrines relating to his life and deeds are popular
tourist attractions. In the capital of the canton, Altdorf, there is a heroic
statue on the site where the apple-shooting is alleged to have taken
place. In Bürglen a chapel stands on the place where Tell is supposed to
have been born, and a museum is filled with Tell artifacts. A richly
frescoed Tell's Chapel is set on the shore of Lake Lucerne, where Tell
presumably escaped by springing from the boat that was taking him to
prison. A tablet marks the spot where he is believed to have ultimately
drowned while rescuing a child on the Reuss River. Schiller's play
celebrating Tell's part in the Swiss thirteenth-century revolt is performed every year in Altdorf, Interlaken, and in New Glarus, Wisconsin. In our time a controversy has developed over the morality of a
legend and play in which a political assassin hides in ambush to commit
his murder.

Rainer Maria Rilke, a solitary poet who sought isolation in the
mountains of the Valais, said of the Swiss: "What sort of an inner life
can take place in a mind which is germ-free and shadowlessly lighted
like an operating room?" Dr. Jung, I'm sure, would disagree. The Swiss
mind is plenty germy and full of shadows, though not of the type,
apparently, that Rilke had in mind.

I lost an inlay on a caramel and the jovial dentist thought it an
extraordinary event to have a patient from New Glarus. He told me
that Swiss teeth, especially in rural areas, are so bad that in some

villages it is the custom to give adolescents a set of false teeth as a confirmation present. A young man anticipating marriage may choose a bride who already has false teeth. As in buying a horse, the groom wants to make certain his wife will have a good bite and that he will avoid the expense of dentures.

Switzerland has the most newspapers per capita in the world and the Swiss are the most avid newspaper readers.

Joe and Mathilda Henley, two innocent Americans, took up root in Minneapolis upon Joe's retirement from business and settled in Glarus, where they do not speak the language. "It's the most perfect place to live in the world," Mathilda said. "The Glarners are the most friendly people we have ever known."

It seems a mysterious judgment. In a country known for its mute laconism, the Glarners are among the most taciturn of citizens. The Henleys were eager to explain:

"We had to get away," Henry said. "America used to be a great country but everything's changing for the worse. Here it is like America once was. There's respect for public property, for parks, and buildings."

"Even if we don't speak the language, we are always communicating by the universal language of love. Everyone is our friend. There's nothing they wouldn't do for us," Mathilda said.

"We don't understand a word in church but it's the only church I do not go to sleep in," Henry said, smiling.

"When our grandson visited he learned about responsibilities and he went home with a new set of values. He learned to care about people," Mathilda said.

"The people are teaching us to see things. Americans never even take time to look at their mountains," Henry said.

"A fool wonders and a wise man asks," Mathilda said. "I ask questions and everyone loves me for it. At the store the clerks show us what to buy."

"We're unwinding, taking a lot of walks. Everyone smiles at us," Henry said, smiling also.

"We went to a yodeling festival and they played their big horns and sailed their flags through the air. It was so beautiful I cried," Mathilda said.

"We must learn the language," Henry said firmly. "We want to be able to speak to these wonderful people . . ."

There is truth in what the Henleys say. The Swiss, in their loneliness, do extend themselves to strangers; they are courteous and friendly. But they need a defense against intimacy with which they cannot cope. In the case of the Henleys, the barrier of language is that defense. I hope the Henleys continue to see Glarners through the mists of innocence. I hope they never learn the language.

9

CONTRASTS

When I arrived in Switzerland Kap was somewhere in the Alps serving his annual military duty. One Saturday night he burst into my apartment in booming spirits and embraced me in a bear hug.

"I'm a bachelor!" he whooped. "Pia and the children are in Spain. I have one more week in the army and then you must come to Elm. I'll take a week off. We'll have a *Chilbi*." The term had the literal meaning of a religious festival, a rededication of the sanctuary, but like many Swiss words it had a corrupted designation, meaning a celebration, a blowout.

We celebrated that evening by going to the opera, a performance of *The Magic Flute*. The small baroque Zurich theater has the cozy intimacy of opera houses in Mozart's time, and a beautiful Greek soprano with a face like Nefertiti's sang Pamina. Afterward, in the opera cafe, Kap described his keen pleasure in military life. "The army's a liberation; for many Swiss, it's the happiest time of the year. You see old friends. You're free of the responsibilities of business and family. It's our annual escape." He spoke of another Rhyner from Elm, Heiri, a member of his company. A compulsive hunter, Heiri Rhyner had gone AWOL on the first day of the deer-hunting season and returned in the evening with his buck. "Now he is famous," said Kap. "A military hero."

75

Kap reviewed the events in his life since our last meeting. The founder of his construction firm had died and Kap had been made partner and manager; his brother, Hans, had returned from Zurich to be his assistant. He had ninety employees, including sixty-three Italians, twenty-five Swiss, and two Spaniards. He was engaged in a "valley Renaissance" which would include further expansion of Elm's soft-drink factory, a new military base, and a hotel with forty rooms, each with a bath. When it was finished Elm would have more bathrooms per capita than all of Canton Glarus. There were also plans for a ski resort and vacation condominiums.

Between the Vorab and the Hausstock was the notch of the Panixer Pass, below which Kap dreamed of tunneling an *autostrada* to Graubünden. The idea had polarized not only the people of Elm but also the politicians in Berne. Visionary parliamentarians, excited by the audacious dream, supported it, and conservatives, thinking of the cost, opposed it.

I did not believe that the highway would improve the quality of life in Elm. Still, I could not help being stirred by Kap's obsession, by the scope of his builder's imagination. It was not that the Panixer was impregnable, or even very difficult for experienced mountaineers. Maps showed a hiker's trail which probably followed the route of Russian General Suvarov's escape from Napoleon's troops in October 1799, an event which the people of Elm look upon as the village's single major participation in history. "Try to imagine it," Kap said. "The first great military crossing of the Alps since Hannibal. Cannon and artillery had to be abandoned; three thousand men were lost. But he made it!"

He was speaking of the exodus as if it were a victory, a triumph of conquest rather than the conclusion of a defeat.

The project to which Kap was currently giving his closest attention was the restoration of the two largest, most historic houses in Elm. One of them, the sixteenth-century Grosshaus—"large house"—in which my Elmer great-grandparents lived before departing for America, was being restored for a historical society. Kap was restoring the second, and grander *Suvarovhaus* as a residence for himself. The six-story manor was built in the seventeenth century, by a governor for his young wife, and was later named after the Russian General Suvarov who, in flight from Napoleon in 1799, billetted himself and his officers in it for two days. In this century the *Suvarovhaus* had fallen into moribund dilapidation and plans were made to tear it down to make space for a dairy cooperative. Instead, Kap had bought the property and, with the aid of a government grant, was returning it to its original elegance. Artists were restoring old frescoes and sculptors were replacing carved woodwork. "There will be an apartment in it for you," Kap said. "It will be your home in Elm."

Listening to him, something was becoming clear. The Suvarov legend had possessed his imagination. Like every citizen of Elm he had lived with it from the cradle. One of his favorite paintings, one that hung in the Elmer Hotel, portrays the Russian troops roasting their own horses for food before the Suvarov House. Now Kap was restoring the house, making it his own. Like a possessed Theseus, he dreamed of conquering the same mountain that Suvarov had conquered, of turning the general's Sisyphean journey into a swift and easy passage for all men. Quite certainly, his preoccupation with the Russian general was a force in his creative obsession, a center of his builder's passion.

The house in which he had lived, where I had had my bath, had been sold and Kap and his family were living temporarily in an apartment he had built over the village power plant. During the four months of deep winter, when paralyzing snows halted construction and his Italian workers went home to their families, Kap taught construction skills in a vocational school in Schwanden.

The dizzying report went on. I sensed a contradiction in it and wondered how he could reconcile the preservation of Elm's archaic pastoral rusticity with its transformation into a booming, prosperous tourist center. He saw no contradiction. Tourists, he said, would come to Elm precisely because it preserved old, classic Switzerland. Because he had in his own life reconciled the polar existences of urban and rural Switzerland, he believed that the Elmer character was strong enough to resist the worldly influences which tourists would bring. The renaissance was a creation of his imagination and energy and he was its patron-builder. I called him "Lorenzo of Elm" and he threw back his head and laughed.

A week later I took the train to Schwanden where Kap was waiting in the station, wearing his usual costume of knickers, pullover, and boots.

"The sun shines in Schwanden," he said. "It's a good omen." The village was known as the sinkhole of the canton because of heavy rains caused by a configuration of mountains; I remembered a depressing fortnight there in another season when the rains never ceased, when the river overflowed its banks and the streets were covered with slimy black snails. "We're going up the Linthal," he said. "I want to show you a secret Switzerland." He was taking me, he explained, to see the new Kraftwerke Linth, an underground power plant in the construction of which he had been a foreman. Hidden inside a mountain, impervious to attack, the plant was designed to provide power for a country in war.

Driving with a wild thrust, Kap started up the larger of the canton's two valleys along the Linth River. "Don't worry; I've never had an accident." Whirring over the narrow winding lane, the small Volvo seemed by a curious osmosis to be absorbing his energy which, like Kap, himself, it seemed hardly able to contain. Kap pointed to a square patch of snow on the peak of the massive Glarner alp, *Vrenelisqärtli,* and he told me the legend of its name.

"Vreneli was a proud, ambitious girl who decided to plant a garden on top of the Glarner," he began. "Everyone warned her against such foolishness but she was stubborn. She was caught in a great blizzard and she put a cheese kettle over her head to protect herself from the storm. The kettle piled over with snow and grew so heavy Vreneli could not get it off her head. She collapsed from the weight of it and died and was covered with snow. So the garden of snow is still there and never melts and the kettle is Vreneli's tombstone. If you look carefully you will see it." I saw the dark fleck in the white patch. "Serves her right, the silly girl," Kap concluded.

Little Verena's little garden! The language was like a mother's to a child, a kindergarten patois of diminuition in which everything was small. Yet it was the language men spoke to one another and I remembered a cabaret comic in Zurich satirizing it, saying, "I will sell my little milk from my little cow for some little francs to buy a little house and a little bed so I can marry a little wife in the little church and she will grow some little beans and little potatoes in a little garden to make a little soup to feed our little children when they come home from the little school . . ."

Kap laughed. "Yes, it's true," he said. "We are pygmies in a pygmy land and to bring everything down to our own size we speak a pygmy tongue." It hardly applied to him. In this Lilliputian land he was a giant. Recognizing him, pedestrians shouted "*A schöne Namitag!*" as we drove by and he shouted back, "A nice afternoon to you!" We passed through Nidfurn, the hamlet from which my maternal great-grandfather, John Jacob Ott, emigrated with his family in 1849 and then we passed through Diesbach, the village of my maternal grand-mother's people, the Hoeslis. Skeins of power wires covered the land like the webs of gigantic Jurassic spiders. The valley narrowed until the rail and auto roads converged in a single bed. We arrived at Lintahl, the largest town in the valley, filled with once elegant and now deserted Victorian hotels, and continued on to Thierfehd, a hamlet at the end of the road.

There we left the car and climbed a foot trail that seemed to lead nowhere until, suddenly, a young man appeared and shouted a greet-ing. A friend of Kap's, his name was Otto; he was an engineer, and was to be our guide. Otto was standing before a steel door, almost imper-ceptible in the mountain wall. After a moment it slid silently open on a deep and brightly illuminated tunnel. We entered and the door glided shut behind us with a muted click. I held back and Kap, sensing my apprehension, urged me on, saying, "There's no safer place in Switzer-land." His voice was not reassuring but disembodied and ominous. We continued on for what seemed a long distance, our echoing footsteps resounding like a roll of drums, and arrived at another door which opened on a great hall of roaring turbines. Walking on the antiseptic parquet floor, feeling the chill of air conditioning, I had the nightmarish feeling of entrapment as in a James Bond movie. Above the thunder of machines Kap and Otto were shouting statistics. Each of the eight turbines cost a quarter-million francs and each weighed more than six tons. Each one required five thousand liters (1,321 gallons) of water per second of ten revolutions. "And the water *comes from Elm!*" Kap shouted triumphantly, grabbing me in his excitement. It came from the snow of the Hausstock alp and flowed through eight miles of tunnel to a mountaintop reservoir that was protected from possible enemy attack by a network of cables.

We went on, moving deeper and still deeper into the mountain and each time a door clicked behind us I felt a wave of panic and moved closer to Kap, drawing security from his presence. Still another tunnel, this one on a rising elevation, led us into a hall of pipes and valves, past doors marked "toilette" and, bizarrely, a wall covered with red-crayon graffiti of nude Rubenesque women. For some distance we followed a coil of twenty cables, each three inches thick, carrying current, said Kap, to factories in Zurich, Basel, and Winterthur. We descended sixty-eight steps, which I counted to distract myself, stopped to admire some more graffiti, and descended twenty-two more steps, arriving finally at another door which opened silently, to my astonishment and relief, on the outside of the mountain, a quarter-mile from the door through which we had entered.

A heavy fog had rolled up the valley and the world was ominously dark. Otto suggested a chair lift through the fog to see the reservoir on the mountaintop but I had had enough of James Bond and declined the invitation. Only then, when we were outside did I remember that I had never on the long underground journey seen any humans other than ourselves. Where, I asked Kap, were the workmen.

"There aren't any!" he replied, exulting in my astonishment. "Everything is automated. There are three watchmen, each with an eight-hour shift, to fill out the day and that is all."

I tried to comprehend. I heard the tinkle of a bell and through the fog I was able to make out the reassuring form of a cow ahead. My mind clung to the image and would not let it go.

The valley was gloomy and chilling but above the fog the sun would be shining. We had a hearty lunch in an old inn in Thierfehd, during which Kap described other redoubts carved out of mountains, underground hangars for fighter bombers behind massive iron doors, military offices, and communication centers from which wars could be conducted; repositories for nuclear weapons and bombs. "They are the most impregnable fortresses on earth," he boasted. "A major nuclear attack could not harm them."

We drove down to Linthal, where we parked the car and boarded the funicular to Braunwald, the canton's highest village and its only resort. There we jerked upward through mists at a dizzying incline and suddenly, like an Orphic resurrection from the underworld, ascended into dazzling sunlight and crisp light air.

Rivulets of snow water irrigated the meadows and cowbells clanged

everywhere. In one of the pastures we met a merry white-haired herdsman from Elm, whose name was also Kaspar Rhyner. The two Kaps
embraced as if they had not seen one another for years. The older Kap
was known as *Hinterberg Kap,* or "Behind-the-mountain Kap" and he
was visiting relatives in Braunwald where, he said, the grasses grew
sweetest in the canton, and the cheeses were the best. We descended
into the village and met a woman working in her flower garden—a
glory of zinnias, asters, and marigolds. The lady was Frau Hessler, a
seventy-five-year-old widow, observing the anniversary of her marriage. "It's a day like in heaven," she said, looking into the skies. Then
she added, "Of course, I don't know how heaven is. I can only imagine
it." She was born down in the valley and had moved into the alps when
she married fifty-five years ago. Her husband had died many years
before, by his own hand, a victim of the depression not uncommon to
alpine people, especially men. Her son also had been depressed and his
death, by cancer, she said, was looked upon as a blessing, since otherwise he might have followed his father in suicide. The day before our
visit Frau Hessler had gone down into the valley for a funeral. "I could
not wait to come home," she said. "This is the happiest of all places. We
are lucky. We have no floods, no tornados, no catastrophes. I am
thankful for my house and for my food, which no one can take from
me, and I pray to God every day to keep me safe from the Russians."
Her abiding fear, that the Russians might sweep over Europe and
conquer Switzerland, was shared by many rural Swiss. "When that
happens I hope they do not find me here," she said. "I hope I do not live
so long." She invited us into her home, into a small whitewashed room
with a ceiling so low I needed to bow my head. "In the winter the snow
is so deep I cannot open the door to get outside," she said. The room
was filled with a tropical growth of potted plants. There were newspapers and magazines in neat stacks, and a radio. "I listen to all the
broadcasts," she said. "I hunger for newspapers. If I were poor and had
to choose, I'd prefer newspapers to food. God be praised I do not have
to make the choice."

Braunwald has a small, modern, glass and wood-paneled Protestant
church. At five o'clock its bells rang out summoning villagers to an
extraordinary event, a pageant performed by children, honoring the
memory of Dr. Martin Luther King. The participants were seventy-five

campers from Basel, six to sixteen years of age, supervised by deacon-
esses, or Protestant nuns, wearing black gowns and white bonnets.
The author of the pageant and its director was Fräulein Pfarrer Hanni
Wartenweiler, one of Switzerland's more than 120 lady pastors. Her
source materials were the writings, speeches, and sermons of Dr. King
and a German-language biography of him written by an uncle, Fritz
Wartenweiler. She was a large, vigorous woman, a type familiar in
Swiss public life, and she had an awesomely commanding voice. In her
presentation, short dramatizations from the life of King were inter-
spersed with spiritedly sung German evangelical hymns. I asked Pastor
Wartenweiler why she had not used the black spirituals associated with
Dr. King and she replied, "We are not capable; it would not be
convincing. We can only express our feelings in our own idiom."

The ceremony began with music by a cello, harpsichord, and flute
trio and then Pastor Wartenweiler, likening Dr. King to Jesus, spoke of
the *Negerpfarrer* who "died for the sorrows of man, who was murdered
for his good deeds." A group of beaming blond children wearing
brightly knit sweaters paraded with placards reading "Parks only for
whites," "Restaurants only for whites," "Churches only for whites,"
"Buses only for whites," and in a resonant voice the lady pastor,
speaking in German, read the words of Dr. King: "To all this once and
forever we must set an end and I will not rest until the Negro is a full and
equal member of human society." She read on, and the repeated word
"*Neger*," sounding so much like the colloqualism "Nigger," rang
harshly in my ears.

Scenes of violence followed. A pink-cheeked boy, playing the role of
Dr. King, led a group of followers onto a segregated bus and was
beaten by police; a man was halted at the door of a restaurant and
freedom marchers grappled with soldiers; and then all subsided and a
youth in the role of a judge read, "The highest court of the United States
has declared the Alabama law on segregation unconstitutional."

There was a scene of jubilation, and the chronicle moved toward its
anticipated conclusion, to April 1968, and the simile changed from
Jesus to Moses as Pastor Wartenweiler read the famous words, "*Denn
ich habe auf dem Berggipfel gestanden und ich habe das gelobte Land
geschaut...*," Even if I had not understood the language I would have
recognized the cadences of the words, "I have stood on the mountain

and I have seen the promised land. . . . For this reason I am happy tonight and I have no worries. . . . My eyes have seen the future. . . ."

The voice of the pastor, softly now, said, "When Mother King had to bring her children the tragic news that a murderer had slain their father, twelve-year-old Yolande replied . . ."

A child's clear voice spoke, saying, "Isn't it so, Mother, we can not hate that man?"

The silence was like a benediction and the children converged into a procession and marched triumphantly from the church, singing:

Now we beseech the Holy Ghost,
For the faith, above all else,
To protect us until our death,
Until we are delivered from this misery . . .

As the last humming voices faded away, the oblique rays of the setting sun filled the church like an annunciation. On the hard wooden benches men and women were weeping. Beyond the window I saw fir trees and red autumn leaves and the crescent of white peaks and sensed, like a mystical pervasion, that in this unlikely place under the mountain snows a beatification by the innocence of children had taken place.

When we returned to the valley the fog lay thicker than ever. By curious coincidence, since the program in the Braunwald church had not been anticipated, Kap had tickets that night for a concert by the Golden Gate Quartet in Glarus. This black American vocal group was greatly admired in Switzerland and the concert had been sold out for a week. It commenced with spirituals such as "I Was Born in Sin and Sorrow" and "I Want to Go to Heaven in the Morning." The amplification was too loud and the singers' mannerisms of snapping fingers, slapping thighs, and folding hands in prayerful attitudes struck me as eccentric. But the audience was transported. The Glarners, who are known for their stoic suppression of emotion, rocked and stomped and clapped with the rhythms and the applause after each song was frenzied. Faces gleamed with sweat and tears. The identification with the alien music seemed complete. I tried to understand this, to find reasons for it. There was no doubt that the mood of the spirituals related to the Swiss Protestant view of life as a vale of tears with its accrued rewards in heaven. But I suspected a deeper, more subtle origin for the extraordinary welling of emotion. Under a mask of conservative capitalist-socialism, Switzerland is essentially a master-slave society, and the songs born out of slavery might be arousing hidden subliminal guilts. For the Swiss, who never cease expressing indignation over the "persecution" of American blacks, see no contradiction to this in their own "master" role over their foreign workers. Nor can they understand that the Italian, Greek, and Spanish migrants, separated from their families and living in ghetto isolation in an unfriendly land, actually may be more oppressed than the commiserated-over American blacks. How much of the solicitude for blacks, I wondered, was really an uncomprehended transference of guilt? Or, practically speaking, was it a matter of economics? Indignation over oppression in a distant land costs nothing, while any rectification of oppression at home might be disruptive and expensive.

What was happening in the shooting hall was certainly an expiation. The singers broke into "When the Saints Go Marching In" and the audience rose and applauded so loudly the music could not be heard. A pair of nuns embraced one another and hopped about in the aisle like American groupies. When the concert finally concluded, with "The St. Louis Blues," the shouting and stomping were tumultuous.

We hurtled up through a fog that our lights hardly penetrated. About midway we were halted by a waving flashlight. On a perilous stretch of road at midnight two policemen were checking automobile tires. They told Kap his were thin and ordered him to replace them. Kap told them to put on their spectacles and look again; that the tires had traveled only 13,000 kilometers. At that moment a car approached from the other direction and the officers stopped it, blocking both lanes in the narrow road, and everyone commenced shouting. A second car rolled down through the fog and, unable to stop, smashed into the rear of the car facing us. A young man got out and began to curse and weep, and the policeman arrested him for drunken driving. One of the officers said to Kap, "You'd better go or you'll get a bump, too." Revving away, Kap shouted back, "Do you think my tires will make it home?" He drove fast, as if guided by radar. "They hire fools for policemen in Switzerland," he said.

We stopped for a drink at The Sun, where young Italian workers were competing with Swiss soldiers from the barracks above the village for the attentions of local girls. At two o'clock we rolled through a flurry of falling snow down a steep slope to Kap's temporary home over the power plant, an utterly appropriate dwelling for a human dynamo.

The Sun was the gathering place. The old, recently redecorated inn was hung with antlers and fading photographs. Its owner was Marta Arnold, a warm-hearted, full-figured maiden lady who, with a brother, had inherited The Sun on the death of their father. Marta was not a Glarner but a native of Canton Uri, across the Klausen Pass from Glarus. Her *Ausländer* status, her Catholicism, and her brusque manner and uninhibited tongue set her apart in the Protestant village. Admiring in her an independence they would not tolerate in their own wives, men came to The Sun to have their sexist chauvinism challenged. Like a Chaucerian innkeeper, Marta joined in their lusty humor and seldom lost an argument. Not many wives in Elm frequented The Sun.

Near the bar over which Marta presides is the *Stammtisch,* or "head table," reserved for patrons with established priority. It is the setting for a never-ending symposium of current events, local gossip, weather, and politics. When a patron arrives he formally shakes hands with everyone at the table and, on leaving, he repeats the polite gesture.

As a friend of Kap's I was welcomed at the table and my presence frequently turned the discussion into a forum on language. The Glaronese I spoke, was not, I discovered, as perfect as I had believed. Though the men of Elm and I spoke with the same nuances and accents, there were troublesome differences in vocabulary and usage. Language is a living force that changes and evolves, but my New Glarus argot was an archaic patois atrophied in the mid-nineteenth century, sealed in that moment of time when my ancestors emigrated from Switzerland. My words were understood only by the old grandfathers, and some were not comprehended even by them. Such a word, which I used constantly, was *dichamal,* meaning "occasionally," and when one old man heard it he laughed and said, "I haven't heard that word since I was a boy." One phrase that I had learned from a great-aunt in New Glarus so amused Swiss friends that they picked it up and turned it to hilarious use. It was *s'wasser ab lu,* literally "drain the water" and meaning to urinate.

Another of my linguistic difficulties came from Swissified American words brought into the language by the people of New Glarus. Among these was *aufringen,* the New Glarus verb for "to telephone," which in Switzerland is *aufläuten.* Another was *triebe a carre* for "drive a car," instead of the proper Swiss *fahren an auto.*

My most troublesome abberation was the use of the second-person pronoun, *du.* In Switzerland the German third-person plural *Sie* is used in all cases except the most intimate ones, such as when addressing a child, a parent, or a beloved friend. Though my ancestors in Wisconsin spoke the old language almost exclusively, the American democratic spirit pervaded their use of it, with the result that in New Glarus almost everyone was addressed in the familiar *du* and *Sie* was seldom used. Though I tried to remember to use *Sie* in Switzerland, I often forgot. In Zurich my mistake was usually tolerated as the eccentricity of an American. But not in Elm, where formality of language is strictly observed.

One afternoon at the *Stammtisch* a careless *du* precipitated a crisis. The six of us at the table included Kaspar Hefti, municipal secretary and official village poet; schoolmaster Heiri Knobel; a construction foreman in Kap's firm named Spälti; a carpenter I shall call Frick; and Kap and myself. We were all drinking beer. The controversial subject under discussion was a proposed *autostrada* that would pass through Elm and into a tunnel under the Panixer alp to Graubünden. This road, strongly supported by Kap, would route the heavy Zurich-St. Moritz traffic through Elm and cut the driving time by half. Hefti, who opposed it, said, "If that ever happens Elm is doomed. Our peaceful life will be destroyed."

"It will bring economic growth," said Kap. "Hotels and new factories."

"And benzine stations and foreigners," said Hefti.

"Elm will grow," said Frick.

"Elm is large enough," Knobel replied. He turned to me. "There are *autostradas* in America. How many autos pass in an hour? I'll bet there must be two or three hundred."

"More like two or three thousand," I replied.

"*Herrgott!*" said Knobel. "Think of the noise!"

"It would be a disaster," Hefti said, his voice rising.

"You cannot stop progress," Frick said. "You cannot hold back the future." The heat of the argument increased and everyone was shouting at once. I wanted to tell Frick that I thought him wrong, that Elm should preserve its rural character.

"Hey, *du* . . .," I shouted, trying to get his attention. The voices silenced. Frick pushed away from the table and, rising to his feet, speaking with Jehovist solemnity, said "Never in my whole life has a younger man addressed me as *du.*"

I apologized for the insult, explaining it was a slip of the tongue, that in New Glarus, where I had grown up, everyone was *du.* The angry dialogue continued:

"New Glarners must be primitive peasants. No one else would be so rude," Frick said.

"In America life is less formal. We prefer not to recognize differences; we think of everyone as *du* . . ." I replied.

"It is rude not to show respect," he said.

"Americans are strange people. They have curious ideas; they do things differently," Knobel offered.

"When a certain intimacy exists, sometimes with younger man, I say *du,*" Hefti said.

"I am not younger than Herr Kubly," Frick retorted.

"Herr Kubly is a professor and he says *du.* How do you explain it?" asked Spälti.

"Ignorance!" Frick exclaimed.

"Among peasants *du* is heard quite frequently," Knobel said.

"Not in Elm. No stranger has ever addressed me in that fashion."

"It requires a certain intimacy," Hefti said patiently.

"*Du* is not used in the Bible," Knobel said.

"Even if it were, it would not be proper," Frick continued.

"I always address God as *du* so why shouldn't I address you in the same way? Are you better than God?" Kap queried.

"I would not permit myself to say *du* to Fräulein Arnold," Knobel said.

"Then I can't say *du* to you since I'm younger than all of you," Marta said.

"We all work for our daily bread; we're all equal," Hefti said.

"When I say *Sie* to a man he replies that he doesn't have lice. So I say *du,*" Marta said.

"Even children in a family should address parents as *Sie*," Knobel insisted.

"In such matters a certain sensitivity is required . . ." Kap said.

Hefti shook his head. "In business it is important to keep a position. *Du* should not be abused."

"To a pastor or a teacher one does not say *du*," Knobel said. "It would be an insult."

Frick nodded. "I know a dentist who refused to finish filling the tooth of a patient who addressed him as *du*."

It went on like that, everyone talking at once, until Marta brought it to a close, shouting, "A beer on the house for all *du* peasants. *Sie* aristocrats can afford to pay."

We had our beers and then Kap said, "Let's get out of this asylum." He suggested a drive up the Kärpf alp to show me the site of the ski area he planned to develop. At his office we picked up a *Haflinger*, a four-cylinder Swiss jeep named for a species of small Tyrolean horse, and in it we commenced a slow climb up a mountain trail.

The jeep coughed and spit and Kap cursed it. We passed clusters of old farm buildings, identified as Barley Kobi's, Goatkeeper Hans', and Stonehouse Blasi's. No one seemed to have last names. Finally we arrived at a house before which a *Haflinger*, like ours, stood in the yard. There we stopped.

"My machine is kaput!" Kap shouted, and a woman came running from the house and offered us her jeep for the rest of the journey. "Wait, I have to put some cider into it," she said, fetching a canister of gasoline. She was a widow, known as Sami's Regi, whose husband, Samuel, had died of a tumor only a month before. She told us she planned to stay on the alp and operate her dairy of six cows because, "most sickness comes from folded hands." She asked Kap about the ski lift, which she and her family looked forward to riding down into Elm. "When will you build it?" she asked. "For what generation?" "For yours," Kap replied. "So you can go to church." The woman laughed.

The path was hardly wider than the jeep and it was slippery from rain. I was sitting on the outer side and felt a rise of vertigo. I closed my eyes while Kap struggled with the gears. When I opened them Elm had disappeared under clouds lying over the valley. At the end of the trail we parked the jeep and continued by foot over clusters of pink autumn crocuses to a plateau where Kap was planning to build the terminus of the ski tow. Facing us on the south was a row of summits named The Twelve Apostles and, to the west, saw-edged peaks known as the Swiss Dolomiti. With one hand Kap outlined a network of ski trails down into the valley.

The anachronism in Kap's plans for Elm continued to puzzle me. "If you are convinced of differences, if you really believe the people of Elm are happier than other Swiss, why bring the outside world into the valley?" I asked.

"You can't stop progress; you can't shore up history."

The setting sun was igniting the snow peaks with coral flame; the light was blinding. We began the descent, rattling down over stones, and came to a clutch of huts clinging together like brown lichen on a stone. We stopped and entered the summer quarters of an absent herdsman. It was a small, dark, odorous room with a dirt floor and a tiny stove. There were a few dishes and tin cups. When we returned to the jeep it was surrounded by a herd of inquisitive goats. "They run wild in the summer," Kap said. "One day soon they will descend and enter into their proper barns and the farmer will say, 'The goats have returned. It is going to snow.' and that night it will snow."

10

THE FALL OF A GODDESS

Swiss are very emotional about hero-gods. There is a strong desire to believe in something ideal, which may turn into adoration. Woodrow Wilson was deified, and the collapse of that ideal after the first World War caused a national trauma. This phenomenon was repeated on a lesser scale with the fall from grace of Jacqueline Kennedy.
—Alphonse Kubly

At the *Stammtisch* a patriarch was saying, "I do not believe that she will marry."

"There's that English lord and the American writer," an unshaven farmer, peering out of a hooded hay shirt, replied. "A widow as rich as she can have any man she wants. Fidel Castro if she chooses." The speaker and one other man laughed. The rest scowled their disapproval.

A young man, looking up from a magazine, said, "It says here she is dedicated to the memory of her husband and to her children." On the magazine cover was a picture of Jacqueline Kennedy, subject of a continuing dialogue in The Sun symposium. Preoccupation with the widow of America's martyred president existed not only in Elm but in all of Switzerland. It was a national obsession, sustained and nourished by the weekly pulp press. No face appeared with such frequency on news racks as Mrs. Kennedy's, no life was chronicled with such minute detail and hyperbolic fantasy, no living person was given so much column space. All of her images—the grieving widow, loving mother, international beauty and social queen, devout Catholic, and celibate vestal—were idealized into a mythic fusion of Joan of Arc, Hecuba, Venus de Milo, and St. Catherine of Siena. The role was not unlike that of a Greek goddess for whom marriage to a mortal man was unthinkable. Explaining the phenomenon, Kap said, "We Swiss need a romantic heroine. Having none we create her; we deify Jackie."

How deeply the deification had taken possession of the Swiss psyche was made apparent on a disquieting October day. A greatly respected villager named Blasius Zentner, a cousin of Kap, had died after a long illness. It was an Elm custom, Kap said, for at least one male representative from each household to attend a funeral and he asked if I'd like to go with him. It was traditional for everyone to wear black and I had only a gray sports jacket. Kap offered to loan me a black tie, which he said would be acceptable. The family would feel honored by my presence.

The funeral was on a Friday. I was awakened early by the tolling of bells—it was the custom to ring them twice, an hour apart, before a funeral service. Through the window I saw black-clothed men and women moving through the town, up toward the Zentner house. The older men were wearing stove-pipe hats and long black swallow coats known as *Anglais,* or "English." A formal suit was bought by every man for his marriage and worn for christenings, weddings, and funerals; and on Christmas, Easter, and Pentecost when communion was served in church. When he died the man would be buried in this same suit.

A car came roaring up the road. It was Kap with a load of funeral passengers. They unloaded and he rushed into the apartment to change into his black suit.

We joined the dark procession moving up through the town. Kap told me that while the deceased man had been considered financially well off, interments nonetheless were paid for by the commune and all deceased villagers, regardless of economic and social positions, were buried alike.

In the upper village men were standing in two lines, one on each side of the road; the lines turned into a lane that led to the Zentner house. We took places in one of the lines. The rows of black-clad figures and the awesome silence filled me with uneasy disquiet. I turned to Kap. His face might have been carved of stone, his jaw jutted more strongly than usual, and I wondered what thoughts, what emotions were passing in such a moment through one so vitally alive.

A tensing in the lines indicated that something was about to occur. In the lane a man appeared, leading a single horse drawing a farm wagon bearing the wreath-covered coffin. The rustic catafalque turned the corner and moved down between the lines so slowly it took several minutes to reach us. Behind it walked the dead man's four sons. The youngest, still a youth, was weeping. Seeing him, the only person showing emotion, stirred a response in me and I wondered how I could maintain the awesome control of everyone around me. I clenched my jaws and looked ahead. Walking behind the sons were the men of Elm, in their swallow coats and Lincoln hats, stepping slowly in rhythm with the tolling church bell. I heard a gasp beside me and turned and saw tears in Kap's eyes.

I felt his hand on my arm, directing me into the procession. Behind us, following the men, were the dead man's widow and daughters-in-law, and after them came the women of the village.

Slowly, very slowly, we moved to the church and when we arrived the coffin had disappeared, carried behind the church to the gravesite. We moved inside and took places in the right half of the church reserved for men; the women followed and filled the left side. The contrast of white walls and black-clad mourners was stark. No color, not a single flower relieved the austerity. The young minister was wearing a white collar on his black robe. Beside him on the pulpit was an hourglass to measure the time of his sermon. The congregation sang a hymn and the minister prayed, rolling "r's" with dramatic sonority. He commenced a chronicle of the deceased man's long illness, dwelling on each sequence, likening it to the suffering of Christ, turning each detail into the jewel of a crown. I understood him clearly for I also had been brought up to believe that suffering was a virtue. The sand trickled down the glass, the pastor spoke of death as a passage into eternal life, and the parish listened earnestly without a flicker of emotion.

The sand ran out and everyone filed from the church. I assumed that we were going to the interment and was surprised to discover that it was over, that the coffin had already been lowered and covered. The wreaths formed a canopy over the grave. The dead man's family gathered for a prayer and then, abruptly, the silence ceased. People gathered in groups, shaking hands, discoursing with friends. I observed a group of women in agitated colloquy and, suddenly, one of them began to wail and the others joined in weeping and sobbing, and I was relieved that the unbearable restraint was finally broken, that at last emotion was being released.

"It is not possible," I heard one wail. "The poor woman," another cried, and still another, "It's a terrible thing!" Several, one of whom was Kap's mother, were keening together. "No, no, no, it cannot be. . . .," and I assumed they were weeping for the widow. They went on with it, freeing a flood of emotion, releasing agonies, and I asked Kap, "Is this the way it is done?"

"What do you mean?"

"The shoaling of grief, and the spending of it at the end."

He looked at me, bewildered for a moment, then said, "They are crying because of news they have just heard from someone who claims to have heard it on the radio. Jackie Kennedy has married Onassis!"

"What?" I tried to comprehend it. I remembered other unsubstantiated rumors of implausable alliances for Mrs. Kennedy and I said with firm conviction, "That is impossible!"

The women crowded around me, pleading for reassurance that the rumors were not true, and I said, "I am certain they are not." Some women took comfort from my words and others listened uncertainly as the news spread through the cemetery.

Eventually the mourners dispersed and Kap and I walked down to The Sun, where men were gathering to drink. A radio was tuned high and we listened to the astonishing report that would remain for the rest of the day the single subject of conversation in Elm. Men huddled before the radio, turning the dial, and on every station excited voices were repeating the news. Against a background of the "Wedding March" from *Lohengrin,* a hoarse broadcaster was saying, "The marriage is a triumph for the Greek government. Bound by marriage to the supernation America, Greece will rise in political status." Rumors circulated. The reason for the swift marriage was the pregnancy of the bride! The newlyweds would establish residence in Geneva where Onassis had property! The bride would give up her American citizenship to accept an appointment as Queen of Greece! On the radio an astrologist predicted a stormy future for the newlyweds and a commentator reported, "The marriage is the bride's revenge on America."

At the *Stammtisch* the anger and bitterness was like that of rejected lovers. A man in a funeral cloak mumbled, "Just think of it! Onassis!" Another raised his glass in a mocking toast, saying, "To the new First Couple of the World—Jacqueline I, Queen of Greece, and Aristotle, Duke of Athens!"

"It will be the same all over Switzerland," said Kap. "The joke is on the media, on the editors and broadcasters who have filled our bourgeois spiritual vacuum with a Kennedy Royal Family, a fairy-tale princess. Now the fantasy collapses; the princess is fallen and everyone feels betrayed. We are back to what we were, a dull middle-class society without a goddess to worship."

"It's all very simple," a man at the table was saying. "It's a *Finanzallianz*. She married him for his money. He'll live two or three years and then she'll inherit it all. She's got a head on her shoulders." Spurred by drink, the men made vulgar jokes and laughter filled the room. It went on until suddenly, from behind the bar, Marta's voice rang out, "Why don't you let her alone? She's tired of belonging to everyone and she wants to go to a warm island and live her own life. It's perfectly clear!"

11

GRANDFATHER
AND GRANDSON

The first time I climbed Basel's steep Pilgrim Street to the red stone house in a rose garden, it was not as a pilgrim but as a journalist to interview the most noted theologian of his century, Professor Karl Barth. But I had prepared for the visit in the Zurich public library and what I learned had filled me with a pilgrim's awe.

I read that Professor Barth was the most highly regarded Protestant theologian since John Calvin, that his 14-volume *Church Dogmatics* was considered a "cathedral" of Christian logic, the most powerful exposition of Protestant thought since Calvin's *Institutes*. I found comparisons to Thomas Aquinas, St. Augustine, and Martin Luther; and I learned that a pope had praised Professor Barth's work and a Jesuit theologican had written a book about him.

When I tried to read from the *Dogmatics* I found the German difficult and the unfamiliar substance nearly incomprehensible. Now, approaching the house on the hill, I felt a presumption in my journalist's role and I wondered how I would be able to speak to such an intellectual colossus.

My appointment was for four o'clock and Professor Barth was waiting in his study. He rose, straight and smiling, to greet me. Puffing on a huge pipe, his white hair in disarray and his glasses low on the tip of his nose, he seemed almost perfectly the archetypal kindly professor.

"I have looked forward to your visit," he said, putting me immediately at ease. "I enjoy American journalists and I have never met one with a Swiss name." With a touch of self-mocking vanity he asked, "Did you know they put me on the cover of *Time*? The reporter followed me on a summer holiday and did not stop talking for three days. He really took me apart." He laughed with pleasure.

The room might have been painted by Rembrandt. The afternoon sun was turning the nimbus of the professor's hair into a halo and it covered the aged leather of books with Rembrandt's glowing light. On the walls were three pictures, a Grünewald crucifixion and portraits of Mozart and John Calvin. There was an old wooden chest and a ticking clock. Roses spilled over the walls outside the windows and birds sang in the garden.

Almost at once Professor Barth asked me if I'd ever heard of New Glarus. I wondered if he might be putting me on. He urged me to sit down. For half an hour he fired probing questions at me about New Glarus's cultural and religious life, about my family and myself, seeking every detail of the sequence of events that had brought me from America to him. He was the interviewer and I was the subject and when I answered him in *Schweizerdeutsch* he shook his head in disbelief and then in merriment.

"Extraordinary!" he said, rocking in his chair. "A transference not only in place but also in time, a nineteenth-century Swiss village in twentieth-century America. Someone must make a study. Why haven't you done it?"

I had written of New Glarus, I said, though not in the penetrating way he suggested. "I don't think I could do it," I added.

"Why not?" he asked, his voice sharply challenging.

"My confounded Swissness," I replied. "My self-conscious inhibition, the voice of my mother ringing in my ears, saying, 'What would people say?'"

He laughed. "You need more time, a few more funerals. But don't forget it. I feel you have been chosen for this."

When I saw an oppportunity to direct the discussion, I said I would like to talk about Swiss religious life.

"Ah, yes," he replied. "We are quite religious but not very Christian.

In the gospels Jesus said man cannot live by God and mammon both. But we Swiss prove Him wrong."

He was speaking seriously and I could not be certain whether he intended a joke or not. I had read that the professor was known for his humor and that it was a characteristic of Baslers to speak ironies in utter earnestness. When Professor Barth was praised by Pope Pius XII, he had solemnly stated, "This proves the infallibility of the Pope."

He drew several puffs from his pipe and his eyes twinkled. "Religion in Switzerland is mostly practical materialism," he said. "An unconscious rationale, a compromise. Following the gospel is not possible in Switzerland, but then it is not possible in the United States either, or in the rest of the Christian world. The whole Western world appears to be returning to the golden calf and we Swiss, like you Americans, are typical Westerners. I cannot believe in the famous piety of the Middle Ages. Human nature stays the same; it gets no better or no worse. In our practical life we Swiss have always been heathens. Those famous paid mercenary warriors who prayed before going into battle for foreign kings were no better than the storm troopers of Hitler.

"Our introverted Swiss character has been built up over hundreds of years by the circumstance of living in an isolated corner of the world's history," he said. "We have been lucky to miss wars to which we have been well-behaved spectators. We have no responsibilities so we need to create them. We are pedagogical. We are the self-righteous schoolmasters of the world. We are the good ones, the virtuous people who have no part in the great evils of the universe. Of course we have sins, small ones. And we like to be reminded of them; it eases our conscience, our guilt. So in our lives religion must play a role. Church attendance depends on the qualities of preachers. A good orator about sin packs them in. A lackadaisical one has empty churches."

He sighed, reflected for a moment and continued. "Our real problem is what happens to Christianity in our religion. We Swiss believe we have the whitest cross. But what does it mean? We do not mention it, of course, but in the background we believe that God is rewarding us for being so virtuous with prosperity and uninvolvement in wars."

"The Calvinist ethic," I interrupted.

"No. It is a mistake to call Switzerland Calvinist. Calvin's great influence has been in England and America. In Switzerland the relationship of Calvin to capitalism is limited to the small area of Geneva and perhaps a bit here in Basel. Switzerland is Zwinglian, which is quite another matter. We are born bourgeois, we believe the greatest sin is not to follow tradition. When I retired from the university my recommendation for a successor was not accepted because the scholar was not a political traditionalist. The job is now filled by a mediocre young man who satisfied the requirements. I am sure that both Jesus Christ and the Apostle Paul would be turned down by the faculty of Basel for a professorship in religion."

He smiled at that thought, and shook his head. "Do not get the impression that I think Christianity is totally missing from the world. It exists, as it always has, but only in isolated personal relations. It is a small seed, like the mustard seed of the parable, and it can never be a business of the majority of the people, of the institutional church. In true Christianity the seed has not disappeared. But almost. We've hidden it too deeply in religion.

"The seed flourished for a time with Pope John XXIII, a simple creature of God who re-created in his sheer goodness the Christian spirit and built an aura of respect for the Catholic Church which it has not known for centuries. By him the Catholic faith became once more a living, vital religion. Pope John opened the doors of faith to young Catholic intellectuals, to my good friend, Hans Küng.* He and I have had many discussions and we are very close in thought; we agree on everything except the infallibility of the Pope and the Mary cult." The professor hesitated and a twinkle came into his eye. "Sometimes I believe I may yet convince him in these matters. The younger generation of priests are open-minded, anything may happen in the next thirty years.** There is a spiritual movement in the Catholic realm which has no equal in the Protestant faith."

Through the open window came the sound of a woman beating a rug.

"You are smiling," he said. "Do you disagree?"

"Oh, no. I was thinking how each morning in my apartment in

---

*The Swiss Jesuit theologian who published a book on Barth and his teachings.
**In 1974 Küng challenged the dogma of papal infallibility.

Zurich I am awakened at six-thirty by a woman beating rugs in the courtyard and here I am in the library of Professor Barth and . . ."

"Ah, yes, without rugs to beat there would be no Switzerland. Swiss women express all their anger and hostilities on rugs." He laughed, and added, "Sometimes it is their bed clothes they are beating in the morning and then the psychology becomes even more complex."

He returned the conversation to an exploration of me and asked, "What things do you write? Do you deal with Christian themes?"

I replied that in my youth I had written a play based on the story of Hosea and his faithless wife, Gomer, and that I had taken the premise for another play from the Book of Proverbs.

"Hosea and Gomer is one of the beautiful parables of the Old Testament," said Professor Barth. "Its theme of forgiveness foreshadows the New Testament. How did you use it?"

I described my play about a navy seaman and his errant wife. "Was it made into a film?" he asked. It was not. "Do you like the Book of Job?" he asked. "*That* is a story. It tells everything there is to know about the relationship between man and God. Do you enjoy American cowboy and gangster films? When I work too hard and feel tired I sneak out to see a gangster picture and it drains my tired brain and relaxes me to begin again."

"When that happens I listen to Mozart."

"Yes, of course. I begin each day with Mozart. Mozart is food and drink. God's voice speaks in his music. *The Magic Flute* is a theological revelation filled with the harmony of the universe, of a creation in which light breaks out of the shadows and joy overtakes sorrow without extinguishing it. This is Mozart's prevailing force, his theological truth, the YES over the NO that is the joy of life."

The professor's eyes twinkled. "I have always believed that when the angels in heaven worship God they sing and play Bach but when they are enjoying themselves it is Mozart they sing."

The shadows were lengthening in the garden and I realized I was lingering past the appointed time. I moved to leave. He urged me to return and said he would like me to meet an American son, a professor in Pittsburgh. Like a patriarch from the Bible, he spoke of his children: two professors, an artist, a daughter married to an industrialist, and a younger son, a theology student, who died in a skiing accident, and of fourteen grandchildren and a great-grandchild. Since there was no mention of his wife I assumed she had died. Later I learned that she was alive but did not live with her husband.

Walking down Pilgrim Street I felt transported, as if a blessing had been placed upon me and its effusion was like a levitation. Tamino's aria, "*Dies Bildnis ist bezaubernd schön*," rang in my mind's ear and I began to sing.

My last visit with Professor Barth was in November 1968. He did not get up from his chair to greet me. He appeared frail and for the first time very old—he was eighty-two. I knew he had been hospitalized with an illness. But the warm curiosity, the affection, the humor had not diminished. He had read my novel, *The Whistling Zone.* "I want you to know," he said, "that I followed it with almost unbearable excitement. I was especially interested in the Christian theme that runs through it."

I told him that because of this book the pastor of the church that I attended as a boy had declared all my books "immoral." Professor Barth sighed with mock despair and said, "It is the tragedy of the church that her greatest Philistines are inside rather than outside her gates. Surely you are aware that to be vilified by the high priests puts you in a very select company?"

He pressed me for insights into the approaching presidential election, and expressed his mistrust of Richard Nixon. "Nixon is a man not in harmony with himself; he does not trust himself and a man who does not trust himself cannot be trusted." In a gently tactful way he expressed his great concern "for the United States which was in danger of losing its influence for good in the world." He went on to say, "I don't feel angry about this, but sorrow, for the world is by its definition imperfect and an understanding of this should move an American president toward a higher moral effort."

He asked if church attendance in America was falling away as it was in Switzerland. "Perhaps it is a good thing to have it so," he said. "Church attendance is no longer a necessary social ritual, something that must be done. Those that go know why they go and for what purpose. They become more earnest and more effective Christians."

He seemed to me a man resigned and free of illusion, a prophet who, firm in his conviction of God's truth, had ceased to shout. He recalled his ten years—from 1911 to 1921—as a parish pastor in the village of Safenwil in northern Switzerland. The reason for this nostalgic mood became clear when he spoke with pride of an American grandson, Peter Barth, who had returned to Europe to earn a theology degree and was serving a small parish in the mountain village of Krinau, in Canton St. Gall. He thought this grandson might be lonely for American company and he asked me to visit him. I promised that I would.

I promised also to send him my new book, advance copies of which I was expecting from America. Early in December, before I could keep my promises, a friend called to tell me that Professor Barth had died.

In April I was able to keep the promise to visit his grandson, the Reverend Peter Barth. It was a bright spring morning and everyone in the agricultural Toggenburg area, including children and grandmothers, seemed to be in the fields spreading manure. In the valleys liquified manure was being blown through pipes and the odor that hung over the land was nauseating and inescapable.

At the road's end I found Krinau spread across a high valley. Two buildings dominated it: a small white church with a bell tower and, across the road, the *Pfarrhaus*. The boyish youth who came to the door so astonishingly resembled his grandfather that I recognized him at once. Though he was shorter in stature, his broad open face, blue eyes, and warm smile were the old man's.

He apologized that his clothes and hands were stained brown. He had, he said, been in the fields helping parishioners spread manure. Speaking English with a slight stammer, he said, "Early in the week I was helping the family of an alcoholic father who neglects his work and this has made other parishioners jealous. They say if I can spread the manure of a man who drinks I can do it also for them. I try to explain to them that Jesus was more concerned with aiding the unfortunate sick than He was with the healthy, but they see it as a moral problem. So I have been very, very busy." Though he spoke earnestly, the shadow of a smile was there in his eyes and I recognized his grandfather's wry humor. I could imagine the great professor faced with a similar dilemma during his own young village ministry.

Though he appeared no more than twenty and seemed in disarming moments like a pink-cheeked adolescent, Peter Barth was twenty-eight and a bachelor. He showed me through the parish house, which had recently been remodeled with an electrified kitchen. "A village minister is the last manifestation of feudalism in Switzerland," he said. "The *Pfarrhaus* is the manor house, the busy center of everything."

Peter had attended the University of Chicago and afterward was a social worker for two years. He came to Switzerland to visit his grandfather and enrolled at Göttingen, the German university at which Professor Barth taught until 1935. He became a Swiss citizen and served his Swiss military duty, during which time he aroused his grandfather's displeasure. A commanding officer had mimeographed and distributed a list of advantages in military life and Peter, challenging each point, mimeographed his own response to the officer's memorandum and distributed it to the company.

"You make friends," the officer had written, and Peter replied. "You can make more lasting and interesting friendships outside the army."

"Military life is good for health," said the officer and Peter responded, "Athletics are better."

"You build bridges for your country," the officer wrote, and Peter answered, "The bridges are poorly built and have no lasting value. Engineers do this better."

"We give our women a vacation from domestic life," the officer observed, and Peter replied, "This can be done by going hunting."

The challenged officer threatened court-martial on charges of insubordination, but public opinion turned the incident into a joke and in the end the charges against Peter were dismissed. He said, "While my grandfather agreed with my ideas he thought it stupid of me to make a fuss. I returned into his good graces when I came here to Krinau. He was very pleased with that."

We talked for an hour in his library. I said that with such a fine house he should have no trouble finding a wife. He smiled ruefully; I had touched on a sensitive point.

"No girl whom I could like would come here," he said. "Life is too remote, too lonely." He thought for a moment and continued, "Besides, a minister belongs to his parish; he has no freedom. Every Swiss village is an extended family. Everyone knows everything, and it's hardly an easy situation for a bachelor minister. My housekeeper acts as an agent for the parish and keeps the people informed of my every move. When I became friends with the schoolteacher, a girl from Zurich, eyes appeared at windows. If I invited the teacher to my house I had also to invite some parish ladies to make it proper. When I invited the teacher for lunch in the *Gasthaus,* it was a great excitement for everyone and the restaurant was crowded. The teacher and I had to be careful never to leave the village at the same time. So you see how it is. I belong not to myself, but to my parish. The time will no doubt come when the people will begin searching for a wife for me and then it will be time for me to leave Krinau.

"My only close friend is a widow who, after the death of her husband, moved permanently from Zurich to her holiday house here in the village. She is fifty-nine years old and being of Jewish faith is not a member of the church. Still, as my friend, she comes to church and, being well off, does much charitable work. Though her bounties are accepted, she herself is not. The people feel that being Jewish she has no right to my friendship. They do not understand that it is only her friendship that makes my life here possible at all."

"What about village girls?" I asked.

"There are none. It is an inexplicably curious thing that three boys to every one girl are born in the village. No one knows why. In other villages the imbalance is reversed. The few girls who grow up here either marry young or they leave. There are almost no young adults in Krinau—my parish is middle aged and old."

Of Krinau's population of 270, two hundred were members of Peter's parish and seventy were Roman Catholics who attended a church outside the village. "Many of my problems concern Catholics," he said. "My parishioners resent the Catholics, who are more faithful than they in church attendance and give them a bad conscience. A Catholic couple moved here from Basel. He works in a textile factory down in the valley and she led a handiwork class for village wives, which they enjoyed. At the end of the class she asked them in a group if they would like to continue and they said they did not. The reason for this was that the lady is Catholic and she made the mistake of asking them together. No lady would admit before the others that she wanted to continue. If the teacher had asked them individually, all would have agreed. Now she is resentful because she has bought supplies for the class and all the women are furious because there will be no class this summer.

"In a social sense I consider myself the pastor also of the Catholics and this is resented by the Protestants. A dairy farmer from my church insists a Catholic lady owes him one hundred francs for milk and she says she has paid him. Such feuds keep the villagers occupied for years; they live from them; feuds are their entertainment. Another Catholic lady, a mother of four children, is having some emotional problems and she left her family and returned to her parents in Lucerne. The husband went with the priest to fetch her and the priest took a stern moral attitude, telling her how she was breaking laws and committing sins and she got more upset than ever. Now the husband has asked me to go to Lucerne with him to see her. I will take a gentler, more understanding position. I will try to reach her in a more humane way.

"My greatest social problem is alcohol. Every tenth man is an alcoholic in the medical sense. I try to help these men by boosting their egos, by spending time with them, by being their friend. I try to keep their families together and when the work is neglected I plow their fields and make their hay.

"Then there are the more subtle moral problems related to my preaching. My parishioners want always to be praised for their virtuous Christian characters." I remembered the grandfather speaking of this, of the demand of Protestant churchgoers to be praised for their piety. "Because of my inability to do this," Peter continued, "I am frequently in trouble. If I say something against stealing there is always someone in the parish who may have stolen some chickens I know nothing about, and he thinks I am referring to him and becomes my enemy. That is why ministers are always changing parishes. After a few years a pastor has offended so many it becomes necessary to move on.

"The people never say what *they* think; they do not tell the truth. This is a characteristic of all Swiss, but it is worse in a village. There is always the evasion of assigning an idea or some gossip to someone else. Without my friendship with the Jewish lady I would never be able to cope with this. She is the only one who speaks directly and honestly, the only one who speaks the truth."

Peter paused and smiled. "You can understand that I am quite busy," he said. "In the winter when the roads are closed and there is no transportation, I am always on skis, going here and there, doing what I can for the people."

It was time for one of his parish duties, to set the mechanism of the church bells. I climbed with him into the open tower, where the wind was blowing. Like a joyful child with a toy, he wound the three weighted springs. The time was almost one o'clock and he said excitedly, "In two minutes the clock will strike. Do not be frightened." We waited. There was a whirr of wheels and the clock boomed like a cannon fire four times and I imagined the tower swaying and felt dizzy. "Sometimes, when I am up here alone," Peter said, "I look over the parish and I try to understand my role; why I am here. Sometimes I even feel the presence of God. That is something my grandfather would have understood and in these moments I feel very close to him."

Two years later I visited Peter again and this time I found him troubled and reflective. His time at Krinau was coming to an end. "My conception of the mission of the church is too different from that of my parishioners," he said. "They wish me to support the status quo; they want me to praise their virtues and not ruffle the waters. They insist that religion and social matters be kept apart and I can no longer support this."

He had applied for a mission post in the Belgian Congo. "In Africa I hope to teach the Christian social message which is no longer acceptable to the European church," he said. An elderly and pensioned clergyman was coming to take over the Krinau parish. "I think he will be better able to please the people," Peter said.*

---

*Peter Barth became professor of theology at the National University of Zaïre in Kinshasa.

12

THE GOOD BROTHERS

Rising above the Niederdorf and dominating the Zurich horizon are the twin spires of the Romanesque Grossmünster. It is dedicated to Zurich's intrepid trio of saints Felix, Regula, and Exuperantius, who in the third century converted the citizens of Turicum, as Zurich was called by the Romans. According to legend, the dauntless missionaries were beheaded by a governor, whereupon they picked up their own heads and carried them to the hilltop where Grossmünster now stands, and there dug their own graves. The Great Seal of Zurich shows them jauntily carrying their heads under their arms.

In the early sixteenth century the cathedral's priest, Ulrich Zwingli, boldly began to preach against the Catholic hierarchy, exhorting his parish to follow Christ's teachings rather than the complex doctrines of Rome. Like Martin Luther in Germany, Zwingli attacked pilgrimages, indulgences, saint worship, celibacy of the clergy, and finally the Mass itself. Admonished by the Bishop of Constance for heretical preaching, Zwingli in 1523 defended his new ideas before Zurich's Great Council. The men of the Council sided with Zwingli, committing themselves to open revolt against Rome, and the Swiss Reformation was born. In 1531 Zwingli led an army against Swiss Catholics in the Battle of Kappel and was killed. The Reformed Church was his legacy.

Five years later John Calvin turned Geneva—which did not join the Swiss Confederation until 1815 but which had entered into a pact of cocitizenship with the Swiss in 1584—into a Holy Commonwealth, in which a majority of citizens were irrevocably doomed to hell by the cruel doctrine of predestination. To a minority destined for salvation fell the role of judging and chastising the damned. Every citizen was forced by law to attend church twice on Sundays and to observe a daily 9 P.M. curfew. Playing cards, wearing jewelry, and eating rich foods were punishable crimes, and public registers were filled with entries such as: "A wife having gone out last Sunday with her hair looser than is proper was put into jail." Calvin's cardinal virtue of hard work and the accumulating of capital became in due time the ethos of the Industrial Revolution. Capitalism and Calvinism became the prevailing faith of Holland, Scotland, and England, and eventually of North America to which it was carried by the Puritans. In German Switzerland Protestantism remained predominantly Zwinglian and Zwingli's doctrines, more humanistic and less fanatic than Calvin's but no less puritanical, continued through history to exert their pressures on Swiss life.

As they did also on life in Wisconsin. In my youth I listened in the New Glarus Reformed Church to German-language sermons extolling piety and warning against sinful self-indulgence. The personality and doctrines of Zwingli became so much a crucible of my life that I wrote a university term paper about him and its tone of uncritical approbation startled my professor.

The house in which Zwingli lived at 13 Kirchgasse is part of the cathedral sacristy. I went there one wintry afternoon to meet the cathedral pastor, the Reverend Hugo Sonderegger, to talk with him about Zwingli and the role of religion in contemporary Swiss life. A sacristan admitted me into a gloomy dark-paneled room. An etching of Zwingli, wearing the low-visored cap with which he is usually portrayed, was on the wall. It showed a full, fleshy face with jutting jaw, heavy lips, and slyly narrowed eyes. In my mind I compared the face to the face of Calvin, consistently portrayed as skeletally taut and bloodless, with fanatic eyes.

I recalled the differences in the two men. Calvin so remote from the world of women that friends had to seek out a wife for him; Zwingli's

well-known traffic with street women and his anguished apology before cathedral electors questioning his fitness for priesthood. "I confess
my weakness," he told them. "I cannot excuse myself. I suffer under it. I
am afraid to go out into the streets for fear I cannot control myself."
Moved by his candor the electors retained him as priest by a vote of
seventeen to seven. Among the Catholic ordinances he vehemently
attacked was the celibacy of the clergy. Unbeknownst to the electors, he
had secretly married a pregnant widow and the marriage was not
acknowledged until Zwingli had openly broken with Catholicism and
had fathered four children. In this matter also his life paralleled that of
Martin Luther, who married a former nun. I wondered to what extent
the Reformation and the subsequent history of the world were directed
by the sexual urges of these two vigorous men.

The Reverend Sonderegger arrived and apologized for being late. He
was a lean, tense, and dedicated man who had learned English while a
student at New York's Union Theological Seminary. He explained he
had been in a Niederdorf mission ministering to drunks, prostitutes,
and homeless derelicts until 5 A.M. "Drunks are the most difficult," he
said. "They tend to be argumentative and not responsive to reason."

"It sounds like a Zwingli commitment," I said. "Wandering dark
streets, reasoning with drunks."

"Precisely," said the pastor. "Zwingli was a people's priest; he moved
with the crowds in cafes and restaurants. He was a very social man who
reintroduced into the church the idea of caring for the poor. He really
originated the concept of social work in Switzerland."

"He looks rather too grim and exacting for compassion," I said,
looking at the Neanderthal features of the alpine peasant face in the
portrait.

"It's probably a fairly accurate likeness," the pastor said. "Certainly
piety was one side of his personality and, probably, in deference to his
memory, he was portrayed as rather unyielding."

"And something of a killjoy." I was thinking of the antipleasure
principle, of Zwingli removing art from churches.

"On the contrary, he wasn't at all," said the pastor. "What we are
shown in the portrait is his warrior side. He was actually a happy,
life-loving spirit. He had a healthy emotional life and attitude. He was
most of all a humanist, a lusty man who sought out pleasures and had

many friends. He loved music and played ten instruments. Most interesting were his relations with women. There's no doubt that his and Luther's decisions to marry influenced the Reformation."

Zwingli, who was born on New Year's Day 1484, was two months younger than Luther; John Calvin, born in 1509, was of the next generation.

"Luther was the prophet of the Reformation," the pastor continued. "Calvin was the organizer and Zwingli its social conscience. His concern was for the communal soul, how the people, having human sins like himself, might escape God's punishment through faith. He differed with Luther in the matter of transubstantiation of the Eucharist. Luther remained closer to Catholic orthodoxy in his belief that the bread and wine *becomes* the blood and body of Christ. Zwingli maintained that transubstantiation occurred in the participant with the presence of the holy spirit. His insistence in this matter resulted in our Reformed Church.

"As a young man he was a chaplain with Swiss mercenaries in foreign wars. This experience turned him against mercenary service, which he concluded was harmful to Switzerland. Once farm youths experienced this life they did not wish to return to their homes. Many had syphilis. If Zwingli had not opposed mercenaries the Reformation would have progressed more easily and more completely. Because of his position the cantons of central Switzerland, which provided most of the mercenaries, remained Catholic. There is no knowing how history might have been changed if Zwingli had lived out a normal life span."

I spoke of a banker who argued that Calvin was a greater force in Swiss Protestantism than Zwingli. The banker called Calvin "the patron saint of banking and business," and he said, "Calvin's view of production of material goods and the accumulation of money as a Christian service has been the dominant influence in the Swiss church."

"That may be the rationale of a banker," the pastor said dryly. "But it has little to do with Christianity. As Zwingli was aware, the Pharisees in the church have never understood Christ."

I brought up the matter of church attendance, about which Karl Barth had said, "When the quantity goes down the quality goes up."

"That is true," said the pastor. "In America you go to church far more frequently. In Switzerland church attendance no longer implies social status and the minority who do attend are brought by a spiritual dedication.

"Though few Swiss attend church regularly, it is virtually mandatory to belong. In the Reformation all church properties were secularized and turned over to the cantons. Church taxes are collected by cantonal governments which maintain church finances. A Swiss belongs to a church—either Protestant or Catholic—by birth as he belongs to his commune and people pay taxes all their lives for the privilege of a socially acceptable funeral. We call these 'four-wheeled Christians' who ride autos to their christening, confirmation, marriage, and burial. I do not think our traditional church structure is viable to twentieth-century society. In another fifty years the church as we know it will have ceased to exist."

An aspect of the Swiss church that intrigued me was its lady pastors. A country that until recently had denied women the right to vote had at least 120 ordained women in its pulpits. I had heard that one of the most dynamic was *Fräulein Pfarrer* Leni Altwegg in the Zurich industrial suburb of Schlieren. I told a mutual friend I would like to meet her and the next day I received an invitation to lunch from Pastor Altwegg herself.

Waiting at the Schlieren station was a petite pretty blonde wearing a youthful pink frock. She picked me out from the disembarking passengers and came to greet me, saying, "You must be Professor Kubly. I am Leni Altwegg." I was surprised. "Perhaps I'm not what you expected?" she asked.

"Well, let's say you're not exactly my image of a *Fräulein Pfarrer*."

She laughed merrily and stopped to speak briefly to a young couple who had arrived on the same train. "I am quite worried about them," Pastor Altwegg said as we drove away in her car. "The girl believes the boy will marry her but he is like all Swiss men. Since he is already sleeping with her he sees no need for marriage. I try to advise them but they will not listen. I don't know what to do."

The unusual confidence so immediately offered indicated that my hostess was neither an ordinary woman nor an ordinary pastor. Driving breezily up a hill, she told me her church had six thousand members and that she was one of three pastors; the other two were men. All three had equal status and alternated for Sunday sermons. I asked how many members attended services and she hesitated. "We don't see many," she said. "Perhaps three to five percent." She performed the parish rites of baptism, confirmation, and burials. "But not many weddings. Brides do not like other women in wedding photos so men are chosen. I don't mind since I don't care much for weddings. Too many people marry in church because a big show is essential but do not come to church again. They say, 'What difference can it make?' And I agree. If they are going to live as they do, it can make no difference." She had, she told me, been a pastor for only three years. A former medical technician, she had begun pastoral studies when she was thirty years old.

Her apartment was an aerie on a hill, with walls of books, green plants, and windows looking out over the rooftops of the town. There was a piano and antique furniture. She offered me an aperitif. I replied that I had not expected to be offered a drink by a Zwinglian lady pastor. "Why not?" she asked, pouring vermouth into glasses filled with ice. "I hope you didn't expect to find me very churchish."

We finished the drinks and sat down to a pleasant lunch of veal chops and risotto, salad, and a bottle of Fendant. I brought up the subject of women's suffrage, which had only recently been approved in progressive French-speaking cantons. "I am ashamed of my country," said Pastor Altwegg. "Though I can't vote I do what I can to influence elections by preaching about issues in my sermons."

How did lady pastors manage in a male-oriented society, I asked.

"It takes a sense of humor. Some men pastors are jealous of each other and more jealous of us women. Though there are thirty women pastors in the Zurich area, when men address meetings it is always 'Dear fathers and brothers . . .' They never address *us*. So once when it came to me to make a report I began, 'Dear mothers and sisters . . .' They still haven't recovered from the shock." Pastor Altwegg laughed girlishly. "The bickering and squabbling at ministers' meetings never ends and I always take a book to read. Later this afternoon I am expected at a pastors' meeting to discuss social problems. We discuss and discuss and discuss and in this way we ease our consciences about never doing anything about the problems."

What, I asked, were the problems. "There are almost too many," Pastor Altwegg replied. "Foreign workers. Sex and marriage. Divorce. Especially divorce. Swiss live in constant fear that their marriage partners will leave them. It is worse for women than for men, who are always running off with younger women. And, of course, abandoned men more easily find someone else." She poured some wine and continued, "I cannot understand how men and women can live together in perpetual warfare. This is a reason I have never married. I couldn't endure a state of constant siege." She spoke of a young priest with whom she sometimes conferred over community problems. "There is always much gossip because he is keeping a mistress. Why should everyone object? He is a strong and virile young man who needs the comfort of tenderness to release him from his passions, to free his time for his work. He is a much better priest because he does not spend his energies in angry battle with himself."

I was sensing a plaintive wistfulness in her ardent defense of the priest, as if she might be speaking of her own loneliness, an absence of tenderness in her busy life.

"Zwingli was a very complicated man," she said. "The Swiss compulsion to work, the antipleasure principle, really came from Calvin. The guilt with which Zwingli endowed us is sexual. To ease his own conscience he had a moral council to punish adulterers. He was preoccupied with sex and the result of his guilt is with us still."

Two weeks later, on a Sunday when Pastor Altwegg was scheduled to preach, Midi Schuler and I went to Schlieren to hear her. On the train we discussed the Swiss attitude toward religion and Midi, who is active in Christian organizations, said, "It is difficult for a Swiss to admit a need for God, for a spiritual design. Our religion is mostly pretense."

Pastor Altwegg met us at the station. She was so hoarse with laryngitis I wondered how she could preach. We drove directly to the church, where the bells were ringing. About a hundred persons, mostly elderly ladies, were scattered through the large sanctuary. Sunlight filtering through four apostle windows glowed brightly on a cluster of forsythia beneath the pulpit and on polished empty pews. The service moved quickly. After two hymns and a prayer Pastor Altwegg, wearing a long black robe, ascended to the pulpit and read as her text the story of the prodigal son from the Book of Luke. Sunlight cascaded over her golden hair. Standing there above us she seemed to have gained stature.

Her voice increased in vigor. Halting now and then for spells of coughing, she related the parable to contemporary life, likening the congregation to the prodigal son's elder brother. "It is about him, the *good* brother, the one who stayed at home, that I wish to speak." The strained voice rang out. "For we are he, the smugly disapproving older brother. All of us sitting here in this church, who believe we are not sinners, who think we are good brothers because we stay at home, living our decent conformist lives, we are really envious of the brother who has gone astray."

As she developed her theme it became clear that the prodigal son was her metaphor for the youth of Switzerland, for protesting students, for young explorers of freer life-styles. "There are no prodigal sons sitting in this church," she told the handful of old people. "Only self-satisfied older brothers. The prodigals are gone. We disapprove of our younger brothers who have left our houses to explore the world, to live a life for which we do not have the courage. We cling to a Christianity which is rather boring; we stay with it because it is comfortable. We are the self-virtuous stay-at-home older brothers who believe we are fulfilling our duties by judging our younger brothers. 'I'm the good boy,' we say. 'I've always worked hard, never gone with bad companions; I've loved my father.' We do not welcome the prodigal; we cannot meet him with forgiveness; we will not say with joy, 'I have a brother!'"

I wondered how many of the pastor's aged listeners were comprehending her words. After twenty minutes the parishioners were becoming restless, thinking no doubt that their *Fräulein Pfarrer* was speaking even more strangely than usual, that she had continued long enough, that it was time to go home to prepare the Sunday meal.

Pastor Altwegg invited us for lunch. But Midi was expected to prepare lunch for her family and had invited me, so we declined. The pastor was disappointed. "It is such a nice day," she said. "I looked forward to it." A cloud was passing over the day and I sensed again her loneliness, her longing for friendship.

It was an hour before our train so we accepted her invitation for a drink. I said how moved I had been by her sermon. "I usually preach of joy for the gospel is joyful," she said, her voice now taxed by pain. She took a deep swallow of her drink and went on. "Sometimes it is necessary to show them some truths. Our people are mostly workers and small businessmen. Not many are rich and there are few intellectuals." She stopped for a moment to rest and took another swallow. "One failing of our church—and I confess I am guilty—is that we have become too intellectual for our people. Sometimes I wonder if they understand me."*

---

*Pastor Altwegg has since transferred to a parish in Adliswil, an upper-middle-class suburb of Zurich.

13

FLOWERS AMONG STONES

The Swiss are little people so God sends them little devils   while, the rest of the world fights big devils . . .
                                                              —Carl G. Jung

I met Yolande Jacobi at a Christmas open house in her apartment on Wilfriedstrasse. It was a large affair and I had little opportunity to speak to the hostess, but her intellectual force and exquisite graciousness captivated my imagination.

Dr. Jacobi was a votary of Dr. Carl Jung, whose response to and effect on women was legendary in his lifetime. He was admired by women, flirted with them, preferred their company to that of men, and was more successful with them as patients. A covey of intellectual women gathered around him, became his patrons, and fought for his attention. Most of them were jealous of Dr. Jacobi for her aggressive zeal and professional reputation and called her "the devil's grandmother." She was the strongest of Jung's "ladies" and, after his death in 1961, was appointed to the *Kuratorium,* which directed the Jung Institute, and became its most famous member.

After the party at Dr. Jacobi's home I went to the Zurich library to learn more about her. She was born Yolande Székács in 1890 in

Budapest to wealthy Jewish parents who were baptized Catholics. The emancipation of women was a controversial issue in Budapest at the beginning of the twentieth century and Yolande had to overcome her parents' conviction that a woman's place was in the home. When she was fourteen she enrolled in a predominantly male high school. At nineteen she married a successful lawyer, Dr. Andrew Jacobi, and had two sons. In 1919, after the communist takeover of Hungary, she moved with her family to Vienna. The move resulted in a serious depression for her husband. In her effort to understand what was happening to him, Yolande Jacobi read everything available on the new science of psychotherapy and she was able to bring about her husband's recovery.

In Vienna she joined the Austrian *Kulturbund,* became its vice-president, and was soon at the center of Vienna's intellectual life. In 1927 she met Dr. Jung when he was in Vienna for a lecture and they became friends. Seven years later she wrote to ask him to train her as an analyst and he replied that she must first earn her doctorate. At age forty-four Yolande Jacobi enrolled at the University of Vienna to study with teachers of the Freudian and Adlerian schools of psychoanalysis. Four months before the completion of her degree the Nazis occupied Austria. After her home was ransacked by the Gestapo she lived with friends and wore mourning in order to cover her face with a veil. In October 1938 she moved to Zurich. When the Nazis occupied Hungary Dr. Jacobi's parents were arrested and committed suicide; her husband died in a concentration camp. One son was studying in Zurich when she arrived there; the other was not permitted to leave Hungary until 1956. Of these tragic years, Dr. Jacobi said, "I owe Jung my life."

With the publication of three books and many articles, Dr. Jacobi became a recognized interpreter of Jungian theory. After the Second World War she lectured in European universities and in America at Yale, Harvard, and Princeton. Her reputation as a psychotherapist grew. She conceived a Homeric view of human nature and its survival as a balance between man's inner and outer worlds, a confluence of introversion and extroversion. It was a genesis of Jungian theory by which she had triumphed over the catastrophes of her own life.

In January, when relations with my Swiss mentors had reached such a culmination of incomprehensibility that I was making plans to go home, I received an invitation from Dr. Jacobi to come to tea. I was eager to talk with her. My own life had been enriched by Jungian analysis and I had just finished reading Dr. Jacobi's work on Jung's concept of individuation.

The afternoon began with a crisis. When I took off my raincoat I discovered that the zipper on my fly was sprung! With careful, self-conscious steps I moved to the chair to which my hostess directed me and sat with crossed legs, turning napkins into fig leaves. If Dr. Jacobi was aware of my dilemma she gave no sign.

We were in the dark-paneled drawing room in which I had been before. Renaissance paintings and Gothic sculpture, illuminated by soft candlelight, gave off a sacerdotal air and when Dr. Jacobi prepared tea and served cakes she might have been a high priestess engaged in mystic divination. Small and slight of body, she moved with fragile, queenly grace. When she spoke her dark eyes flashed and the strength surging forth from her dominated the room. With her Circean intuition she could hardly have helped sensing some need in myself.

"How are you finding the Swiss; what do you think of them?" she asked.

"At the moment I am not thinking especially well of them," I replied.

"That's understandable. They are not a lovable people."

"What I resent most are the qualities they are bringing out in me. A touch of paranoia, for instance, the feeling that people are against me."

Dr. Jacobi smiled. "That's the difference between you and me," she said. "You think they may be against you. I *know* they're against me. Paranoia is a part of Swissness, and living here one cannot escape it."

I remembered from my own therapy that in paranoia other persons became threats and potential enemies and that this was rooted in a sense of inferiority, a battered ego. I spoke of the outbursts of hysteria in the Swiss offices with which I was associated and my subsequent awareness of the rise of paranoid reflexes in myself.

"I understand very well," said Dr. Jacobi. "The legendary Swiss efficiency about which one hears so much is real enough when they deal with inanimate materials, with controllable objects like chemicals, fine instruments, machines. But the 'efficiency' falls apart completely when it is confronted with the uncontrollable human factor, with people. Not having a healthy ego to sustain his position the paranoid cannot endure being challenged or opposed. Contention becomes persecution and logical behavior is abandoned to emotionality, and hysterical outbursts.

"This is a national trait. Everyone has a trace of it; everyone feels himself constantly observed and judged. And of course everyone is, because every Swiss is constantly observing and judging every other Swiss."

As she spoke I remembered my own childhood and youth in New Glarus, for she seemed to be describing how it was—and in some measure still is—in my Wisconsin village. I recalled a never-ending preoccupation with the behavior of others and I could hear my mother's worried voice whenever my own behavior deviated from her rigid code: "What will people say?" That single question, repeated over and over, became the abiding stricture of my life for I was always doing things about which people might talk and I believed myself the most talked-about person in town.

"It begins with jealousy," said Dr. Jacobi. "The Swiss are jealous of everyone who dares to step outside the confines of their own lives. Jealousy is one of their two strongest emotions."

"What is the other?"

"Fear. They are frightened all the time and they never escape their fears. They are afraid of life and the world; they are afraid of one another and especially of strangers. Everything is a threat."

I remembered this too, a childhood fraught with fears of lightning and high winds, of water and boats and all conceivable disasters, fear of the dark and every imaginable supernatural phenomenon.

"They fear nature," Dr. Jacobi continued. "The dangers of alpine life, the memories of violent deaths in avalanches and floods make them superstitious and wary of evil spirits. All Swiss, even those urban ones who pretend to sophistication, are primitive rustics ruled by an unknown demonism. It is a mistake to assume they are a twentieth-century people living in the modern world. They live still in the dark centuries of demonology. Even more than nature, they fear people. Centuries of life in the narrow, snowbound valleys have made them hostile and suspicious. They see everyone as a poacher on a domain, as an enemy. Always suspicious, they mistrust and hate one another. Their fears have made them deeply introverted, have given them a crushing sense of inferiority. They care mostly for creatures inferior to themselves, for children, animals, the aged, and sometimes the poor. With equals they cannot cope because they feel inferior to them and fear them."

The candle flame beside Dr. Jacobi lit her face and eyes and gave her a youthful glow. She continued:

"With a sense of inferiority there is a loss of self-respect and emotional disturbance is inevitable. The typical Swiss smugness, the arrogant conviction that the world is wrong and they are right is not the anachronism it may seem. It is a defense set up against their own fears. Everything is a threat."

I recalled a newspaper editor who blamed anxieties and fears for the Swiss obsession with insurance. "Everything is insured and premiums come to a quarter of one's annual income," he said. "When a baby is born a procession of insurance solicitors arrive at the door. To purchase skis means insuring them and yourself. Insurer lobbyists have a great influence on government and are a predatory influence in Swiss life."

I spoke of something which puzzled me: the Swiss habit of suggesting social engagements and never following through, speaking frequently and vaguely of inviting me to their homes and never setting a date. I recalled a young writer who stood me up on a dinner date and a month later phoned to inquire why I never called him. When I reminded him of the broken appointment he replied that the anesthetic for an operation six months before had affected his memory and he had forgotten.

"It is one of their greatest problems," Dr. Jacobi said. "And fear is the reason for it, fear of opening their house to you, the fear that you may learn the secrets of their domestic life. Having a very bad conscience about their social manners, they must pass the blame. They will ask you why you haven't called when in fact, as they well know, it is they who should have called. And because of this they are very, very lonely."

As Dr. Jacobi went on I sensed how my visit was stimulating her, how she was being spurred by a sympathetic listener. I even detected a hint of impish mischief as she continued with unerring intuition to touch on matters submerged deep within me.

"One of the greatest fears of the Swiss is sex," she said. "The revulsion goes back to what Jung called 'group incest,' which was once so strong in mountain villages and huts. No Swiss is free of it because everyone, no matter where or how he lives, has parents or grandparents who were village peasants. It is the Lord's curse on a people. There is an absolute lack of communication on a physical level. There is none of the sensitivity of the French, the healthy lust of the Italian, or even the sentiment of the German. It is all crude bestiality, an act of hostility. Attitudes about sex are completely unnatural. It's either sacred or profane—the wife or the whore—and both are unrealistic. When a man approaches a woman it is with crudeness and vulgarity, with the puritanical attitudes of shame and fear. The men's long refusal to give women the vote was a matter of revenge; the vote was the one thing they had to withhold. Women worry so much about voting when they should earn the right to it in bed first. The vote has been the last male prerogative, the men's final bastion of superiority over the female in a losing battle. In turn women have taken their revenge by dominance and family control. I attribute this in part to a lack of femininity in women who have become masculine and bossy. Swiss men do not get the sense of beauty and feminine refinement from their mothers that would prepare them for a healthy and balanced sexual relationship.

"So denying sex they have replaced it with money. The acquisition of money and what it can buy has become their emotional life. This is the real source of what we call *malaise suisse*. They are unhappy and they don't know why."

I said, "I have been thinking of Dr. Jung's theory of race memory which quite certainly is exercised in me for I recognize what you are saying."

"But you are fortunate," Dr. Jacobi said. "You don't know how fortunate you are. You have the recognition without the being. You have escaped the greatest of the Swiss psychic perils: the repression of the imagination and the negation of human instincts. Swiss men strive for success in the world of things, in banking, commerce, the manufacture of machines and chemicals. But being introverted they have a deep, dark imagination which must be repressed. Anything dealing with imagination they cannot accept. This also is a fear—a fear of opening up the caves of demons in themselves. Of course, the fear of demons is an unconscious one—they do not *believe* in them, their science no longer permits men to accept the supernatural, so the demons have been internalized and that is why they are so dangerous. There are many families in Switzerland that have at least one member tucked away in an asylum. Sometimes I think of the country as, in effect, one great asylum."

"I have had exactly the same thought," I said. "There are times when I even question my own sanity."

Dr. Jacobi laughed softly. "I know," she said. "I know. But there is your strength, your knowledge that you *are* sane. When everyone else is wrong, you will cling to your conviction that you are right."

For two hours that afternoon, with her enchantress's insights, wit, and poetry, Dr. Jacobi dispelled my melancholic mood, restored my humor, and healed my bruised ego. When I left her it was with a euphoria of shimmering elucidation and joy in the gift of friendship she had conferred upon me. With hardly an awareness of conscious deliberation, a decision had been made. I would stay in Switzerland.

During that winter in Zurich I saw Dr. Jacobi frequently. We attended the opera together; I was invited to her house and sometimes we went out to lunch. One Sunday in February we lunched at a popular downtown restaurant that she favored. A line was waiting for tables. Dr. Jacobi, who was recognized, moved through it like a queen and led me to a table. The restaurant was famous for its dessert buffet to which guests returned after a heavy meal to fill large plates with pastries, ices, and fruit. At a table near ours three enormous old ladies who wore identical fur hats and probably were sisters, chomped heartily from stacked plates. Their conversation, punctuated with eating, consisted almost entirely of one word:

"*Schön . . .*"

"*Ja, schön . . .*"

"*Schön, nid?*"

"*Sehr schön . . .*"

"*Schön, schön . . .*"

"Three graces on an orgy," I said. Dr. Jacobi's merry laugh rippled through the hall.

"A perfect description," she said. "One needs only to look at them to see that eating is the only sensuality possible for them." We touched our glasses of sherry and she said, "Orgy excesses are very important to the

Swiss. Their festivals are pagan surfacings of race memory turned into orgies of release from repressions and puritanical negation. In a week they will begin carnival and you will be puzzled by the transvestism, by an apparent passion for Swiss men to dress in women's clothes. They do so not out of a desire to become women but as a rebellion against women.

"Festivals are necessary safety valves for releasing the dangerous tensions. By parodying their fears they are able for a moment to escape them. Dressing in women's clothes gives men complete license; they feel free to do everything that is forbidden. Wearing masks is a kind of therapy and I know doctors who send shy, inhibited patients to the carnival artists' ball. One man was shocked to find his wife there, behaving as licentiously as himself.

"The most interesting festival is not carnival but the *Sechseläuten*, which comes later, in April. That is the one day that the men of Zurich are permitted to feel like men, when they are completely freed from the dominance of women. For a day and a night they celebrate their rebellion and women throw them flowers from windows. But the women triumph in the end. At four o'clock in the morning they wander through the streets and appear at the clubhouses to collect their drunken husbands and take them home. The wifely controls and repressions are reaffirmed."

Dr. Jacobi asked me if I thought I could live in Switzerland. I replied that I did not think so but that I had come to look on my year in Switzerland as a necessary self-discovery, a time for more deeply understanding my own Swissness.

"I understand that," she said. I asked her a question which did not at the moment seem presumptive. "Are you happy here?"

"I have been here forty years," she replied. "My life has been disrupted several times by the tragedies of Europe and I have experienced too much. Here life is comfortable and easy. It has taken all of forty years but I have become quite fond of the Swiss and feel a mother's tenderness toward them. They are so, *so terribly* unhappy."

She was thoughtful for a moment and her eyes glowed. Speaking softly she said, "Knowing and working with Dr. Jung has been my great fulfillment. Switzerland was as necessary for me as it was for him. Where else but in the human laboratory of Switzerland could his greatness have emerged? Only a Swiss with his Swiss awareness of the soul's suffering could have developed as he did. By opening up the avenues of the spirit, of myth, art, literature, and religion that are the genesis of his vision, by exploring the light and dark rivers in the souls that he knew, he was able to show the way toward a happier life for all people. He said it best himself: 'My flowers blossom only among stones.'

"Where else," she wondered, "could I have found so vast a field for studying the human problem?"*

---

*Dr. Jacobi died unexpectedly on April 1, 1973. She was eighty-three years old.

14

UNKNOWN TERRORS

Dr. Jacobi's image of the fear-haunted Swiss character would not let me rest. I saw a play by Friedrich Dürrenmatt, *Der Meteor,* the theme of which was fear of eternal life; and I remembered that all the plays I had seen or read by Switzerland's two renowned playwrights, Dürrenmatt and Max Frisch, dealt with unknown terrors. In *Der Meteor* an aged Nobel Prize dramatist, Schwitters, is on his deathbed unable to die because he cannot believe in his resurrection. While Schwitters continues to live the persons around him who are awaiting his death—his physician, his pastor, his wife—all die. Dürrenmatt's terrifying irony is that those who wish to continue living perish, while the only one who wishes to die must live on. As a Salvation Army chorus plays and sings hymns the old man cries out in anguish, "When will I finally die?"

I discussed the psychology of the Swiss character with journalists and bankers, with artists, professors and students, and from the conversations some patterns emerged which supported the insights Dr. Jacobi was giving me.

A journalist invited me to call at his office. He was a small, soft-voiced man, younger than myself, who apologized for publishing a negative review of one of my books, explaining it was not the book he found wanting but the translation. He spoke of an older brother of whom I reminded him, who had committed suicide, and he attributed Switzerland's high suicide rate to the fears, in a small country, of largeness, of things unknown and uncontrollable.

"Everything is so controlled that anything not controlled, anything unknown, becomes a terror, like a dark room," he said. "I am a good swimmer. In my youth I was able to swim across Lake Zurich. Now I am unable to go into water in which I cannot see the bottom."

Zeit ist Geld—time is money—is an aphorism I've heard all my life, and one day at lunch I discussed it with Peter Studer, an editor of the newspaper *Tages Anzeiger*. He told me that most Swiss, whether they admit it or not, are driven by this Calvinist maxim. "It is responsible for the guilt a Swiss feels for every minute not usefully spent. It turns a holiday into a frenzied pursuit of as many places as it is possible to see in a single day, as many miles as it is possible to drive. It is responsible for the *Putzwut* or 'cleaning frenzy' mentality of so many Swiss women. They must be doing something all the time; they are constantly running like Olympic racers. It has much to do with some women's disinterest in suffrage. They fear they don't have time."

A young architect I knew spent twelve hours a day in his office, was seldom home before eight o'clock, and then usually worked several hours more on a design. "I am not happy when I am not working," he said. "I love my children but it bores me to be with them." His wife understood his fear of not working and managed their household to support it.

A banker spoke of the inability of the Swiss to make up their minds, of long and agonized indecisiveness which made every business negotiation seem to last forever. This was something I understood, for indecisiveness was one of my own torments. The banker said it was based on a fear of the unknown, the inability to substitute for a familiar situation one that was unfamiliar.

A Catholic painter from the Italian-speaking canton of Tessin blamed the unhappiness of the Swiss on Protestantism. "Catholics find their release from guilt in confession," he said. "The Swiss Protestant is forever carrying his burden of guilt which grows and grows and can never be absolved."

A professor who lectured on American literature described Switzerland as "a matriarchical, materialist land of indulged happy children and unhappy adults." He said, "Children are the perfect materialists; they identify with the things we urge upon them. But with maturity the passion for things becomes either obsessive or unfulfilling or both, and the worried expressions set in." Making more or less the same point, an elementary teacher blamed Swiss discontent on the pampering of children. "Indulgent, dominating mothers sow the seeds of frustration and self-centered isolation," he said.

I kept encountering striking examples of parent-dominated men. A successful bookseller, thirty-five years old, lived with his parents because whenever he spoke of getting his own apartment his mother had a "heart attack." He dreamed of escaping to Tangiers and opening a shop but it was obvious he never would. An extremely nervous thirty-one-year-old lawyer, the only child of doting parents in Davos, lived in a room in the apartment of an elderly woman who kept a close watch over him and reported his activities to his mother. He had a German fiancée of whom his parents disapproved; because his parents insisted he visit them every weekend that relationship was foundering. The young lawyer seemed to be living in a variety of cages, cages provided by his parents, the zealously watching widow, and by his army lieutenant, a Zurich hoteliere, who kept a close guard over him. "Switzerland is so small," he said one night over a drink after a performance of *La Traviata*. "I should like to invite you to my house but it is impossible. Whenever we plan to have a guest my father is in a bad temper for several days because his routine is upset. So we never have guests."

Sometimes when I thought the Swiss judgment of themselves too harsh I would take issue with them. Once a businessman quoted André Gide to the effect that the Swiss had icebergs for hearts, and he himself added, "We are a cold people unable to comprehend human needs." I asked how he could reconcile that view with the Swiss reputation for humanitarian benevolence, for their founding of the Red Cross, their welcoming of thousands of political refugees from Nazi Germany and more recently from Hungary and Czechoslovakia, of their support of a children's village in the Canton of Appenzell for 250 world orphans, and of a refugee village in the mountains north of Zurich in which displaced Tibetans live according to their Buddhist traditions. He replied that these well-known generosities rose out of guilt over prosperity and uninvolvement in the world's wars. "Call it a pretense of idealism to mask our materialism," he said cynically.

One evening after my lecture at the university I brought up the subject of fear to some students whom I had accompanied to a cafe.

"We are afraid of people," said a girl named Sabina. "But really, I think we are most afraid of ourselves, of our inability to communicate emotions. We fear the exposure of intimacy so much that we cannot give ourselves to people."

I spoke of instances of kindness from strangers, when persons had seemed to reach out to me. The conductor on a city funicular, the *Dolderbähnli,* had shaken my hand when I entered and left his little train; a clerk in the foreigners' registry in City Hall had invited me, on a first meeting, for a weekend at his vacation house in the mountains. I recalled the middle-aged woman, of whom I had inquired where I might take a certain tram, insisting on walking, ponderously, five blocks out of her way to show me. How, as we walked, she spoke of her visit with relatives in Chicago and how, when she delivered me to the tram stop, she shook my hand and wished me a pleasant evening.

"Yes, that is how we are," said a tall red-haired girl named Margaret. "We long to be friends but only when it is safe, when it does not involve or commit us, when we do not feel the threat of real contact. Because we fear that, we keep everyone at a distance and this makes us rather ill-mannered. I'm sure you've noticed this."

"Because we are afraid," said Sabina. "We want to see people and so we speak of doing it but when the time comes we are too frightened."

"We are afraid of pleasure," said Walter, an economics student preparing to be a banker. "Everything enjoyable is forbidden. We are even afraid to laugh because in laughing we are guilty of pleasure. When a foreigner laughs on a train we look at him reprovingly and when someone asks, 'How are you?' we reply '*Ja, es gaht*'—it goes— and never '*gut*' because to have a good life implies something sinful."

"We're entirely too self-centered," said Peter, a good-looking blond youth who was going into medicine. "We think of no one but ourselves; we cannot comprehend another's emotions. It's the heritage of our history, that we be concerned only for our own survival."

"We cannot rise above our village mentality; our instincts have been atrophied," Walter commented. "Except for our bankers, Switzerland would be an archaic curiosity like Lichenstein. We cannot differentiate between little things and big things and it is the little things that dominate our lives. Only bankers think big."

We spoke of marriage and the relationship between the sexes, subjects in which the students had a keen interest. Margaret said, "There is an attitude against educating women. My father is not very pleased that I am going to the university. He says men are prejudiced against educated women and he is right."

"That is true here in German Switzerland but not in the French-speaking cantons," said Peter. "In Geneva there is freedom in these matters. Boys and girls meet in the university and they fall in love and they marry. But in Zurich this does not happen."

"Educated men deliberately marry inferior girls," said Sabina. "They want housekeepers and childbearers and have no interest in sharing an intellectual life with a wife. Isn't it so?" she asked, turning to Walter. "You can't say it isn't."

Walter blushed. "I don't think it's that way with all young men. I have friends who married girls who are not Swiss because they could not find Swiss girls that were intellectually interesting." What he was saying did not surprise me. I knew a young minister in Glarus who had a Swedish wife and I had two friends, both newspaper editors, one of whom was married to an Australian wife and the other to an English woman.

I spoke of something else I had observed. Unlike American men, who consider a chic and glamorous wife a professional and social asset, Swiss businessmen retained glamour for themselves. They wore eye-catching tailored clothes, had coiffeurs care for their hair, and expected their wives to launder, starch and press to keep up their self-images for a business-social life which excluded their wives. The wives, on the other hand, dressed with unfashionable simplicity, often in drab colors which were oddly enough, however, frequently enhanced by expensive and striking jewels.

"It's true," Margaret said. "Men want their wives to be busy mice and they dislike them to be chic because it takes the attention from themselves. The diamonds and pearls are an investment and they want their wives to wear them to show they can afford them."

The hour was late and a waitress was clearing tables, letting us know it was time to leave.

"We like to complain," said Walter. "We are always saying how unhappy we are, how dreadful life is, how unfriendly people are. Yet we stay. We do not leave."

"Our loneliness is like an illness," said Sabina, whose soft eyes were pools of pain. "We don't know the way to the doctor and if someone shows us the path, we are too shy, too frightened, to follow it to the door."

15

HIDDEN WEALTH

It was snowing hard and the train to Winterthur was running late. I checked my watch and counted the minutes. The invitation in my pocket said I was to be allowed exactly one and a half hours, beginning at 10:30 A.M., to view a private treasure trove of art which an art historian described as "one of the secret wonders of Switzerland."

It's a hushed truth that the Swiss own more art masterpieces per capita than any other people in the world. Switzerland, which has neither import nor export duties on works of art, is Europe's most active art market. Art in private collections is a hidden national wealth which, with few exceptions, is like numbered bank accounts, concealed from the public.

The mania for collecting is a retaliation to history. The Reformation banished art from Switzerland at the time that the Renaissance was in its final burst of glory in Italy, Spain, and the Netherlands. Zwingli, who believed paintings and statues to be idolatrous, stripped the churches of art, turning them into the austere gray gothic temples that most of them remain to this day. "Zwingli killed art," a museum director said. "We had no kings or dukes or popes to collect for us. So we diverted our creative energies into sciences, technology, and theology."

Quite suddenly, at the beginning of this century, a passion for collecting broke out in the small industrial city of Winterthur and spread out over the land. It was engendered by a feisty, strong-willed lady named Hedy Hahnloser-Bühler. In 1907 Hedy bought a nude by the Swiss-born French painter Felix Vallotton, which shocked the good Protestants of Winterthur. Through Vallotton, Hedy met the artists of Paris and began buying their works. This was the time that the school of painters known as *les fauves* was bursting forth in the Paris art community, and Hedy bought up the "wild beasts' "vivid, dissonantly colored canvasses as quickly as they produced them. To be near the painters she rented a villa in Cannes, and invited them to Winterthur. She organized a Tuesday *Kaffeeklatsch,* called "the revolution table," at which she urged the wives of such rich industrialists as Reinhard (machines and locomotives), Sulzer (Diesel engines and turbines), and Bühler (textiles) to buy art. The "revolution table" turned into a movement. A new class of wealthy industrialists, bankers, and businessmen quickly recognized that art was an investment, and collecting spread to Zurich and other cities.

Hedy Hahnloser was not a rich woman. But fortunately, her husband, an oculist, was able to support her compulsion. Trusting her intuition, and bargaining shrewdly, Hedy assembled one of the most massive collections of French art in the world. After her death, in 1952, her thousands of paintings and engravings were divided between her two children, Lisa Jäggli-Hahnloser and Dr. Hans Hahnloser, a Berne professor of art. Professor Hahnloser moved his collection to Berne and Frau Jäggli kept hers in her mother's house, where she continued to live with her husband, a retired banker. It was from Frau Jäggli that my invitation had come.

I urged the taxi driver to hurry and arrived only four minutes late. The house, called Sur Flora was so unimposing that I wondered for a moment if the driver had made a mistake. The modest family home, built in 1840, had been enlarged by the purchase of a similar house next door and the two were joined by a corridor. The Jägglis greeted me graciously. Frau Jäggli had white hair and was wearing walking shoes and a wool skirt and sweater—clothes worn in winter in underheated homes. The house was spacious but, except for the paintings, without luxury. There were no formal galleries. Pictures had been hung everywhere, not a foot of wall space seemed uncovered, and others were stacked on floors.

Herr Jäggli excused himself, and his wife at once took me on a tour of the labyrinthian rooms, which were on varying levels and joined by steps. The rooms were poorly lit by ceiling bulbs. Still they glowed with the paintings' lights, the bright warm French flush of Bonnard, Cézanne, Matisse, Renoir, Vuillard, and Roussel. On and on it went, each room devoted to an individual artist and every one with pictures overflowing into corridors and on staircases. It was too much to take in, too much to believe that such a hoard could exist outside a museum.

"Mother was a fighter," Lisa Jäggli said in excellent English. "In her time people were against French art—it was considered decadent and shocking. My brother was beaten in school because the children were told our pictures were sinful. When mother paid five thousand francs for a Renoir, her brother, a banker, saw the check. He and my grandmother put on their Sunday clothes and paid us a call, ordering my mother to stop her madness. When she refused, my uncle said, 'If you ever need potatoes for your children, don't come to me.' Naturally there was a family rift, and when my mother persisted in what her relatives considered throwing money away, they threatened to have her declared incompetent and appoint a guardian. It was true; we were often deprived of necessities because all the money my father could earn went to artists. We were never allowed more than one small piece of meat and the butcher let it be known that we were undernourished, that working people ate better than we did. Life was never easy with mother but it was always exciting. We loved the summers in France with the painters."

We were in a room filled with Bonnards, paintings of graceful Parisiennes by an artist known in his time as the *enchanteur*. Lisa Jäggli said, "Bonnard was our neighbor, as were Vallotton and Manguin. Each artist saved his paintings until mother arrived in the summer so she could have first choice. She had the idea to follow through each career, to acquire a full documentation of an artist's development, and she bought fifty Bonnards." I was looking at a large and lovely painting of a family group, with a dog seated in a boat. It was called *Promenade en mer*. "The family in the boat is our own," said Lisa Jäggli. "For years mother had begged Bonnard to do a painting of us and he kept promising but never did one. Then one day he saw us sailing with the dog and he took out his sketch pad and began to draw. He loved to include dogs in his pictures and mother was wearing a light blue coat which came out a perfect Bonnard blue."

We passed into a room filled with sculptures, including Rodin's bust of Balzac made ten years after the author's death. "Rodin shows Balzac as a strong, muscular man when he was actually quite the opposite," said Lisa Jäggli. "What Rodin had in mind was Balzac's spiritual strength and the brute-beast he sensed lived in Balzac. To the beast's strength he added the head of Balzac, the spirituality. It was as Rodin saw Balzac, as he felt about him."

Near the Rodin was a bust of Hedy Hahnloser by Marini and it had a strong, high forehead and a firm, determined mouth. It looked, I said, like the head of a Roman senator. "You're quite right. Mother *was* a Roman senator. She did not like the piece at first but I daresay Marini did not see her incorrectly. She was sick much of her life and several times near death, but her passion for collecting healed her again and again. Her fear, that in dying she would miss out on something new, something great, kept her alive. She was a friend to all her painters and took a keen personal interest in them. Sometimes she would say, 'Now he's gone too far; I won't follow him anymore.' But follow she would and much of what she collected shocked the people of Winterthur. In her later years she took immense pride in her astuteness and boasted how each artist had been ahead of his time and a prophet."

One of Hedy's greatest enthusiasms was for Felix Vallotton from whom she bought fifty paintings and two hundred engravings. The most enchanting was a portrait of two children, a seated boy and standing girl who were Frau Jäggli and her brother. "He didn't like to paint children, but he was intrigued by the composition possibilities of our black stockings." In the background of the picture the artist had painted a detailed copy of another of his paintings, the original of which was hanging in the next room. This was a picture of the Seine emptying into the sea, entitled *Embouchure de la Seine.*

We raced from room to room, trying to cover everything in the designated time, passing walls of Cézannes, Corots, Daumiers, and Renoirs. One bedroom was filled with Matisses; there was also a stack of them against the wall behind a chest. And there were some erotic paintings, including one of nude ladies bathing in the sea, by Maurice Denis, a painter who became a monk. Another artist whom Hedy supported through his entire life was Henri Manguin. "He lived with us during the First World War and painted right here in this room," said Frau Jäggli. "Winterthur was Germanophile and Manguin's children were so tormented in school we had to send them into French Switzerland." There were several nudes of the artist's wife. "Madame Manguin was one of the few wives of artists mother liked. One she especially disliked was Madame Vallotton, whom she called 'the tigress.'"

Halting before the pictures, Frau Jäggli held a folded newspaper above her eyes to shut out the glimmering highlights. We saw early and late Van Goghs, flower paintings by Odilon Redon, a room of Utrillos and Vlaminks, some of which were hanging over a sink. A laundry room in which a maid was doing a steaming wash was filled with Rouaults. "In 1913 mother went to a show in Paris and saw Rouault for the first time. He was poor and unknown and she bought forty pictures in one afternoon. Then years later, when he was famous, Rouault tried to buy them back but mother was not to give up any and the friendship cooled.

"As children we were kept busy nights cataloging the collections. I began to slip in school and had to get up at five o'clock to do my homework. We were always short of money. In spite of our poverty mother managed a never-ending open house for artists."

There was no accurate record of what the collection had cost Hedy, nor had it been professionally appraised. Certainly, its original cost was infinitesimal compared to its current value. Before her death Hedy Hahnloser herself directed its division between her two children. "It was well she did," said her daughter. "It saved us a lot of strife."

Three weeks later I called Professor Hans Hahnloser to ask if I might see his half of the collection and he graciously invited me to lunch. The professor was a short, dynamic man in his sixties who had just returned from a skiing holiday. His house on a hill had a superb view of Berne's Gothic cathedral set against a horizon of snow-covered alps.

My immediate impression was that Professor Hahnloser's collection was even more striking than his sister's but this judgment was probably due to the more advantageous presentation of the paintings against white walls in well-lit rooms. The first paintings facing me as I entered were Van Gogh's *Girl With Straw Hat* and a large Gauguin nude, *Anna la Javanèse.* The Gauguin figure, deep purple against a mauve background, was illuminated by a bright pink monkey at the girl's side. In the same room were Utrillos, Matisses, Toulouse-Lautrecs, three Cézannes, and six more Van Goghs including the famous *Night Cafe.*

There was a room of Bonnards, among them a larger, more detailed painting of the Hahnloser family in a boat for which Frau Jäggli's version appeared to be an original study, and pictures by Utrillo, Matisse, Manguin, Vallotton, and all the other artists I had seen in Winterthur. The grandchildren's playroom upstairs was filled with the works of Ferdinand Hodler, Switzerland's first modern painter, whose works Hedy collected when he was considered a controversial and dangerous revolutionary and who became, in her lifetime, Switzerland's most esteemed artist.

In the professor's house also there were paintings stacked on floors because there was no place to hang them. Crates of engravings were awaiting shipment to an exhibition in Germany. I asked about the problems of insuring such a Herculean collection. "If I worried about such matters as fire and theft I would not be able to sleep," the professor replied. "Besides, stolen paintings almost always come back." He recalled how, when he was a child in Winterthur a Christmas tree had been ignited by candles and extinguished before any paintings were damaged.

Professor Hahnloser's son, Bernard, a lawyer, joined us for lunch. Bernard remembered his grandmother as a nervous, energetic old lady who was always at a typewriter preparing articles on art. "She had eleven cats who crowded around her typewriter and which she kept pushing off her manuscripts," he said.

At least three of Switzerland's private collections have been opened to the public. In Winterthur I saw two collections assembled by Oscar Reinhard, the bachelor son of one of Hedy Hahnloser's coffee-table friends. The first, housed in a converted schoolhouse, included five hundred nineteenth-century pictures of the Swiss and Austrian and German schools of mountain-landscape painting. The second collection, housed in Reinhard's villa, Römerholz, known as "Switzerland's

National Gallery," is divided between French impressionists and masters of the Italian and North European Renaissance, including Rembrandt, Holbein, Rubens, Breughel, Bassano, and El Greco.

In Zurich I saw the Bührle collection of Rembrandts, painters of the Venetian Renaissance, and French artists from Van Gogh and Cézanne through Braque and Picasso. The Bührle fortune was derived from the manufacture of machine guns and munitions and the day after I saw the collection students in the square outside my apartment were demonstrating against Bührle's sale of arms to warring African countries.

My friend Jenny Brenner was vexed. "Why do you spend all your time in cemeteries?" she asked. "Don't you realize that what you're seeing is finished, is dead? Art must be a living, a contemporary experience."

Jenny and her husband, Hugo, a businessman, were collectors. Their home was a gallery of abstract paintings and sculptures. The Brenners were part of an affluent middle class for whom collecting was an avocation with social prestige. Life for the Brenners and their friends was made up of *vernissages*—literally "varnishings"—the name given to receptions for artists held in Zurich's seventy exhibition galleries. There were sometimes several of these in a day and I attended one at 11 A.M. on a Saturday for a young Bernese named Rolf Iseli. "One of our most important artists," said Jenny. "Any collection of consequence includes him."

A large crowd was drinking white wine and chattering rhapsodically over a curious display. On the walls were large drawings of clothes pins and the rooms were filled with gigantic wood and aluminum pop sculptures, including several huge wooden feet down the slopes of which children were sliding as in a playground. The largest foot was priced at 6,500 francs. There was also a sculptured tooth at the same price and the clothes-pin drawings ranged in price from 1,200 to 2,500 francs. I could not help wondering whether the artist, a jolly, good-humored young man busily discussing his work, might not be secretly laughing at the earnestness of his patrons and thinking of the checks they were going to write.

"What's the matter?" Jenny asked me. "Don't you like it?" She introduced me to an art professor named Stolz, an intense little man who, she said, would educate me. He commenced at once, leading me to a structure of four squared beams bolted into a quadrangle. "You see, the artist has not assigned its function," Dr. Stolz said. "That is the beauty of the piece. You can put flowers on it, sit or sleep on it, or throw your mackintosh over it. Therefore, by assigning a function, you are participating in the act of creation." He directed my attention to the children sliding down the foot. "See what I mean. The foot is an amazing defunctionalization of a functional object and the children are turning it into a slide. Isn't that wonderful?" Sensing my Philistine bafflement, Dr. Stolz became bored and wandered away. In minutes Jenny returned and said, "I must tell you in a very friendly way that you did not make a good impression on Dr. Stolz. He found you rather stupid."

I went to the wine table and opened a conversation with an attractive young woman who turned out to be a French art critic named Claire, and I discovered that she shared my reservations. "It's all infantile and absurd and cannot be taken seriously," she said. "These people are *arrivistes, nouveau riches* who have to collect something or they would go crazy. They are socially ambitious people not accepted in the rigid Zurich society. So they create a kind of exclusiveness of their own, a life of *vernissages* and viewings. They're playing a masturbatory game with one another, supporting and compounding the absurdity. The best one can say of them is that they are children with toys."

A type of art for which there is a great Swiss fad is "kinetic sculpture" containing moving parts, a functionless and sometimes fascinating by-product of Switzerland's watch and fine-instrument industries. The most famous collector of kinetics is a Berne department store owner named Victor Loeb who invited me to a "room-opening party" in the Berne suburb of Muri. The new basement gallery in his house had marble floors and ceiling spotlights and was filled with fantasy machines plugged into wall sockets and all were in motion. One had ten cogged wheels turning a myriad of semaphore flags. Another had balls bumping around on a revolving disc. A silver mesh disc undulated and pendulums swung inside glass cylinders. Everything was in motion and I had the eerie feeling of being trapped in a Martian toy store. The guests marveling over the devices were a combination of bohemia and Berne society. Women were wearing knee breeches and leather boots, young men's eyes were shadowed blue, and a tall Polish artist with burled hair and beard and a long fur coat looked like an unwashed Mongol. A stereo blared rock recordings entitled "It's All Meat" and "Mama Told Me Not to Come" and guests danced among the moving machines. I watched a trembling object that seemed to be breathing, and a government cultural officer, almost weeping with excitement, said, "Isn't it fantastic to get such an effect? This is art for the masses, for everyone to enjoy."

My purpose in Berne was to see an exhibition in the *Kunsthalle* of which Mr. Loeb was a director and which is the most innovative and controversial public gallery in Switzerland. The current show, entitled "Live In Your Head," was a *succès de scandale* which had aroused the entire country. It was sponsored by the Philip Morris Europe Company, whose president wrote for the catalog, "We at Philip Morris feel it is appropriate that we participate in bringing these works to the attention of the public for there is a key element in this new art which has its counterpart in the business world. That element is innovation . . ." About half the exhibitors were American.

In the first room some wilted flowers were sprayed with liquid mica. Straps hung from wall hooks, as in a harness room. A swatch of rotted burlap hung from a wire. The corners of the room were spattered with some yellow stuff that looked like beaten egg yolks. From the next room I heard two voices engaged in a nonstop argument:

"*Ja, ja . . .*"
"*Nai, nai . . .*"
"*Ja, ja, ja . . .*"
"*Nai, nai, nai . . .*"
"*Ja, jaaaaa . . .*"
"*Nai, nai, naaaaai . . .*"

I moved into the room and saw a crowd gathered about the strangest display in the gallery. Some layers of rectangular gray felt were piled on the floor, forming a kind of mattress in the center of which was a white stain—presumably orgasmic—and beside the felt was a tape recording producing the voices endlessly uttering "Yes" and "no," changing in tone and tempi from sighs to anger, from excitement to exhaustion, from pleading to rebuff, sometimes whispering and sometimes bellowing like bulls.

Beside me a fat man, mesmerized by the phenomenon, asked, "How long does one have to wait until they finish?" I laughed and some young people looked at me as if I'd desecrated a temple. I wondered if the whole thing might be some perverse put-on but the piety of the viewers refuted my suspicions. There were two guards in ill-fitting uniforms, looking rather like dull-witted postmen, and the thought occurred to me that they might be part of the hoax.

I wandered through more rooms, passing burlap bags of potatoes, beans, rice, and charcoal. Walls were smeared with what appeared to be offal and covered with scrawled graffiti. I climbed over piles of old boards and ducked under clumps of bamboo. There were nasty little heaps of brown foam rubber and uninsulated electric wires labeled "*Nicht berühren,* high tension." Bricks were embedded in paraffin, crumpled chicken wire looked like tumbleweeds, and a small copper plate was engraved, "This is the final point of a 391,193-mile-long straight line."

Suddenly the scene turned comic. At the reception desk people were picking up catalogs and opening them without paying the price of 12 francs and in the second room children were leaping and down on the felt mattresses. The two guards ran back and forth like Mack Sennett policemen, grabbing up the catalogs and racing back to shoo the children from the mattresses. The fat man was still there, laughing, holding his stomach, saying, "They can't pull it off; you'd think they'd get tired," and the thought occurred to me that he too, along with the harassed guards, was part of the exhibition. In this place where I was so obviously a Philistine I remembered uncomfortably that when Hedy Hahnloser was assembling her great collection in Winterthur she also was considered a Philistine.

16

THE GNOMES

"How do you like us gnomes?"

The man who asked bore no semblance to a gnome. He was Alfred O. Hartmann, tall and robust manager of the Swiss Bank Corporation, one of the giants of Swiss finance of whom George Brown, Chancellor of the Exchequer of Great Britain when the pound descended to a record low in 1964, had said, "The gnomes of Zurich are at work again."

Brown's appellation entered into the language of international finance and Zurich bankers turned it into a joke, using it to refer to themselves and their associates. An American of Swiss descent, T. R. Fehrenbach, wrote a book, *The Gnomes of Zurich*, in which he said, "Very few people have ever met a Swiss banker—but a great many who never have don't like them."

I met many and I liked some of them a great deal. Liberated from Switzerland's confining parochialism by their wealth and status and broad travel, they were urbane, sophisticated, humorous, and friendly. "To be a Swiss banker," one of them said, "is to breathe the air of the world." Some were educated in America and other served early apprenticeships in New York or San Francisco banks. Most were enthusiastically pro-American.

I had read Fehrenbach's book and had the uneasy feeling I should not like the bankers as much as I did. My relationship with them was entirely social. Several actually suggested I might like to open a secret account and when I replied that I had no money to invest the subject was dropped but not the friendship. Lunches with them were leisurely repasts beginning with martinis, continuing with wine, and concluding with *Kirschwasser.* At first I was puzzled by the effusive hospitality which I had not experienced from any other group in Switzerland. It was apparent that they liked the society of Americans. Though all of them spoke English, most of our dialogue was in Swiss dialect.

That I was a writer was certainly a reason for their friendliness. In both America and England, Swiss bankers, since the end of the Second World War, had been the subject of a controversial press and they were sensitive to public opinion. In Washington the United States Senate was trying with minimal success to investigate the Swiss banking code. An American ambassador to Switzerland charged that financial negotiations through Berne facilitated narcotic traffic from China to the Western world and that Communist espionage in the West was being financed through Switzerland. The French government accused Swiss banks of financing arms deals with Algerian rebels. The most frequent charge was that Swiss banks provided a hiding place for stolen and looted money and helped tax evaders conceal income and assets. News stories reported that deposed dictators, Peròn of Argentina, Batista of Cuba, Arbenz of Guatemala, Trujillo of the Dominican Republic, and the late, exiled King Farouk of Egypt and murdered King Feisal of Iraq had all concealed enormous fortunes in Switzerland. Sometimes dirty deals went wrong. The wife of Clifford Irving, author of the bogus Howard Hughes biography, was caught when she tried to transfer a handbag of currency from one bank to another, and Louis Cirillo, a Bronx bagel baker, was apprehended attempting to hide a $4-million heroin-smuggling fortune. Both ended in the slammer. But such cases are the exception and respectable Swiss banks remain the most secure money-stashing and money-laundering places on earth.

Swiss preoccupation with the manipulation of money has its moral authority in John Calvin's principle that gold belongs to God and men are His stewards to husband and not squander it. The most controversial issue of the banking ethic is the famous bank secrecy law which makes it impossible for foreign governments to gain access to records. The secrecy does not apply if a foreign government can show that an account violates a criminal offense under Swiss law. The frustrating catch for U.S. officials is that in Switzerland tax evasion is not a crime but a civil or "gentleman's" offense. Whenever there is publicity about this in America, Swiss bankers are inundated with inquiries from Americans wishing to open accounts.

The most ingratiating of the bank czars whom I met was Eberhard Reinhardt, president of the gigantic *Crédit Suisse*. Dr. Reinhardt, born to missionary parents in India, was a banker in the Medici mold with an exuberant interest in art, literature, history, and Swiss folklore. A short, roly-poly, blue-eyed man with boundless vitality, he was an economic theorist who, according to his executive secretary, ran the bank like an artist and hired the best financiers and logicians. Dr. Reinhardt had ties in my state of Wisconsin, where a brother was a dairy farmer and where he himself owned vacation property on Lake Tippecanoe. He was interested in Wisconsin Indians and boasted of his friendship with the late Emil Wanetka, owner of Little Bohemia Lodge, the resort where, in 1934, John Dillinger shot it out with the FBI and escaped.

Dr. Reinhardt came to fetch me one summer Sunday afternoon for supper in his home on the fashionable Zurichberg. He was driving his unpretentious Citroën, a comic-book car that resembled a bullfrog about to swallow on-coming traffic. The party was in a garden with a pool and birds singing in hemlock and fir trees. I met Mrs. Reinhardt, a pretty blond who appeared younger than her husband. He called her "the real financial genius of the family" and explained that she speculated profitably in real estate. My fellow guests included diplomats, a Minnesota professor of medicine, and bankers, the best known of whom was Dr. Erne Spitz, president of the government-controlled International Exchange Bank.* A retired ambassador to the United States at the party described Dr. Spitz as "a financial wizard who maintains close relations with the Federal Reserve Bank of America."

---

*Dr. Spitz and the International Exchange Bank have been so named for this report.

At the moment the wizard, a bachelor in his sixties, was seated at a table reading the palms of lady guests. One lady refused to submit to a reading because, she said, "he sees too many embarrassing things." I asked Dr. Spitz if he read palms of depositers in his bank and he looked up and said, "Of course. You'd be surprised what I learn."

Dr. Reinhardt bustled about introducing guests and looking after drinks, at the same time sustaining with many interruptions a summary of Swiss industrial history for a Turkish banker. "The invention of the turbine was the most important single event in Swiss history," he said. "Modern Switzerland commenced when we learned to harness our waterfalls." He stopped for a moment to supervise a maid and his student son melting *Raclette* over an open grill. "The second important event was Napoleon's blockade of England," he continued. "Europe was importing weaving machines from England and during the blockade Switzerland manufactured them and began a textile industry."

Dr. Reinhardt helped the maid serve the *Raclette,* folding the melted cheese over boiled new potatoes, and the simple peasant meal was excellent. To drink there was a choice of Mosel wine or peppermint tea with grappa liquor, at least one of which was necessary to digest the cheese, Dr. Reinhardt explained. The former ambassador was speaking of contrasts in America and Switzerland. He said, "In the American West you see signs that say, 'Last chance for gasoline in two hundred miles.' In Switzerland the signs say, 'Last chance for gasoline in ten kilometers.'" During the meal Dr. Spitz was called to the phone and when he returned he excused himself, explaining his mother was unwell and needed him at home. He left and the ambassador said, "His mother is well over eighty and is the only wife that exists for him." A banker told how each morning before he went to his bank, Dr. Spitz shopped in the market for food and each evening returned from his office to cook supper for himself and his mother. Someone told a story, obviously apocryphal, in which David Rockefeller telephoned one morning to ask Dr. Spitz whether he should devaluate or escalate the dollar and Dr. Spitz replied, "Just a minute. I will ask *Mutterli* (my little mother)."

Later, when most of the guests had left and the night grew chilly, the Minnesota professor and I were invited indoors to see Dr. Reinhardt's print collection. The house, furnished with French period furniture and oil paintings and brightened by bouquets of delphiniums and gladioli, had a patrician elegance. Dr. Reinhardt poured sixty-year-old brandy and brought out cabinet drawers full of engravings by Dürer and Altdorfer and etchings by Rembrandt, some of which had once been in the collection of General Rommel. There was also a collection of rare books and Dr. Reinhardt selected some first-edition volumes of Jules Verne. From *De la Terre à la Lune,* he read:

> Two hundred and fifty-seven francs was the modest contribution of Switzerland to the American venture. You have to see it bluntly, the Swiss could not comprehend the practical use of the operation. It did not appear to them that the action of sending a ball to the moon would be helpful in establishing business connections with the heavenly body of the night and they considered it rather unwise to invest their money in such an uncertain enterprise.

He had, he said, read the same passage at a meeting of Crédit Suisse directors whose attitude toward foreign investments he felt was too conservative.

Three days after the party a secretary from Dr. Reinhardt's office telephoned with another invitation. The reason for it, she explained, was a call from Dr. Spitz in which the palm-reading president of the International Exchange Bank expressed regret at having to leave the party and wished for another opportunity to meet me. To accommodate him, Dr. Reinhardt was arranging a "small supper" at which only Dr. Spitz and I would be guests.

When I arrived on the designated evening Dr. Spitz was not there. A half-hour later he phoned and offered his distressed apologies. His mother was having "an attack" and he would not be able to come. The next week a third appointment to bring Dr. Spitz and me together was made by Dr. Reinhardt* but this was canceled in the morning. His mother, Dr. Spitz was sorry to report, was unwell and could not be left alone.

---

*Dr. Reinhardt died unexpectedly in October 1977.

A week later I received an invitation to lunch with the most powerful man in the Swiss banking structure, Dr. Alfred Schaefer, manager of the mighty Union Bank of Switzerland.

Dr. Schaefer was a living legend, a banker that other bankers held in awe. He was called "the pope of finance," "the most powerful man in Switzerland," and "*der Haifish.*" The epithet means "shark," a fish which Dr. Schaefer was said to emulate with his cool sagacity and ruthlessness. A widely quoted statement of business philosophy attributed to him was, "Nobody can be his brother's keeper." Stock values rose and fell with Dr. Schaefer's public pronouncements and foreign bankers came to Zurich like courtiers seeking advice and favor.

Since he was known to be a stern man not given to social frivolities the invitation mystified me. A possible explanation was that word had reached his office of an American writer hobnobbing with his banking peers and he wanted to find out why. The anticipation of lunch in a private dining room of the bank filled me with apprehension.

I was greeted at the gray fortress on Bahnhofstrasse by a junior officer into whose custody I seemed to have been assigned. The officer, whom I shall call Hugo, escorted me into a palatial dining hall where a table was set for eight and a bar was supplied with Jack Daniels and Chivas Regal. Two English bankers wearing gray and blue flannels arrived and introduced themselves as Cross and Barnes. I was relieved that there would be other guests and that English would be spoken. A haughty German appeared, wearing a blazer with silver buttons, and then three officers of the bank. One asked what bank I represented and when I replied I was not a banker there was a long silence during which the other guests seemed to be wondering, as was I, what in hell I was doing there. After a half-hour of explorative conversations and two drinks each the door opened and Dr. Schaefer entered. He was a small, slight man with a large head and sun-tanned face. His gray suit hung loosely on him and in the meticulously tailored company he seemed almost shabby. He moved through the group, shaking hands and coolly surveying each of us through pince-nez spectacles. "It was good of you to come, Professor Kubly," he said.

A conversation about money began almost at once. There had been distressing news that morning: the price of the dollar had risen and Dr. Schaefer was annoyed. "Those sophisticated New York bankers simply can't go on loaning money," he said. "If they insist we shall have to take it from them."

"You're absolutely right, Dr. Schaefer," Cross said fawningly and the German echoed, "Absolutely." The dialogue concerned "Eurodollars," which I understood to be masses of dollars floating about Europe and outside of Federal Reserve jurisdiction. They were controlled largely by London and Zurich banks which loaned them at substantial interest to international corporations and investors. With the rise in the value of the regulated dollar on the international money market, returns on Eurodollars declined.*

"One way to dry up Eurodollars is to stop loaning them to London banks that loan them to American banks," Dr. Schaefer said. The Englishmen looked distressed.

The table was set with place cards and my name appeared opposite Dr. Schaefer and next to Hugo who, when we were seated, described for me the bank's kitchen and food facilities. "At eight o'clock there is breakfast for the bank employees," he said. "At noon two thousand lunches are served which are ordered by menu a week in advance. In this way there is cooked exactly what is needed and there is no waste."

I heard Barnes ask Dr. Schaefer if he had taken his holiday yet.

"No. I shall be taking it in two weeks," Dr. Schaefer replied.

"And where will it be?" asked Cross.

"In Ninfa."

There was a silence during which everyone seemed to be deliberating where Ninfa might be. Finally the German asked.

"It's in the hills forty-five miles south of Rome," said Dr. Schaefer. "A medieval village which was abandoned during a seventeenth-century plague of malaria."

"It's been restored then?" asked Barnes.

"No. Nothing. Only ruins and roses. An excellent place to meditate."

There was another silence. "How fascinating," said Barnes and the German said, "It's very important to meditate."

---

*The original designation of Eurodollars has since been broadened to "Eurocurrency" to include any away-from-home currency.

One of the Swiss asked where in Zurich I lived.

"In the Niederdorf," I replied. There was a silence, during which everyone seemed uncertain whether I might be joking. "I live in an apartment a few doors from that of Dr. Schaefer's son."

Hugo jostled his knee against mine to hush me up. Dr. Schaefer gave no indication he had heard.

"Are you having any strikes in Switzerland?" Cross asked. "We have so many in England."

"Our workers consider strikes obsolete, an outdated process," said Dr. Schaefer sharply. A lunch of curried veal, asparagus, and a salad was served and everyone murmured how excellent it was. The conversation turned to food.

"The best restaurants in Europe are in France and Italy," Dr. Schaefer said. "But they are expensive. Only in Switzerland can you go to an inexpensive restaurant and eat well." The German praised the Swiss diet, responsible, he said, for the good health of Swiss workers. It was a subject on which I had some knowledge and I spoke of the extraordinary good health of the peasants in the Lötschen Valley who lived almost exclusively on bread, cheese, and milk and who, unlike most Swiss, had no need for either doctors or dentists. Dr. Schaefer turned to me. "Chocolate destroys Swiss teeth," he said. He asked if I lived in New York and I replied that I no longer did.

"My favorite city in the world," he said. "So vital and exciting. If I were in New York, if I could afford to live there, I would reside in the heart of the city, high up in a skyscraper. It would be stupid to commute when you can live on a thirtieth floor and have it all to enjoy, the glorious views, the fantastic culture." He reflected for a moment. "For New York you need to be young in spirit," he said.

The dialogue returned to the more urgent subject of finance and Cross said, "The last time I saw you, Dr. Schaefer, the market had just dropped thirty points."

"The American economy causes it," Dr. Schaefer said. "It's been in a very dangerous situation for more than three weeks and it's not over yet."

There was a rustle and, with no warning, as if he'd received a sudden secret signal, Barnes said, "It's been very pleasant to visit with you, Dr. Schaefer, and we thank you very much for having us."

We all stood up. Dr. Schaefer moved around the table, shaking each guest's hand, and when he came to me he said, "I hope you will enjoy your stay in Switzerland." At the door he turned back for a final pronouncement. "Today I feel quite optimistic. But the Americans will have to be shown. They cannot be allowed to continue cutting the market." The bankers smiled with relief.

The most untypical banker that I met was a younger man named Emil Hirt, a junior officer in a renowned private bank. We became friends and sometimes met at the Tailors' Guild, a medieval trade union turned into an exclusive men's club. I had not seen him for a month and a week before my departure for America he left a note at my hotel inviting me for dinner. He came to call for me after work, at five-thirty, and we drove up the south side of the lake to his old house in a vineyard at Thalwil. With boyish enthusiasm he showed me his rose garden and fruit trees and introduced his daughters, three beautiful schoolgirls who, responding to a childlike, often clownish quality in their father, appeared to adore him. We had drinks and Emil played the guitar and he and the girls sang Swiss folk songs. I saw his joyous nature was real and I tried to reconcile it with his profession. Many bankers were hearty, even jolly men, but Emil's elation was something else. It was touched by the fine madness of an artist or saint and one could not resist it. His wife, Renata, seemed to understand this and was indulgent and protective as a mother.

We drove around the lake to a restaurant operated by a fisherman on a peninsula called Hurden. There we ate fresh perch cooked in butter and drank the light dry Riesling of the area. It was an Orphic setting. Silvery mists creeping up the lake clung like veils to the poplars, and turned the green waters to cobalt. Emil described his feeling of melancholy because I was leaving Switzerland. I was, he said, his best friend, his brother. I credited the hyperbolisms to the wine for I had not taken our Guild association so seriously and our friendship, while warm, had not seemed to me an intimate one and I was surprised that he considered it so. Renata sensed my confusion and when Emil went to settle our account with the innkeeper, she said, "He always wants things to be ideal; he wants to have them perfect. He wishes to change things, to improve them, and his enthusiasms and ideas are not always understood and make enemies for him. He is easily hurt and that is why he has not called you. He was afraid of being rebuffed."

I understood what she was saying for I had been lonely in Switzerland myself. In a somber land, where joy is suspect, a nature such as Emil's would be looked upon with suspicion and a measure of envy. I understood how his jester's role was a reaching out for friendship, that behind the clowning was a clown's melancholy. The dilemma of a feeling man was universal and most societies had their subculture havens of art, social service, and scholasticism. But in Switzerland, more than in most countries, feeling was suspect and had to be suppressed. Being oneself was something to be avoided. I felt remorse and uneasy guilt for not recognizing the measure of Emil's friendship until so late. I had been put off by his position as a banker, by an aristocratic lineage, even by his handsomeness and fastidious grooming. The brotherhood of tailors, which had seemed to me a childish game, was suddenly meaningful. We were indeed brothers and this was something Emil had recognized and I had not.

We drove back through the mists to Thalwil, where he presented me with a copy of a thick book that he had written, entitled *The History of Swiss Banking*. While I did not expect to read it, it became a meaningful gift.

17

CARNIVAL

Switzerland is full of demons and the people are frightened. They live in pagan times and the middle ages and this is the source of their anxieties. Science no longer permits them to believe in the supernatural, so the demons have been internalized into the unknown fears of the subconscious. Their festivals are pagan exorcisms of demons, a surfacing of centuries-old race memories.

—Dr. Yolande Jacobi.

I was in the center of the action. Niederdorfstrasse, which passed my apartment, was the main avenue of carnival merriment, and Hirschenplatz, on which I looked down from my windows, was a place of assembly. Sometimes in moments of exasperation or impatience I had in months past thought of Zurich, or even all of Switzerland, as a vast and controlled asylum. Now, suddenly, that part of the city in which I was living was an asylum gone berserk.

It began the week before carnival with the constant cacaphony of wandering *Guggenmusiken.* A doctor of linguistics explained to me that the strange word derived from the verb *guggen,* which means to blow a horn badly. In the context of carnival it referred to groups of masked and costumed itinerant musicians who strolled about the city

blowing horns and beating drums for at least eighteen out of each
twenty-four hours. For a week I lived with the ear-shattering din, which
continued all night, sometimes until 6 A.M., and resumed again at 10
A.M. An architect named Luzius, and his wife, were leaders of a large
troupe called *Mondchälber,* or "moon calves." They were a charming,
cultivated young couple at whose house I'd had pleasant dinners. Now,
suddenly, they seemed possessed as they marched all night through the
streets, with forty musical friends who had clown-white faces and wore
bright red pajama suits with fins and wings and fantastic headgears
including antennas and flickering lights. *Guggis* would invade bars and
restaurants where managements were obliged by tradition to serve
them free drinks. Their antics inevitably grew more frolicsome and
unrestrained as the evening progressed. By midnight each group had
collected a retinue of followers, mostly drunken men, who flapped
about and danced to the music. Two of the most popular carnival cafes
were the *Malatesta* (The Headache), a student rendezvous on Hirschenplatz, and a homosexual enclave beyond Zähringerstrasse, which
I called the *Doppelgänger.**

For carnival the *Doppelgänger* turned into a center for transvestism.
But the predilection for wearing women's clothes was not limited to
homosexuals. The hordes of men wearing dresses included business
and professional types, foreign laborers, shopkeepers, and visitors
from the country. A young banker who lived in my apartment house
had a practical explanation for the mass transvestism. "There are
always women's clothes about in a household so for most men it is the
easiest costume," he said.

In the area in which I lived preparations had gone on for a feverish
month. Many earnest carnivalists felt impelled to wear a different
costume on each of five nights. Peter, a television salesman who
delivered a set to my apartment, warned me what to expect. The entire
Niederdorf would be an uninterrupted revelry lasting a full week of
days and nights. Bars would be open all night. "It is necessary to wear a
mask," Peter said. "Then you are able to do all kinds of naughty things
you can not do if you are recognized." Rural Catholic cantons cele-

---

*The name of the cafe and the names of most persons in this account are fictive.

brated their carnival before Ash Wednesday; in Protestant cities it began on the following Monday. "So all Catholic men come to town for a second carnival," said Peter, a Protestant. "They steal and pick pockets and you have to be very careful."

On Saturday night the uproar in the square was so horrendous I could no longer stay in my rooms. As I debated what to do the phone rang. It was Karl, my barber, calling from the *Doppelgänger* where the crowd was so thick they were about to close the doors. He was saving a place for me and I must rush right over. When I got there an angry group of elegant ladies was shouting loudly in deep voices and pounding large brown fists on the door. I opened the door and was pushed out by two security officers who slammed it in my face. I opened it a second time and the officers apologized, saying they had just ejected some "low types" and had concluded I was one of them. I paid an eight-and-a-half-franc admission charged to patrons not in costume. I found Karl at the bar and took the empty stool beside him.

The long hall, extending between two streets with entrances on both, was jammed, mostly with extravagantly costumed "ladies" dancing either with each other or with men. Surprisingly, few in the crowd wore masks, and the first impression was one of propriety. But most of the elegant "ladies" were excessively tall and their voices were raucous. They wore flamboyant evening gowns, huge beehive wigs sparkling with diamond dust, and monumentally padded brassieres. Even some of the bartenders were dressed as women. One, a black man, was wearing a gold lamé gown.

The most hilarious costumes were parodies of the traditional cantonal costumes of Swiss women. A large brawny worker wore the bright red-and-orange costume of Appenzell. Appenzellers are small people and this strapping fellow had blue eyelids, was six feet tall, and weighed at least 200 pounds. The black lace butterfly wings of his cap were greatly exaggerated and as he danced with men smaller than himself they fluttered like limp sails. There were also male costumes: Roman senators, a Robin Hood, toreadors, country rustics, and astral invaders with bizarrely painted near-nude green-and-blue bodies. A half-dozen security officers controlling the revelries appeared incongruous, as if they were celebrants in policemen's costumes.

"Wait until the Spaniards come," said Karl. "Then you will see something." Switzerland's foreign laborers were enthusiastic carnivalists. Spaniards and Italians, especially, welcomed the opportunity for abandoned escape from the oppressive lives of their noncitizenship status and strove to upstage the Swiss.

A group of gray-haired men in business suits arrived, wearing domino masks to hide their eyes. They were, Karl said, "professional and businessmen," voyeurs like myself. What they had come to see was the "grand procession" of costumed "ladies" on top of the bar. For this our stools were ringside seats. Each "lady" in turn climbed up a stepladder and strolled with Ziegfeld pomp down the long bar. Some of the dresses were so tight that it was necessary for the paraders to hop, rabbit-style, up the ladder and proceed with tiny mincing steps. Behind the bar a young woman wearing leather trousers was the official photographer and each of the performers stopped to pose for her. Burly faces, heavily made up, peered out from under exaggerated wigs; false lashes fluttered; fur and feather stoles covered thick shoulders and arms. Freezing for the camera, the subjects placed rough hands on hips, flexed legs, and pointed bulging feet in oversized golden slippers, and the crowd applauded the grotesque parody of womanhood.

The performance on the bar was interrupted by the arrival of a group of Spaniards dressed as a wedding party. There was an elaborately veiled mincing bride with a lewdly magnified bust and a toreador groom whose black hair was flecked with silver dust. There were weeping mothers and coy bridesmaids and a Spanish band to which the group began to dance with passionate abandon. More foreigners arrived, Greek Evzons, Turkish harem girls, three Hindu maharanis, and a few Japanese samurai. The invasion of aliens seemed to inhibit the Swiss, making them self-conscious. The Spaniards and Italians grew more hilarious. To recapture attention away from the foreigners a hand played "Yes Sir, That's My Baby" and the "ladies" began moving up and down the bar as if it were a treadmill. An elegant Cleopatra, weighted by her costume, seemed about to collapse and had to be assisted. A new group of surrealistically costumed Venutians arrived, their faces invisible inside large tinsel balls shaped like the tops of old-fashioned refrigerators. It was one o'clock and I decided to leave. In the street the scene was much the same. I went to my rooms and tried to read. The din in the square continued until 4 A.M. One night of carnival had plunged me into depression and there was more than a week to go.

The next evening I escaped to the opera, to a performance of *Lohengrin* sung by a youthful Swedish tenor and the thrust of the opera, the destruction of innocence by evil, was poignantly real. As the days passed it became increasingly apparent that very real demons were loosed in the land. Arab guerrillas shot up an Israeli plane at the airport and a fire, set in the central telephone office, put telephones out of commission in a third of the city. Three respectable housewives named Clara, Ursula, and Sabina, created a flurry in the Niederdorf by setting fire to the apartments of several prostitutes patronized by their husbands. They told the newspapers they intended to continue their campaign of smoking out whores and the police were morally perplexed.

The weather turned unseasonably warm, the result of high-pressure *Föhn* winds that create an illusion of spring and which, it is popularly believed, have the power to drive people mad. Each morning for about four hours it was quiet enough to sleep. At all other times Hirschenplatz was a bedlam. In one afternoon I counted twenty-eight *Guggi* groups. One band of thirteen youths on bicycles, dressed as red devils, swooped and swerved their wheels in an elaborate drill while blowing on horns American melodies such as "The Battle Hymn of the Republic," "When the Saints Go Marching In," and "Camptown Races." A group of enflamed fire-breathing dragons snorted on tubas and barked like dogs and some women dressed as fruits, including one encased in a papier-maché banana the size of a canoe, played accordions. A group in courtly Maria Theresa gowns, like a *Rosenkavalier* chorus, played pipes and flutes. Another fantastic group, called *Groteskas,* had their faces painted gold, pink, blue, and green and wore bizarre headdresses of bird cages containing live birds, naked dolls with blinking eyes, and neon tubes with illuminated liquids gurgling through them. At one point six groups competed in the battle of sound. Through the midst of them wandered an earnest young man in a red shirt bearing a sign reading, "Attention: Jesus died for your sins; He renews your life." The crowds jeered him and some Italians made a broadly parodying sign of the cross. The youth began shouting, "The Bible says . . ." and his words were engulfed in laughter. A bearded old man wearing a gold-tasseled stocking cap shouted to the young man that he was a fool. Clutching his sign, chain-smoking cigarettes, the youth outshouted him, saying, "The people of Zurich are doomed!" The red devils swirled around him and the crowd roared. I felt compelled to defend the youth but when I approached him he backed away, believing me to be one of his tormentors. At that moment church bells began to ring over the city and I realized it was five o'clock on Saturday, the time for weekly vespers. I saw the youth clutching the sign begin to weep and I fled from the square.

It was the night of the Artists' Carnival Ball, for which I had two tickets. I telephoned a Swiss girl, Antonia, to invite her to go with me and she declined, saying, "It is absolutely essential that you go separately and alone so you may lose your identity completely. Even my girl friend and her fiancé are going separately." I had heard that psychiatrists sent their socially inhibited patients to the ball as therapy. One doctor said, "A patient's choice of costume and mask is of great significance. The suppressed self is released; the individual's true nature is permitted for a moment to surface."

Masked and wearing a Venetian gondolier's blouse and hat, I went alone to the *Kongresshaus,* where four halls were filled with hundreds of costumed figures. If any psychiatrists were present I wondered what they might make of the display. Wandering about was a huge orange penis bearing the sign, "Christ's Cock." One group, calling themselves "the pantswetters," picked at the noses of their papier-maché heads and dripped pools of water from tubing hidden in their pantaloons. Another group, bearing signs reading "Greco-Roman 69," wore short white togas and carried upside-down pink papier-maché female figures with legs swooping over their heads like antlers, and the bearers were pantomiming cunnilingus on the upside-down figures and rolling their eyes ecstatically. The rooms were steaming hot and the bands blared deafeningly. Wandering through the insanity I was, by an inexplicable irony, haunted by the memories of my two Swiss grandmothers, the queenly dignity of one and the loving gentleness of the other, and when a band of masked "prisoners" in red-striped suits began lowering their zippers to display their genitals I decided it was enough and I left.

The warm moonlit town was a surrealist phantasm. I crossed a bridge back to the Niederdorf, where drunken musicians were blaring dissonant wails from their horns. Police were ejecting costumed drunks from bars and they rolled up like caterpillars on the pavements. Several shrieking "girls" began an impromptu striptease before auto lights. Though everyone seemed dazed from drunkenness and exhaustion no one seemed willing to go home and it went on until dawn.

Though the Zurich bachanalia had continued for a week, the Basel carnival, one of the most famous in Europe, did not begin until the next Monday, and on Sunday I took a train to that city. In my hotel I found a message to call friends, a young couple named Berthol, and they invited me to meet them for supper in the *Kunsthalle,* an artists' restaurant. Galla Berthol was a beautiful and impetuous artist who had been my friend before she married Damon, a quiet, good-looking young man from one of Basel's aristocratic families. Their marriage had vexed Damon's friends, who felt he had chosen beneath his class. I had seen Galla only once since her marriage and had been astonished as always by her lean, vibrant beauty. Now her hair, which I remembered as black, was a tawny cascade; her face as flawlessly delineated as a cameo. She was wearing a russet taffeta dress that enhanced her radiant glow. With an exuberant flow of words she reviewed the years, telling me about her two small daughters, Victoria, aged six, and Olga, aged three; of her studio in Paris; of a year in New York where Damon had been sent by the chemical firm where he was employed. In New York she had switched from painting to garden sculpture which involved the welding of discarded fire-escape ladders. In pursuit of old ladders she had met a demolition foreman named Joe with whom she climbed over old buildings. "One time on top of a roof Joe took me in his arms and said he loved me," she said. "I am thinking very quickly and I say to him it is not very comfortable up there and I invite him next day to my apartment. I invited two friends for tea and we all put our hair in curlers and had six dirty children among us and as I expected Joe lost interest. But I succeeded in making him feel guilty and I got twenty ladders for only one hundred dollars. I finished the sculpture and now there is a dispute between the Metropolitan Museum, which wants it for Central Park, and Damon's company, which wants to fly it back to Switzerland." I suspected the story, like many of Galla's narrated adventures, was exaggerated, but it was true to her character, to her love for excitement and drama. She and Damon spoke of the "mystery" of the

Basel carnival that, unlike Zurich's, had a traditional format unchanged through the years. "At three o'clock in the morning everyone will move silently through the hushed, dark streets to the *Marktplatz*," Galla said. "You will hear silent noises, like a secret invasion, like rats attacking, and you will not know what it is."

"The morning starts something," Damon said. "The spirit is released; your troubles are forgotten." They were taking their little girls who were then in bed. "They were happy to go to sleep for they are very excited about getting up early," Galla said.

My hotel was quiet and in my inside room I had the first good sleep in a week. At 3 A.M. the phone rang. It was Ernie, a young man from the Basel tourist bureau, waiting downstairs to take me to the *Morgestraich,* a drum reveille which officially opens carnival. The city was dark; not a single light was burning. Barely audible soft shufflings and murmuring voices were the only indications of the rivers of humanity flowing toward the heart of the city into the marketplace. Exactly at four o'clock the lights of the dark town flashed on and a great swell of sound, of pipes and drums playing a single melody, the "Morgestraich" march, rolled over the city. From every street appeared processions of lanterns, gigantic lamps borne on men's shoulders and thousands of small ones carried by hand. The eerie corteges were thirty-seven men's clubs known as "cliques," each with drummers and fife and tambourine bands, and more than a hundred improvised groups, including *Guggenmusiken.* Among the 20,000 masked and costumed marchers were shoals of rustic clowns called *Waggis,* a name given by German soldiers to Alsatian farmers who came to the Basel market to sell their produce during the Franco-Prussian War. The carnival *Waggis* were parodies of country bumpkins wearing white trousers, blue smocks, wooden shoes, outrageous masks with lewdly huge noses, and wildly clumped wigs in a variety of colors. In addition to the organized *Waggis* there were independent *Waggis* who, Ernie said, "are wild creatures who behave eccentrically and never stop talking." Ernie's father, a tobacco merchant whose name was Alois, was one of the most famous of the independents. "Being a *Waggis* is the most important thing in his life; it is his religion," said Ernie. "He spends weeks preparing his mask and during carnival he never appears at home. He is ordinarily a quiet man too shy to speak to anyone. But something happens when he puts on the mask; he becomes an opposite creature. I can never believe it when I see him behave in this ridiculous manner. It is sometimes quite embarrassing." The week before Alois had been sent by the Swiss Tourist Office to London to publicize the carnival. He was introduced to a member of Parliament who had recently published a book asserting that the Swiss lived in immaculate houses but were less fastidious in their personal hygiene; that they did not wash their bodies as frequently as their homes. Before he shook the lord's hand Alois had dashed into a washroom to wash his hands and then, after he had shaken the hand of the lord, he dashed back into the washroom and washed his hands again. The incident, publicized in Switzerland, had turned him into a folk hero. I had the impression that Ernie, a somber youth, did not approve of his father's conduct. He told me that masks frightened him and he himself was unable to wear one; that he did not enjoy carnival and this affected his relationship with his father.

What had begun ceremoniously now turned intemperate. The procession of lanterns wove in and about one another and the din of drums and pipes was ear-shattering. The governor of Canton Basel was playing a flute with the *Chutläbutzer,* the tripe-cleaners' clique. A blithe, youthful woman in a leather coat joined us. She was Ernie's mother and appeared younger than her son who, at twenty-three, was gaunt and sallow-faced. As we were being introduced a *Waggis* leaped into our midst, shouting, "Where is that damned American professor of milking cows?" The sepulchral voice emerged from a mask with a gourdlike nose twelve inches long and huge wooden teeth, from one of which hung a rubber fish. The head was covered with a snarled thatch of horse hair and around the neck was a flowing red-and-white checked scarf. "It's him, my father," Ernie whispered. The creature continued to insult me, shouting, "He says he is a professor from America but he is a fraud!" Whirling like a demented dervish, he knocked over children, kissed women, beat men with a gnarled stick and then, as quickly as he had appeared, he vanished.

It was five-thirty and time, Ernie said, for *Mehlsuppe,* a creamed soup of roasted flour and onion with which the Swiss traditionally conclude heavy drinking. Women were selling cups of it from canisters. Officials and guests were having theirs in the Helm restaurant on the edge of the square, where Ernie's mother had a table reserved for us.

The crowd was so thick we could not get near the door and Ernie found a back door through which we squeezed. Ernie's mother was waiting at a table with a journalist from London, a professor from Basel University, and a mild-mannered man in his forties who was wearing a spotted kerchief. The gaudy scarf was familiar and I realized its wearer was Ernie's father, the demented *Waggis*. He smiled shyly when we were introduced and did not speak. The strange repast began with onion pie and coffee and then the soup, which was too salty for my taste, and I drank beer instead. When it was over, Ernie's father disappeared and in a moment reappeared wearing his mask, transformed back to phrenetic lunacy. He climbed a dividing wall, on the other side of which the Basel city council was having its soup, and shouted, "Here is the Basel Kindergarten!" Indicating an elderly city father who had recently married a young woman he announced, "His wife has given me her private phone number!" Scrambling down the wall, he sniffed at the journalist and shouted in English, "He stinks; he hasn't had a bath in a week."

Word spread through the rooms that it was raining outside and the celebrants, who had been congratulating one another on the weather, now began to wail. Rain on a parade was a catastrophe and people speculated whether the weather would clear by noon. Fuzzy-haired, phallic-nosed *Waggis* were chasing after women and insulting men, and the crowd was dispersing throughout the city.

I walked through the rain to my hotel and went back to bed. When I got up at noon it was still raining. I returned to the marketplace and saw a restaurant called *Gifthüttli*. The idea of eating in a "little poison hut" intrigued me and I went inside.

I found a place across a table from a blond young man wearing a military uniform covered with Nazi military decorations and ribbons and medals fashioned from beer bottle caps. He listened to me ordering my lunch and then introduced himself. His name was Bernard and he was a printer from Berne who had returned for carnival in his hometown. He complained of the control of the event by cliques. "In the past," he said, "it was a matter of individual participation. It used to be a *Strassäfasnacht*—street carnival—and now it is an organized theater for television and tourists. The real spirit is gone and young people are unhappy."

I had been invited to watch the parade from the Berthols' apartment on *Aeschenvorstadt,* the main business street, and since it continued to rain this was a good fortune. When I arrived the parade had been going on for a half-hour and the apartment, two floors above the street, was filled with Galla's and Damon's friends. In the street below, on lorries under transparent sheets, *Waggis* pummelled onlookers with pig bladders and grabbed the hair and clothing of women, dragging them along, showering them with blizzards of colored confetti and pouring it inside their dresses. Many of the shrieking women seemed to be enjoying the abuse and others escaped by slipping out of their raincoats. The confetti disintegrated in the wet streets into ankle-deep pink and purple mud.

In the open windows of the Berthols' apartment heavy burlap awnings had been hung and I soon discovered why. Parade floats were loaded with oranges which the *Waggis* threw at crowds and into windows that were natural targets, especially when pretty girls watched from them. Almost immediately I was struck by a flying orange; my glasses flew off and my nose began to bleed. Oranges pelted against the tarpaulins like cannon fire. The floor of the apartment was soon covered with oranges and walking on them was like roller-skating. Now and then Damon and his friends would gather them up and there were always several baskets. The sidewalks below were rivers of oranges which, pulped by the traffic, made walking perilous. I remembered a carnival at Patras, in Greece, when it also rained, where the crowds were pelted with chocolates, and I reflected on the curious anachronism of a chocolate war in a land where oranges grew and a battle of oranges in the land of chocolates. Why, I asked, was it oranges? "Because they are fun to throw," Damon replied, and added, "They are cheap oranges from Italy."

The plastic-covered procession went on. Each of the cliques had its float, drum and fife corps, lantern bearers, *Waggis,* and horse carriages, and each was accompanied by *Zettel* bearers who distributed thousands of colored papers printed with original doggerel insulting politicians and public figures. It went on for five hours and when it was over I trudged through the confetti mud back to my hotel. The entire event was to be repeated two days later.

In the evenings each clique had a banquet and I was invited to that of the "Olympiads." When I arrived in the upstairs hall the noisy hilarity was like the revels of a student society. Many members were drunk. Some were dressed as sixteenth-century burghers with starched white ruffs. Wives wore evening dresses and their hair was speckled with confetti. A group of pipers wore red robes like neophyte cardinals. Each clique had its own piping school, for which boys were chosen for training in their eleventh year. An annual piping contest was held every January and the current Basel champion was an Olympiad, a twenty-two-year-old mathematics student named Urs. Urs piped for a quarter-hour like a bewitched Papageno. A gentleman beside me whispered, "Of course, we are very jolly but when he plays we are silent because we appreciate good piping." Urs was joined by a dozen other pipers and the chorus of piping was like a flock of trilling birds. "They are playing a piece called 'The Knocking Ghost,'" said my informant. "The ghosts of past carnivals are knocking in the city and we are about to join them."

It was the custom after the dinners for cliques to parade behind their pipers and drummers until dawn, stopping frequently for drinks, but because of the rain it was decided to march only two hours. One of the ladies invited me to walk with her. It was raining hard and her umbrella did not quite cover me and the water dripping from it rolled down inside my collar. We passed some masked men who were stripped to the waist and the lady on my arm said, "Men who are not decently dressed are not from Basel. They are from Zurich or Italy or someplace like that." The dripping caravan reminded me of a grotesque funeral procession. My feet were wet and I was hoping for a chance to escape.

My opportunity came when a policeman would not permit me to enter a ballroom because I was not in costume. I excused myself and trudged in solitude through the wet town. A solitary masked figure, riding on a bicycle under a huge beach umbrella, covered me with confetti and it stuck to my clothes like adhesive. I heard the clacking of wooden shoes and saw a *Waggis* pursuing two shrieking girls. I began to sneeze and, though it was only midnight, I went to my hotel to bed.

In the morning it was still raining. I checked the prediction and it was for continued rain so I decided to return to Zurich. Walking down *Freiestrasse* I saw, inside the open door of a department store and lying against a display of women's underwear, a man's body laid out like

Scarpia's in *Tosca,* with candles at its head and foot and bouquets of flowers and bunches of carrots and onions. A circle of shoppers was looking down on it. I moved in and when I saw the viewers laughing I realized that the man was not dead but dead drunk. Someone had lain the fellow's *Waggis* mask over his loins and the huge nose stood up like a phallus. Around him business was going on as usual.

I stopped at the tourist bureau to say goodbye to Ernie, and when I told him about the drunken *Waggis* in the department store he said, "Oh, my God, it must be my father!" We went back to check and it was not. Salesgirls were selling underwear across the prone body and Ernie said that the man was allowed to sleep in the midst of the bustle because the people of Basel were especially tolerant toward drunks during carnival. I suspected there was more to it than that. Looking at the leering circle around the incredible spectacle, I sensed an element of cruelty in the hilarity.

I passed two hours at the Basel Museum, restoring my equanimity with Holbein portraits and collections of Picassos and Chagalls, and in the afternoon I took the Zurich train. When I returned to the Niederdorf the *Guggis* were still blaring on Hirschenplatz. They continued the next day and it was several days and nights before the demons were subdued.

18

CHECKING REFLEXES

Sometimes in summer a faintly coral cloud hovers over Basel. The nimbus mists are not, as they seem to be, a celestial aura on the lovely old city on the Rhine which, since the Renaissance, has been Switzerland's center of learning and culture. They are the alluvium of chemical factories and when the wind is right they have a faintly acrid odor.

Chemistry was brought to Basel in the eighteenth century by refugee Huguenots from France who continued their trade of ribbon dyeing. The modest cottage industry has grown in two centuries into the greatest aggregate of chemical production in Europe; today a sixth of employed Baslers work in dye, perfume and medicine factories. In the company of a Swiss journalist, Rudi Kraft,* I visited a chemical conglomerate's biological research laboratory. Kraft was a patrician Bernese bachelor who was fond of cats.

The laboratory building on the Swiss border looked out over the Rhine into France and Germany. We were greeted by a public relations man who introduced us to the laboratory director, a German scientist named Dr. Karl Holzer.* He was a thin, small man wearing a striped

---

*Kraft and Holzer are pseudonyms.

bow tie and a blood-spotted white jacket. Holzer was deferentially servile, an attitude I attributed to my journalist's credentials. He never stopped smiling. In excellent English he told me that his researchers devoted at least half of their time to their own experiments, "as in your American universities." He led us through a corridor, where he opened a door and stepped aside so we might enter. Rudi Kraft looked briefly inside and then stepped back and refused to go farther. The public relations man remained with Kraft and I went on alone with Dr. Holzer. The first thing I saw was a cat stretched on its back on a scaffolding to which it was taped and wired so it could not move. Only the heart pulsations visible on the shaved stomach indicated it was alive.

As we stood over the spectacle, Dr. Holzer, laughing with pride, explained the experiment, "to check the angina results when the heart does not receive adequate oxygen." I was too appalled to comprehend the medical details which he explained, saying, "The blood of four other cats is being pumped through the cardiovascular system of this cat. This means four blood donors, four cats must be sacrificed." He smiled and went on. "The experiment is rather an expensive one because we have a low supply of cats. Our supply has been coming from Holland and now Dutch cats are having an epidemic of rabies so we cannot import any more. We have had to begin breeding our own."

As in a bad dream I followed him into another room where men were operating on the kidneys of white rats. "The purpose," explained Dr. Holzer, "is to prevent adequate blood from flowing through the kidneys thus producing renal hypertension. The rats are treated for the hypertension with drugs and we have some very amusing results." Dr. Holzer laughed. "Some rats become quite kinetic, very active and sometimes even amorous. It is the beginning of a chronic pharmacology and very amusing."

In the next laboratory a variety of impaled living animals were cut open to expose their organs. "Every new drug has to be tested for its effect on isolated organs, kidneys, liver, uterus, heart, everything," said Dr. Holzer. I moved on, helplessly propelled toward still more animals stretched upside down. Were they rabbits or cats, I asked, and Dr. Holzer laughed heartily at my good joke and replied, "You reach under and feel for the ears." He reached under one. "A cat," he said. "It is under deep anesthesia and the graphs are recording blood pressure, heart frequency, and respiration. These are lethal experiments and the animal is finally killed. The brain is damaged so of course it would be impossible to permit it to live." He was smiling.

I was hoping for an end, but more lay ahead. In the next room I saw a cat that, I thought, must surely be dead. It was mounted on a skewer with its spine exposed. The flesh had been hacked away from the bloody vertebrae which were visible as the bones of a filleted fish. "No, it is not dead but decerebrated," said Dr. Holzer. "We are studying spastic diseases, the action potentials from the anterior to the posterior roots of the spinal cord. The result will help us in the treatment of nervous diseases." Nearby was a rat, strapped with one leg free and on it a tiny metronomic hammer was hitting the knee "to check reflexes."

"I think," said Dr. Holzer, "I have been able to show you a small part of our experiments in endocrinology. Now I will show you some parabiotic experiments."

We moved through another door, into a room where a row of men were joining pairs of rats together by surgery, turning them into Siamese twins, joining all their organs. "Here we are trying to establish whether pituitary patterns have an effect on sexual characteristics," Dr. Holzer said. "The joined specimens sometimes become very like marriages." He giggled. "Sometimes one rat gets quite fat and the other very thin, just like in some marriages." He was so overcome with mirth he could not go on. I wondered if he might be mad. "In this parabiosis," he said, "they have the limited common circulation as very often in marriages. They become quite sensitized to one another and they arrive at a kind of compatibility. Sometimes when two females are attached we find an increase in ovaries. Very, very amusing."

I felt a wave of nausea and asked to be excused. "But don't you wish to see more experiments?" Dr. Holzer asked, obviously disappointed. I replied I had seen enough. "Our labs fill twenty stories," he said proudly. "Even so, they are not large enough."

Finally we were on our way out. "No doubt you have noticed a strange thing," Dr. Holzer was saying. "There are no women working in our labs. Swiss women are not very interested in this work. In Germany you would see many women in the laboratories."

"All named Ilse Koch," I said, thinking aloud, hardly aware that the words had slipped out. Dr. Holzer frowned. It was apparent that my humor was as alien to him as his was to me. I was thinking if he had been born a generation earlier of the pleasure he would have found in human experiments, with what abandoned joy he could have detailed the convulsive agonies. Without my realizing what was happening he had guided me into still one more laboratory. "Here we have the life tissue experiments," he said. "These are more economical. We can supply the whole laboratory with one animal, one litter of embryos." I refused to look. "Please take me out," I said.

He bowed graciously. "I hope I have been able to give you a picture," he said. "You will have noticed the quiet, almost religious quality of the laboratory atmosphere, the reverence for life."

19

Auntie Jemima's Swiss Journey

In June 1863 a North England Baptist evangelist and temperance leader named Thomas Cook led a small band of fellow teetotalers on a "temperance excursion" into the mountains of Switzerland. Little was known about the curious expedition until 1947, when a tin box discovered in the rubble of a blitzed London warehouse was found to contain two red notebooks filled with an account of the Swiss journey handwritten by a mysterious "Miss Jemima." Because the manuscript included no surnames, the identities of author and travelers remained a secret. But the significance of the chronicle to the history of Swiss tourism was apparent.

Before the French Revolution, travelers to Switzerland had pursued culture in Basel, made pious pilgrimages to Calvin's Geneva, and languished on the gentle shores of the lakes of Neuchatel and Biel. Mountains were considered insurmountable obstacles and the Swiss, struggling to wrest a livelihood from the intractable and sterile landscape, looked upon them as enemies, a monstrous excrescence of nature invested with a mythology of dragons, witches, and demons causing avalanches, thunderbolts, and landslides.

In the nineteenth century the writings of John Ruskin introduced adventuresome Anglo-Saxons to the allure of mountains. After the

Congress of Vienna had politically tidied up Europe in 1815, Britons commenced traveling to Switzerland to fulfill the new yearning. Wordsworth made a visit and glorified the Alps in poetry. British climbers ascended the forebidding Matterhorn and turned mountaineering into an international sport. Mr. Cook's first organized tour was followed by an exodus of English to the Continent and by the swift rise of Thomas Cook & Son into an international travel agency. The British-spurred growth of Swiss tourism continued through this century until it has become Switzerland's second largest industry.

In 1963, on the centenary of Thomas Cook's first group tour, "Miss Jemima's"* account of it was published. The book was read by a family in Yorkshire who identified the author as a great-aunt named Jemima Morrell who, at the time of the journey, was a thirty-one-year-old maiden lady from Selby. To celebrate the centenary, the Cook Company, in collaboration with the Swiss National Tourist Office, organized a recapitulation of the first tour as it was reported by Miss Morrell. On June 26, one day short of a century after the arrival of the first tour on June 27, 1863, a troup of English actors, impersonating the original party of five women and four men, arrived in Geneva and began a two-week expedition on foot, muleback, and sedan chairs, and in steam trains, stern-wheel paddleboats, and horse carriages resurrected from transportation museums. They were accompanied by members of the Cook and Morrell families and were joined in Geneva by ten guides and press agents from the Cook and Swiss Tourist offices and fifty international journalists. As a representative of *Life* magazine, I was invited on the journey and, emulating Miss Jemima, I kept a journal.

JUNE 26
*Sunday morning was ushered in by peals of thunder arousing us by its heavy artillery . . . Yes, we were really in Geneva, that tried citadel of Protestantism!***

I arrived in Geneva by train from Zurich at noon. The Hôtel du Rhône, where I'd been assigned, had no record of a reservation and it was an hour before it was discovered my name had been misspelled. In

*Miss Jemima's Swiss Journal, Putnam, 1963.
**Quotations are from Miss Jemima's Swiss Journal.

the meantime my bags had disappeared and two more hours passed before they were discovered in the room of a Danish journalist.

Because of the confusion I missed the first event of the journey, a Swissair flight over Mont Blanc and the Mer de Glace. To fill the time I read Miss Jemima's account of the expedition up Mont Blanc by carriage, mule, and finally on foot, an undertaking apparently considered too strenuous for twentieth-century travelers. The climb, reported Miss Jemima, "at first tried somewhat the nerves of some of the lady members as yet unaccustomed to dizzy heights."

The *Journal* was written in a self-conscious literary style with quotes from Wordsworth, Ruskin, and Longfellow; and filled with the feminine preoccupations of clothing and food. The pages revealed Miss Jemima to be chauvinistically English and Protestant (Catholics were "Mary worshippers"), primly straitlaced and keenly observant.

The "Dramatis Personae" includes:

Miss Eliza)	
Miss Mary)	Sisters, itinerant Calvin worshippers.
Miss Jemima:	Artist.
Miss Sarah:	Continental traveller, cousin to Miss Jemima.
Mr. William:	Paymaster.
Mr. Tom:	*Professeur.* Interpreter in the German cantons and Hon. Physician to the expedition (Homeopathic).
Mr. James:	French interpreter and Poet Laureate.
Mr. Cook:	The Excursionist.
Mrs. H.:	The solitary companion accompanying Mr. Cook.

At five o'clock a message from one of the Swiss tour guides summoned me to a press conference. The room in the Hôtel des Bergues was filled with thirty men and five women. I was seated between two attractive, and quite probably the youngest, persons in the room. To my left was a pretty fair-haired girl wearing harlequin sunglasses. Her name was Penelope Lars* and she was from a Swedish press associa-

---

*The names and characters of Penelope Lars, Peppi Rosato, and Gretel Dobish are fictitious.

tion. On my right was a handsome youth with black curly hair and long-lashed dark eyes who gave his name as Peppi Rosato and said he was from an Italian travel magazine. Aside from the large numbers of Swiss reporters and TV crews and British journalists curiously eyeing one another, there were correspondents from Germany, Sweden, Holland, Austria, Italy, Denmark, and France. There was one other American, Robert Deardorf of *The New York Times.*

We were greeted by the tour manager, a dark-haired, kinetic man named Albert Kunz, who was director of the Swiss Center in London. Speaking English with a Swiss accent, he explained that the urgent meeting was called to refute a story in the *Tribune de Geneve* denouncing our expedition as a publicity stunt and suggesting that Miss Jemima had never existed. To refute the accusation we were shown Miss Jemima's red leather copybooks, the pages of which were filled with a clear strong handwriting. Displayed with it was a daguerreotype of Miss Jemima, showing her to have a rather plain round face with strong features—a firm mouth, a large nose, and penetrating eyes— and thick dark hair swept back into a knot. Other items of evidence included the passport of Miss Jemima's brother, William Wilberforce Morrell, the "Mr. William" of the tour. Robert Deardorf said, "The *Times* was a bit worried, of course, about the authenticity of the journal but when I read it and saw how unprofessional it was I knew it was no fake."

Dinner in the baroque ballroom of the century-old hotel might have been a banquet scene from Dickens. Seated around a great table in a flood of TV lights were twelve attractive people dressed in the height of eighteenth-century fashion. Nine were actors and the other three were Thomas Cook, great-great-grandson of the original excursionist; his wife, Virginia Cook; and his sister, Hazel Cook. The tightly laced girls wore lavishly brocaded skirts, gold-braided bodices with bishop's sleeves, small Empress Eugènie hats, and slippers above which showed flashes of frilled pantaloons and colored stockings. The men, all with sideburns and some with beards, wore stovepipe trousers, bright weskits, high collars with brocaded foulards, and Prince Albert coats. On a huge buffet near the table was a display of viands recreated from an 1863 menu recorded by Miss Jemima. To accommodate the cameramen the group at the table were raising wine glasses in a toast to Miss

Jemima, enacted by a pert twenty-seven-year-old brunette named Janet Edwards. Though prettier, her face had a marked resemblance to the image on the daguerreotype.

Hungry journalists crowded around the buffet to admire the gastronomic glory and a tourist office clerk ushered reporters to small dining tables outside of camera range.

"My goodness, what a fuss," a lady taking a place beside me said. "It's only dead salmon!" We introduced ourselves. She was Mrs. Morrell and, seated beside her, was her husband, grandson of Jemima's brother, William Morrell. She seemed a classic English matron, fine-skinned, pink cheeked and blond, dressed in simple good taste.

"The journalists seem rather a mixed bag, don't you think?" said Mr. Morrell, the advertising director of a network of provincial newspapers. Also at our table were Robert Deardorf, a jolly Dane named Hakon Mielche, and Westcott Jones, an Englishman who said he was "a railroad writer" and had joined the trip solely to ride the nineteenth-century steam trains reactivated for our journey. A waiter served us wine, a white Dezaley.

"I'm not really sure the wine is appropriate," said Mrs. Morrell. "Auntie Jemima was a teetotaler and so was grandfather."

"And so was Mr. Cook," said her husband.

"To Auntie Jemima," I toasted. Deardorf laughed, and I explained why "Aunt Jemima" had a comic connotation for Americans.

"I don't think Jemima would fancy that," said Mr. Morrell.

"It's a sheer accident that we are here," said his wife. "They didn't know who Jemima was."

"The book was already printed," said her husband. "Not until February, when we found a small diary from which the book was written, did we discover it was *our* Jemima."

"Of course we let Cook's know and lucky for us we were invited to come along," said Mrs. Morrell.

Her husband went on: "Mr. Cook invited my grandfather, who was a teetotaler, on this temperance tour and my grandfather said, 'I'll bring my sister,' and that's how it all started. Very lucky for the Swiss, I'd say! Five years after the trip Jemima married a wealthy widower. Her husband was a sporting fellow so they lived in Yorkshire for the hunting. She died in 1909 so I never knew her."

A waiter refilled our wine glasses. "She was a tough old Jemima," Mrs. Morrell said. "She did dozens of very bad watercolors. All Morrell women were tough nuts. Opinionated, prejudiced teetotalers. Lord, how this drinking would have horrified them."

Two journalists joined our table. One was a Hollander named Van Dolden; the other was a tall, elderly Englishman and Mrs. Morrell whispered to me that he was John Steel of *Sphere* magazine, the most distinguished journalist in the room. He was an angular storklike man and his heavy tweed suit with folded cuffs might have been a costume for the Jemima group.

At a quarter past nine Albert Kunz announced, "Now it is permitted for everyone to eat. You may take all you wish and have no regrets." Like starving locusts, the journalists leaped to the festive board. "The bill of fare," Jemima wrote in 1863, "reads like a cookery book."

Vegetable soup (mild)
Salmon, with cream sauce
Sliced roast beef with brown potatoes
Boiled fowl, served on rice
Sweetbreads
Roast fowl with salad
Artichokes
Plum pudding, steeped in brandy
Sponge cakes and stewed fruit
Sweet pudding in iced custard
Two varieties of creams
Ripe cherries

"My paper will pay me two hundred guilders just to describe this dinner," said Van Dolden. More bottles of wine arrived, a red Dole and a Pinôt Noir. The hall tinkled with clinking glasses. Journalists returned for second and even third helpings of the sumptuous food.

"Auntie Jemima could have made the plum pudding herself," said Mr. Morrell. At the head table a buxom member of the Jemima group, Thomasina Thornton, lit a cigar and puffed away like a Restoration wife.

"Mercy," said Mrs. Morrell, "wouldn't that have caused a flap! The

Morrells were also opposed to the weed." A man named Cormack, public relations manager of Cook's, introduced Sir Thomas Cook: "Great-grandson of the original Thomas whose face is known to you from your travellers' cheques." Sir Thomas, a pink-faced, white-haired old man who looked like a vicar, said, "I must make some things clear. I have nothing to do with Cook's. I am a country squire and a member, sometimes defeated, of Parliament . . ." Westcott Jones explained that the Cook family sold its interest in the company to Wagons-Lits, Ltd. in 1928. Mr. Cormack read an exchange of congratulatory messages between England's prime minister and the Swiss president.

"Gracious," said Mrs. Morrell. "Jemima did start a fuss, didn't she?" A choir sang "Auld Lang Syne."

JUNE 27

Let us charitably draw a veil over the recollection of our night . . . at four A.M. we were wide awake . . .

At nine in the morning three harried young men from the Swiss Tourist Office—Peter Suter, Helmut Klee, and Theodos Boni— collected our bags and dispatched us into buses. I took a seat beside Penelope Lars, still hiding her blue eyes behind huge black lenses. The long-lashed Italian took a seat in front of us and turned, smiling roguishly. He gave each of us two cards. One said, "Pietro Cavalino, Giornalista," and the other, "Peppi Rosato" with a Rome street address. "It is my duty to test hotels and sea stations," he explained. "When I visit a hotel and say it is disgusting they look who wrote. That is why I have a pseudonym. They see it is Pietro Cavalino and they can't find. The hotel in Geneva was disgusting."

The driver tuned the bus radio to a blast of country rock and, with this accompaniment, hurtled us through the Geneva countryside to a turreted chateau in the village of Dardagny. Not until we arrived did we realize that the occasion was a wine-tasting. "My God!" said Penelope. "It's only nine-thirty o'clock!"

"The Group," wearing full-hooped skirts of heavy woolens and satins, and thick tweed suits, were drinking glasses of dazzling white wine for photographers while Albert Kunz, leaping about like a dervish, shouted, "Smile! Smile like you did a hundred years ago!" We were given tumblers of *Goût du Prieur*. "Drink! Drink!" Kunz commanded. "It is the wine of the country." The silver vintage shimmered in the sunlight and struck like lightning on morning stomachs. "I know wine causes gout," said Westcott Jones. "But whoever heard of advertising it on the label?" A band of schoolchildren filed out on a terrace to observe the wassailing. "I don't understand this," said Mrs. Morrell. "Jemima would be mortified!" There was a peal of horns and a dozen huntsmen galloped their horses over the terrace. They wore the pink jackets, white pants, black boots and caps of English hunting prints, and they blew brass horns. "It's a private society to maintain the tradition of riding," Kunz explained. "In Switzerland we do not hunt in this manner." The Group sang "My Bonnie Lies Over the Ocean," which was said to be Jemima's favorite song. I made a note to check its date and found it was written by one Charles E. Pratt in 1881.

Assuming we would take the same bus back I had left my briefcase containing baggage keys, travelers checks, and passport on the seat beside Penelope's handbag. When it was time to return we found the old bus gone and a new one in its place. Peter Suter assured us the briefcase and the handbag would be waiting for us at the hotel.

After lunch—with more wine—the case and handbag had not appeared. We saw the first bus parked beside the hotel and in it we found Penelope's handbag but not my briefcase. There was no need to worry, Peter Suter assured me. Helmut Klee had taken it ahead to the next hotel.

This was the Beau Rivage in Ouchy. Built two years before Jemima's trip, the lavishly elegant hotel had baroque halls with frescoed ceilings and sweeping staircases. My bags were waiting in my room but not my briefcase containing the keys to open them. There was also a large box of Nestlé chocolates, a bowl of fruit, and several bottles of mineral water.

The day had grown hot and Penelope, Peppi Rosato, alias Pietro Cavalino, and I decided to swin in Lake Geneva. Unable to open my baggage, I rented trunks. When we arrived at the beach we found the water, which had appeared so inviting from the hotel, soupy with muck. Since none of the local swimmers seemed concerned, Penelope and I plunged through the mire out into clearer water. Peppi-Pietro strolled on the beach, inviting admiration.

"Quite a pretty boy," Penelope said. "Rather young to be a journalist."

"He has credentials," I said. "He must be old enough."

"We have been arguing about your age," she told him when we joined him on the beach.

He sighed. "It is my problem. No one believes I am old enough for anything."

"I daresay," Penelope said.

"So I have had to develop a great cleverness to fool people."

"How old are you then?" Penelope insisted.

"Twenty-seven," he said.

A storm was rolling in from the mountains across the lake and we took a taxi back to the hotel. Before the entrance were two flower-decked stage coaches waiting to take The Group on a tour of Lausanne. Horses arrived on trucks and a crowd gathered to watch. The horses, not accustomed to bouncing skirts and flower wreaths, were skittish. A costumed young man of The Group named Kenneth Beck was helping his wife, Enid, into the first coach, while Albert Kunz and Peter Suter pushed back the crowds. There was a rumble of thunder and in the same moment a flare from a photographer's flash. One of the horses reared and kicked a hotel maid and she began to scream. The horse kicked through the dashboard and alarmed its mate. The team, now out of control, took off down the street with a fearful clatter, crashing the carriage into a parked car. Kenneth Beck leaped from the coach and, with heroic speed, ran ahead of the horses, caught them by their bits and halted them. Like a proper Victorian lady, his wife refused to go on, and plans for the procession were abandoned.

My briefcase had not yet appeared. Still worse, according to Peter Suter, John Steel's bags were lost and he was distraught. Helmut Klee was returning with him to Geneva to search for them. I went into the hotel bar for a drink and was asked to leave because of my soiled jeans, sports jacket, and sneakers. Peter Suter offered to send for a locksmith.

I went into the press headquarters and searched for an hour, moving stacks of press releases and files, and under one I found my briefcase— which apparently had been there all day. I rushed upstairs. While I was showering, an Italian maid entered my room. She lowered her eyes demurely and handed me still another box of chocolates.

In the lobby I saw Helmut Klee returning from Geneva with Mr. Steel and his bags and I heard Mr. Steel say he was going to bed. Penelope Lars, with whom I had an appointment, was gone. I taxied to the Château Mon Repos, headquarters of the International Olympics Committee, and arrived at another wine-tasting. I saw Penelope with Peppi Rosato. He gazed at me with a cool smile. I joined the Morrells at another Victorian buffet. "I do think," said Mrs. Morrell, "that all this quaffing is coming quite out of control."

We were hauled across town in buses to the bell tower of Lausanne's medieval cathedral, where we were served *Kirschwasser*. Members of a student dueling society saluted us with clanking steins of beer. Most of our assembly were too spent for the climb of 184 steps into the tower to hear the watchman call the midnight hour. Four of The Group and five of us journalists were sufficiently coordinated to undertake it.

A supply of wine had been sent up into the tower and the jolly old watchman who had been drinking from it showed us his pinups of Brigitte Bardot and Elizabeth Taylor and asked Miss Jemima to instruct him in English. The lights of the city went out. Coveys of alarmed pigeons swirled about. In the garden below, dueling boys broke into a traditional "Midnight Hymn," a mighty basso carrying the solo. When the song was finished the watchman lurched to the parapet and his amplified voice covered the city, shouting for the first time in English: "Twelve o'clock and all is well!"

JUNE 28

Now, there is one impact that these mountains make upon all travellers alike, and that is thirst!

The next morning was stormy and sojourners were hauled in buses to the Ouchy Yacht Club to hear a cannon salute by the admiral of the Swiss Navy.

No one believed such a character existed, but there he was waiting on the dock, a crinkly-faced merry old officer of the *Lac Leman Flotilla*. When everyone was accounted for he invited us to an upper deck where the cannon, a small electronic apparatus hardly larger than a Fourth of July toy, was set in an open window. The "navy" consisted of eight young men in blue jeans and yellow slickers. Bottles were uncorked and wine poured. The admiral toasted Queen Victoria. "The Group!" Albert Kunz shouted, herding the actors around the cannon. Suddenly, when no one expected it, the cannon belched forth a feeble little pop. The TV crews said it had not recorded on their sound equipment and Kunz ordered it fired two more times.

On the dock below a crowd had gathered to watch our embarkation for Vevey on a nineteenth-century steam barge that was bobbing in the mists. Fog covered the lake and green waves lashed against the dock. Several journalists said they would not sail on the old barge in a storm and the admiral offered to summon a modern diesel launch. "But," said Kunz, "The Group must first embark on the barge to be authentic for photographers." With nervous squeals, four of the actresses stepped down into a small dinghy and were rowed away. Miss Jemima, her red skirt whipping in the wind, was the first on the barge and the crowd applauded. An actor, who the day before had helped capture a runaway horse, went next. Climbing up the ladder, he caught his trousers on a nail and ripped a rent in the seat. In an effort to extricate himself he lost his balance and fell into the lake.

The maneuver was abandoned. The diesel boat, decorated with red geraniums, arrived. As we sailed away the jolly admiral waved a bottle of wine and the cannon offered a hollow burp.

"Now we are going to a big picnic," Albert Kunz announced. As our journey progressed, his energy and enthusiasm seemed to increase in inverse proportion to the mounting exhaustion and confusion of the journalists whom he was shepherding like errant sheep. The storm ceased and an hour later, when we docked in the harbor of the Nestlé Company, the sun was shining. Costumed musicians led us into a reception hall where Nestlé officials waited by a table set with bottles of whiskey and gin and a Lucullan board. A bearded young chemist, impersonating Henri Nestlé, nineteenth-century founder of the company, commenced a speech. "*Herrgott,*" I heard a husky voice saying. "He is going to give the history of the chocolate factory."

I turned and saw a pretty young woman. The speaker droned on like an inept actor, saying, "I am sure this first Cook's tour will be remembered one hundred years from now." The lady beside me rolled her eyes. She was smartly dressed. "Do you know," she whispered, "that there are no more Cooks with Cook's and no more Nestlés with Nestlé?" Her name, she said, was Gretel Dobish, and she was a Viennese women's magazine correspondent who had joined the pilgrimage that morning.

The speeches ended and waiters poured drinks. Peppi Rosato and I each had a Scotch. "I have decided to drink everywhere the same Johnny Walker," he said. Penelope Lars had vermouth and Gretel Dobish a gin fizz. The buffet included cold ham, turkey and roast beef, stuffed eggs, and a dozen salads. "Haven't had a hot meal for three days," complained Peppi Rosato, heaping his plate. "And always strawberries for dessert." A local crowd gathered outside the glass walls to watch us eat.

In the afternoon buses took us to Montreux. In Territet we passed a statue of the Empress Elisabeth of Austria who was murdered in 1898 on a steamer dock in Geneva. I asked the driver to stop and he replied there was no time.

"It becomes increasingly clear that we are embarked on a lunatic journey," I said to no one in particular.

Peppi Rosato shrugged. "How is serious viewing a possibility when the brain is constantly drinking?" he asked.

"Rather exhausting, isn't it, this swooping over geography without purpose?" said Penelope Lars.

"You wish a purpose?" replied Gretel Dobish. "It is turning five kilometers of film into a hundred thousand photographs. In Switzerland nothing is done without a purpose."

There was hardly time in the hotel for a bath and change before the bus took us to an old wine cellar, *La Cave a Fanchette*. Gin cocktails were served and white wine drawn from barrels. "When we can't take it orally they're going to give it to us intravenously," said Hakon Mielche. Vernon Jones, an actor, boasted, "I have drunk twenty-four glasses of wine since breakfast." A German-type band was playing and Albert Kunz called The Group to waltz for the cameras. Vernon Jones and Janet Edwards began to swoop gracefully.

Something happened. A lunacy swept over The Group and Miss Jemima threw herself into an abandoned Charleston. Young Mr. and

Mrs. Cook began to twist and since he was tall and slender, their writhings were serpentine. Thomasina Thornton, smoking a cigar, flipped up her skirts in a can-can. "No! no, no!" Albert Kunz shouted. "Dance like you did a hundred years ago!" Unable to halt the paroxysms, he ordered the cameras and music to stop and summoned the buses to take us to the Castle of Chillon.

It was a lovely evening. Mists rose up from the mountains like steam from volcanos and the Romanesque old edifice standing in the water was like a castle in a dream. Nine years before, when I was a student at the University of Geneva, I had swum around it on a dare.

Inside, from its deep windows I watched the sun settle over the Alps and a gleam of light flow toward me on the water. Beside me Peppi Rosato looked down a dizzying depth to the lake and told Penelope Lars that it reminded him of parachute jumps of which he had made forty-seven. Behind us Miss Jemima was reading from Byron's poem:

> A double dungeon wall and wave
> Have made—and like a living grave.
> Below the surface of the lake
> The dark vault lies wherein we lay . . .*

She was interrupted by the entrance of two uniformed officers arriving to enforce a regulation against photographs in the castle. There was a noisy altercation between two sets of Swiss bureaucrats, our own tourist officials and the police of canton Vaud. To the great relief of everyone our men lost. For the first time since we had embarked on our comic-opera pilgrimage, we were freed from the tyranny of cameras. Miss Jemima continued to read:

> At last men came to set me free,
> And all my bonds aside were cast . . .

A fanfare of trumpets summoned us into the Hall of the Knights for a banquet. Sides of oxen were roasting on a spit in a great fireplace and

---

The Prisoner of Chillon, Lord Byron

dripping blood spattered in the flames. Three wine glasses and a brandy inhaler were set at each place. I saw Peppi Rosato switch his place card next to Penelope Lars and heard an Englishman whisper nastily in my ear, "I think the little Italian boy is stealing your Swedish girl." I found my place between Gretel Dobish and the Morrells, who were expecting their fourteen-year-old son by plane in Lausanne. A Cook official named Edmund Swinglehurst Jones had been dispatched to fetch him.

The long meal began with trout fresh from the lake and continued through several courses to the beef, with a different wine for each course. I saw several journalists nodding over their food and now and then a fork clattered onto the stone floor.

For dessert there were *Cygnes du Leman,* swans of flaming ice cream borne on the shoulders of waiters, and an ice cream model of the castle. A British vice-consul was interrupted in a speech by the entrance of Nicholas Morrell, a smallish, cooly disposed lad who had evaded Mr. Jones at the airport, taken a train to Montreux, and taxied from the station to the castle. I excused myself, slipped out of the castle, and took his taxi back to my hotel. On my bedside table I found a box of chocolates, on the foil of which was printed, "*Bonne Nuit, Gute Nacht, Goodnight!*"

JUNE 29

We saw from our casement the women of Sion sitting on the kerbstones and offering cherries for sale.

At nine the next morning I was awakened by a hotel clerk who ordered me to be ready for departure at ten. I passed a leisurely hour breakfasting on my balcony facing Mont Blanc, shrouded in coral clouds. When I arrived downstairs at ten I learned that everyone had departed a quarter-hour before for the train, which was leaving in three minutes. A cab was summoned, a Mercedes with a lady driver who whisked me to a second suburban station where the train was just arriving.

In the second coach I found Peppi Rosato, in custody of *both* Penelope Lars and Gretel Dobish, telling them about his sad life. "My father has a mistress who is a dramatic actress, so there was never any happiness for my sisters and me, only quarrels. Now my father is divorcing my mother to marry the lady. Of course, as a man I have sympathy for him, but it was a mistake not to do it fifteen years ago when my mother was still young enough to find another husband."

"Why didn't *she* divorce him?" Gretel asked.

Peppi sighed. "She loved him," he said. "It is very tragic."

We were moving up the Rhone Valley, following the river toward its source, passing terraced vineyards and old castles. In an hour we were in Sierre, which boasts the sunniest and driest climate in Switzerland. It was a local holiday, the feast of Sts. Peter and Paul, and the town was draped with banners. At the station was a costumed fife and drum corps from the Val d'Anniviers, where musicians play in the vineyards during the harvesting of grapes. They led us in procession to the garden of the Hôtel Bellevue where, under the chestnut trees, tables shimmered with bottles of local wine ready for tasting. A large wheel of cheese was roasting over an open fire, being prepared for *Raclette.* In one corner of the garden men were playing zithers, striking the strings with small hammers, filling the garden with cascades of lovely sound. I found a place with Hakon Mielche and the three English Joneses: Vernon, the actor, Westcott, the railroad expert, and Swinglehurst, the Cook ombudsman who said he was descended from South American Indians. John Steel, the man from *Sphere,* who after the first day never permitted his baggage out of his grasp, had departed in the morning for England. The day was warm. Within a half-hour everyone had returned to the usual state of exhileration. Costumed waitresses served lunch, *Viande sechée* (dried raw beef) and *Pain de Seigle,* year-old rye bread that had to be broken with an ax, a denture hazard which had the rich flavor of dried nuts. The main dish, *Raclette,* was scraped from the roasting wheel with wooden spoons and served with potatoes and pickled onions and gherkins.

Albert Kunz announced a prize of a case of wine to whomever ate the most servings of *Raclette* and several of the English entered the competition with gusto. Westcott Jones said that, unless a glass of white wine were drunk with each serving of *Raclette,* the cheese would harden into a lump in the stomach and remain there. Worrying over the health of The Group, Edmund Jones so warned its members but they were into the contest with abandon and paid him no heed. The zithers tinkled.

The contest was finally won by Miss Hazel Cook, who was reported to have eaten five servings of *Raclette*. Swinglehurst groaned. Waitresses brought dessert, great bowls of lush black cherries, and Westcott Jones warned that the combination of any pit fruits with white wine was a digestive disaster. Several of The Group departed for the rest rooms.

It was time for speeches. I left the garden and walked into the town. Coming to a church, I entered and lay on a pew and slept in cool darkness for an hour.

When I returned to the park an unsteady procession was weaving its way to the railroad station to catch the train for Leuk. A tour guide was making a head count. "Where have you been?" he asked, and added, "The Italian boy is now also taking the Viennese girl from you." Ahead I saw Peppi Rosato walking between Penelope Lars and Gretel Dobish. On each seat of the train coaches there was an assortment of press releases put there for the journalists by the tourist office boys. Westcott Jones and I gathered up armfuls of them and from the platform of the train offered the curious crowds copies of speeches, histories of the Nestlé and Cook companies, and biographies of Miss Jemima, and before the train departed we had distributed most of them.

The short ride to Leuk was rough. "Roaring rails," said Westcott Jones. "Flat on wheel. I'm very shocked." We passed through Pfyn-Wald, a forest of stunted pines marking the boundary between the French- and German-speaking areas of Canton Valais. Crossing the Rhone to Leuk station, we changed to a narrow-gauged electric train for the trip up to Leukerbad. The little cars stopped briefly on a bridge of the Dala Gorge where Albert Kunz directed us to gaze down into a vertiginous canyon where an electrical plant was providing the power for our train. We chugged slowly up eleven miles at an incline of 2,500 feet to the spa of Leukerbad.

The scene at the station might have been from Hieronymous Bosch. The costumed crowd and crush of invalids in wheelchairs was so great no one could move. A band was booming. St. Bernard dogs woofed and women threw flowers. Albert Kunz shouted, "Make a *Zug*!" and Swinglehurst Jones explained to the bewildered Group that a *Zug* was a parade. Two wheelchairs overturned and their wailing cargoes had to be picked up. A German lady in our party slipped into a puddle of mud and I remembered that Mark Twain, after "wading" through puddles in the same place, wrote, "They ought to either pave that village or organize a ferry."*

In the lobby of the Hôtel des Alpes I purchased a local history book and went to my room to read it. I learned that Leukerbad's twelve hot saline springs have been famous for curing rheumatics since Roman times; that a cardinal who frequented them had the bathhouses built in 1501. A sixteenth-century writer, Johannes Stumpf, described the water as "hot enough to boil eggs and stew fowls."

A mountain outside my window was casting an early dusk over the village. The formidable 2,000-foot vertical wall appeared inviolable. Miss Jemima's party had taken half a day to climb it by foot and on mules; our own ascent would be made in suspended cable cabins in a quarter-hour. Looking up into the perilous cliffs I was filled with disquiet.

When I went downstairs for still another 1863 Jemima dinner I found I was not alone in my jitters. Few of the non-Swiss travelers had ever been so close to an alp before. Four days of too-swift traveling, of too much eating and drinking, and too little sleep appeared to have exhausted everyone. The Group, pleading fatigue, was wearing contemporary clothing for the first time. Nerves were frayed and in some cases on the edge of hysteria. Gretel Dobish was accusing the Swiss factotums of censorship—she said a story filed in Sierre, criticizing the logistics of our journey, had not been sent on the teletype. Mrs. Morrell reported that her bathroom had "an Aunt Jemima tub. I'm sure she had a bath in it." In the middle of dinner Penelope Lars ran out of the dining room weeping.

The long meal, which had not pleased Miss Jemima in 1863, had not improved over the century. The trout was fair, the chicken stringy and tough. The greatly heralded main course, roasted chamois, was tough and gamey and a rumor spread that it was not chamois, which were protected by law, but goat.

The only traveler still bounding with energy was Albert Kunz.

---

*A Tramp Abroad, 1878.

Merrily he distributed Victorian bathing costumes to the actors for a morning immersion. The full-bodied pajama-type garments of striped materials with tasseled caps looked like clown suits. To cheer the apathetic gathering Kunz selected a bright red nightshirt for himself and put it on.

Too restless for sleep, I set out on a walk. The great mountain leaned over me like a threatening tower. A strange disquiet seemed to fill the night; the darkness rustled with soft footsteps and voices. I recognized two girls from The Group passing and from the shadows I heard a man's voice murmuring, "Oh, those lovely English peaches, those sweet ripe fruits of love." The unknown speaker passed and I was alone. I heard what sounded like a quarrel, a woman gently wailing and a familiar voice impatiently saying, "Sex and love is a mèlange I cannot support." I saw the girl going toward the hotel and in a moment Peppi Rosato stepped out of the night and, recognizing me, said, "Women who weep are an exasperation. You accommodate them; you *luf* them and they weep! One has to be ruthless; they demand it." He invited me for a coffee and we went into the hotel cafe. He continued his lament. "First it is the Swedish girl wishing for my attention. I am willing but when the Austrian is demanding I be faithful to her I say that is an absurdity that I cannot, as a man, comprehend. To make her calm I have agreed to be understanding and she has gone to compose herself."

The role of confidant that he was assigning me was uncomfortable. If it was true, as I kept hearing it said, that Peppi looked on me as a rival, I wished to persuade him I was not. "How can anyone on this trip have the time or energy?" I asked.

He frowned. "Sometimes I have not energy for other things. But for this always. Is absolutely necessary I have a woman every day and better two or three. In Rome I have three, four girls I see and a country girl who comes once a week. I am catching up my lost time. For five years I was impotent."

"I can't believe it."

"A result, of course, of my unhappy family life, my poor mother for whom I suffer such a great compassion. Three years ago I recovered and unless I have at least one woman a day I become very nervous. You can see, in such a régime, it is necessary to be very ruthless."

"And very busy."

He shrugged and blinked his long lashes. "The secret is not to commit, to keep always a solitariness of protection. It is the only security against situations like now."

His striking handsomeness seemed in that moment repellent and a little pathetic. Perhaps he sensed that his exhibitionistic confessions were not, as he intended, arousing my envy. He drew out his wallet to show me some photos. They were all of himself: at the wheel of a new Porsche, in the gear of a parachutist, in a bikini on a yawl, on water skis. And in each photo he was alone.

JUNE 30

A lady was taking her meal up to her shoulders in water . . .
A moustached gentleman was cutting leather work on his floating
table. Other bathers were preparing for a game of draughts . . .

Like Miss Jemima and Mark Twain, I chose the voyeur's role. When I arrived in the steaming chambers at 8:30 A.M. the antic scene was as Jemima had described it and little changed from the one witnessed fifteen years later by Mark Twain, who wrote, "The water is running, and changes all the time, else a patient with a ringworm might take the bath with only partial success, since, while he was ridding himself of his ringworm, he might catch the itch."

Immersed to her neck, Janet Edwards was reading *The Best of the Reader's Digest.* Mr. Beck and Mrs. Cook were playing chess. Hazel Cook was knitting—her skein was a soggy mass. Mrs. Beck was reading *The London Observer* and Thomasina Thornton was playing solitaire and humming a song. Others were being served breakfast by waitresses in black dresses and white aprons, reaching out over the water. Vernon Jones fastidiously balanced his tray with one hand while pouring coffee from a silvered pot with the other. A Swiss television producer was playing *Jass* with his wife and she, trumping his ace with a thud, upset the tray and spilled the cards which bobbed away. Wearing his red nightshirt and cap, Albert Kunz thrashed about, shouting, "*Enjoy! Enjoy* like you did a hundred years ago!"

The steamy revelries ended when Peter Suter ordered everyone out of the tank to prepare for the Gemmi ascent. When the travelers gathered a half-hour later at the cable car station they were ominously quiet. A few complained of being unable to sleep in the altitude. An English lady refused to make the ascent under any conditions and arrangements were made for her and a cameraman suffering from an intestinal indisposition to drive around the mountains by car to Kanderstag. Peppi Rosato and Gretel Dobish were the last to appear. The day was gray and a misty rain was falling. An assembly of natives and bleating goats had gathered to see us off. Photographers were assigned the first cable car and The Group the second. The rest of us were divided into four cars. Of the fifteen people jammed into mine I was acquainted only with the Hollander, van Dolden. He was pale and perspiring.

The car jerked forward and commenced gliding smoothly upward. I faced the rear of the cabin and carefully avoided looking either down or at the precipice ahead. Everyone was silent except van Dolden, who suddenly began recalling newspaper reports of cable-car disasters, spreading his anxieties through the cabin. I closed my eyes and held firmly to a pole. I heard van Dolden begin to laugh and others commenced laughing until the cabin was filled with manic mirth. Laughing like fools we arrived at the top.

"We hailed our first snowfield," Jemima wrote, reporting a snowball fight in which the professor's glass eye was knocked out. For us also wet snow was falling and Albert Kunz, mindful of the scenario, shouted hoarsely, "Make a snow fight!" The Group dutifully complied until one of the girl's hats was knocked off. "Don't make so hard," Kunz rasped, his voice strained with laryngitis.

A caravan of seven "Gemmi wagons" waited to convey The Group over the Gemmi pass and into the canton of Berne. Each of the open two-wheeled carriages was built for two passengers facing backward on a seat that swung level no matter how steep the incline. Costumed drivers, wearing garlands of anemones and gentians, walked beside the carriages, holding the horses' reins in their left hands and braking the carriage with their right hands. For the rest of us the nine-mile six-hour journey through an Apocalyptian tundra was by foot. A spell of spiritless gloom cast itself over the weary travelers. Clouds covered the mountains and the promised view of alps from Mont Rosa to the Matterhorn did not appear. Looking ahead at the slowly moving single-file procession I remembered that Mark Twain made the formidable journey in the other direction and described a "hideous desolation."

The snow turned to rain. The Victorians in their wagons were bundled in blankets and the girls unfurled frilly parasols. We trudged past naked cliffs and glaciers and a tiny black lake. In two hours we arrived at the summit of the pass where the Jemima party planted a British flag for photographers, hoisting it for Queen Victoria.

As we moved out of the pass, shafts of sunlight shone through the clouds. The air was clearer and the path drier. We had begun the descent and walking was easier. Between patches of snow and ice, meadows bloomed with a botanical profusion of unfamiliar flowers. One of the Swiss journalists, an amateur botanist named Toni Peterhans, identified wild pansies, anemones, primulas, tiny pink orchids, blue and white forget-me-nots, purple gentians, asters, Daphne, and *Frauenmantel,* a tiny blossom which mountain people dried and boiled for tea.

Another hour brought us to the Schwarenbach Hotel, an old hospice that was the only habitation in the pass. We entered a low-ceilinged room where flower-decorated tables were set for lunch. Here we quenched our parched throats with jugs of white Fendant to which our empty stomachs and tired bodies responded quickly and soon the room rang with gaiety. Peppi Rosato plucked a gentian from a centerpiece, filled it with wine, and offered it to Gretel Dobish; everyone applauded and began drinking the golden wine from the tiny blue cups. We ate thick hot soup, cold meats, hard cheese, coarse bread, salads, and a variety of fruits. Outside steamed windows the horses munched oats from nosebags.

It ended when Joseph Blatter, secretary of the Canton Valais tourist office, who had traveled with us since Sierre and was now to return alone through the gloomy pass, stood up and said, "Yesterday when you came to Valais the sun was shining. Today when you leave the heavens are weeping . . ."

His simple eloquence touched off an emotional response from weary souls. Some people laughed and others wept and the applause did not stop. Not fully understanding the nature of the outburst, Blatter himself began to weep. I stood up and congratulated him for the shortest and most moving speech of the journey and he asked me to write my comments on a postcard so he might show them to his wife.

We resumed our long descent, crossing the border into Berne, passing from bleak tundra into a landscape of trees and meadows with lupine, columbines, daisies, and poppies. In two hours we arrived at the cable-car station of Stock, from which we descended through thick fog to the village of Kandersteg. I avoided a welcoming procession of schoolchildren and walked to my hotel and to bed.

JULY 1

The days spent on foot, or by the side of a mule, gave us the greatest pleasure.

I awoke in agony. Fatigue was like a serum in my veins, my throat was swollen, my head ached. I looked at the program of our journey and found it was Monday and that our itinerary for the day over the Bernese Oberland included fifteen departures and arrivals on five buses, two horse carriages, two trains, and one boat.

The first of the carriages, drawn by four horses, arrived to take us to the station where a *Lokalzügli,* a "little local train," waited to haul us to Spiez.

The toylike steam train rattled merrily down the Kander Valley through a classic Swiss landscape of green meadows, dark chalets, and brown cows. In an hour a fanfare of trumpets welcomed us at the Castle of Spiez. After a collation of wine and cheese we sailed on an 1871 steamer across the Lake of Thun and took motor coaches to the Staubbach Falls. Lacy veils of water leaping out from a ledge a thousand feet above fell over us in a mist. Under the falls I saw Peppi Rosato walking hand in hand with Penelope Lars. Gretel Dobish was following them and they paid her no attention.

The coaches took us to another waterfall, the Trümmelbach, where water from the Jungfrau shot out in horizontal jets from cliffs. On this spot our program promised Jemima's lunch of "trout caught by local boys in the river." Laughing lustily over the foolishness, a grizzled old man dangled a dead fish from a pole for photographers while we ate delicious precaught trout on the terrace of a hotel.

From Trümmelbach we rode to Interlaken in stagecoaches resurrected from various museums. Each coach was drawn by four horses wearing bells and reined by two drivers. We jangled down the Lütschine gorge, through dark cool forests, passing nostalgic old men and women who waved and wiped their eyes.

A huge and impatient crowd which had been waiting an hour surrounded our carriages so that we could not move. The people offered bouquets and women who once worked as domestics in England engaged the actors in conversation. Frantic policemen were trying to clear a way so The Group could proceed to a service scheduled in an Anglican church.

I got out of the carriage and walked alone to the Victoria Hotel where I soaked in a hot bath and then slept. At seven I went into the bar and joined English journalists, who were complaining of exhaustion, for a drink. After a time Peppi Rosato appeared and commenced for me an account of his tribulations with Gretel Dobish, saying, "I wish to dispose of her but she will not dispose. She thinks because I *luf* her twice I must all the time. She is boring and hysterical. I believe the Swedish one would be less annoying."

I said that I thought his treatment of both women was reprehensible.

"I have no scruples," he replied.

Dinner that evening—another 1863 men —was a disaster. Service was slow, the fish might have been fried cod and the duck was stringy and tough. Peppi and I shared a table with Mrs. Morrell and her son, Nicholas, the only sojourner still in buoyant spirits. Mrs. Morrell, whom I had discerned to be typically English, informed us she was a German who had married in England after the war. Life in Yorkshire was not entirely to her pleasure. "Yorkshiremen cherish discomfort," she said. "It gives them a feeling of strength to consider central heating decadent."

In the evening there was music. I asked Penelope Lars to dance. When Peppi saw us on the floor he disappeared and I did not see him again.

JULY 2

At Grindelwald we began to feel very tired . . . We had a fracas with the porteur who, at the landlord's instigation, was bent on making an overcharge.

In the morning I was awakened by a Swiss voice at the door

informing me that if I did not rise at once I would be late for departure.

After breakfast our band of travelers took the train to the Alpine resort of Wengen. Familiar faces had dropped away and new ones had appeared. The excitement and friendliness of the first days had run down. Instead there was a remoteness, a withdrawing of everyone into himself. One reason for this change of spirit was certainly fatigue. Another was a loss of orientation. Moving too swiftly, drinking too much, we seldom had a clear sense of exactly where we were or what day it was. The result was a nearly catatonic suspension of will, an acceptance of forces over which we had relinquished control when we began the journey. We were experiencing the ultimate conditions of that which we were celebrating—of group travel, a "Cook's tour."

The company was roused from its torpor for a moment when Gretel Dobish entered the car searching for Peppi Rosato. When she found him with Penelope Lars, he got up from his seat and passed into the forward car. Everyone watched quietly as she followed him, a stricken Ariadne pursuing a faithless Theseus.

We arrived at a meadow of haycocks facing the glistening Jungfrau. Brawny herdsmen blew alphorns and yodeled. The sonorous alphorns and falsetto voices melded with echoes into a reverberating choir. On sawdust courts muscular youths were competing in Swiss wrestling. In this stylized and not very perilous sport, grunting athletes clutched at the loose canvas trunks of their opponents, attempting to throw one another to the ground; their slow movements might have been a Stone Age dance. Next there was rock throwing, a Swiss version of discus hurling, in which young Atlases with biceps like thighs heaved boulders weighing 160 pounds. The distances were gravely measured by an old man who drew marks in the sawdust with his furled umbrella.

A punch of white wine and cider champagne was served and Albert Kunz urged The Group to join in the games. Soon bustled girls were tumbling one another in the sawdust. Peter Cook blew into an alphorn and was able to produce a plaintive trill; and an Englishman, attempting flag throwing, unbalanced himself and collapsed on the ground. The flag fluttered over him like a shroud.

From Wengen we rode a jerking rack-and-pinion train ten miles up the Wengernalp and at the end of the line The Group mounted horses and the rest of us walked for two more miles. Janet Edward's horse kept halting to feed on lupine and Albert Kunz, his voice reduced to a whisper, rasped, "Please, someone help Miss Jemima with her horse." In a half-hour we arrived at an inn called Kleine Scheidegg, facing the north wall of the Eiger, where more climbers have lost their lives than on any other Swiss mountain except the Matterhorn. Two young men from the hotel rolled out a small cannon and prepared to shoot it. "Please," whispered Kunz. "Please be quiet so the TV can hear the echoes." The reverberations of the cannon shot rolled like thunder for almost a minute. "Now, maybe, we have started an avalanche," said Kunz.

We picnicked in the sun on barbecued mutton and jugs of red wine. For dessert there was lemon ice floated in champagne and coffee with Kirschwasser; and then we clattered on a special train down the steep decline to Grindelwald, a journey that the 1863 party had made on foot. On the way down Westcott Jones explained that our train was on its gravitational descent, operating dynamos that generated power for its return ascent.

Grindelwald was our nadir. Like Miss Jemima, we were billeted in the Hotel Adler, operated by the great-grandsons of its 1863 manager. Jagged nerves and tempers, throbbing heads and aching bones, were taking their toll, and few journalists accompanied The Group on the foot journey to a glacier. The completely English-speaking resort was in high season; the food was bad and the service rude and deviously mercenary. Penelope Lars fought with a concièrge over a 12-franc charge for pressing a dress and I made a row over a 6-franc overcharge for a 60-centime telephone call to Berne. An overwrought lady in The Group announced she had fallen in love with a handsome young mule driver who had accompanied her to the glacier and was urging her to remain with him in Switzerland.

One thing had become irrefutably clear. We twentieth-century travelers did not have the stamina and endurance of our nineteenth-century predecessors. Day after day Miss Jemima recorded rising at 4 A.M. to hike over a pass or climb up a glacier, all the time carrying a case and an umbrella. For us, eight o'clock risings were torture and most of the difficult passages made by the Jemima party, either on foot or on muleback, were effortlessly covered in railroads, cable cars, or motor buses. Still our vigor corroded as theirs had not. The evidence was undeniable. Debilitated by twentieth-century luxuries and life-styles, we were sad emulaters of our vigorous predecessors; we are a diminished race.

Certainly, a decimater was alcohol. Miss Jemima and her indomitable temperance companions drank quantities of tea. We were unceasingly saturated with wine and liquor. In Grindelwald that evening one of our Swiss cicerones began to weep uncontrollably, and had to be helped to bed.

JULY 3

You have waked me too soon, I must slumber again.

The descent by train to the Lake of Brienz was subdued. Many slept until we arrived at ten o'clock and embarked on a boat for Giessbach.

It was another dazzling day. After an hour we docked at the foot of Giessbach Falls, a series of seven successive cascades leaping, step by step, out of terraces of green meadows and dark fir forests. In a funicular we ascended halfway up the elevation of the falls to the Giessbach Hotel, a romantic castle set on a terrace next to the tumbling waters. We lunched in the garden on ham and tongue, mushrooms and spinach, and apple tarts swimming in cream.

I disdained the wine for it was apparent I was gestating a virus and I swallowed with mineral water some pills given me by ladies in the party. An accordionist and a clarinetist wandered among the tables and stopped to serenade Peppi Rosato and Gretel Dobish, sitting together at a table in silent alienation. After lunch we walked through a spray of mist into a gallery under the falls and the view through a curtain of water was Wagnerian.

A fifteen-minute boatride took us to Brienz, a village of woodcarvers. Only old people were on the quay and a tiny, wizened woman clutched Janet Edward's hand and, speaking English, said, "I was in England when Queen Victoria died. It was one of the most beautiful days of my life." Another old lady, sobbing uncontrollably, said, "I still mourn for the Queen." Brienz is in an area in which it is a tradition for young women to travel to England to work as housemaids and nannies, and the old women were recalling their youth in service. One old man looked at my khaki pants, blue denim jacket, and ascot scarf, and asked, "Is that an old-fashioned English costume?"

We boarded a northbound train across the Brünig Pass and descended toward Lucerne with a screech of brakes through dark fir forests. Over the eastern mountains dark clouds were gathering and in terraced fields barefoot women were feverishly raking hay into cocks. In less than an hour we were in Alpnachstad on the *Vierwaldstatsee,* "the lake of the four forest cantons," also known as Lake Lucerne. A children's procession led us to a fir-shaded grove where a modern Wilhelm Tell was waiting to shoot an arrow through an apple. He was a small dark man named Xaver Schön, a thirty-five-year-old house painter who had won the Swiss crossbow championship when he was twenty-nine and three years later won an international competition. With one knee on the ground, the other supporting his twenty-pound weapon, he waited for the crowd to quiet. Then, bracing the bow with his left foot, he drew back the thong, slid the steel-pointed wooden arrow into the groove of the stock, and carefully aimed. Seconds passed during which no one seemed to breathe and then I heard a whirr and a soft smack and saw the apple shattered on the ground.

"*Es war ein Meisterschuss!*" I murmured, quoting from Schiller's play, and a small boy in front of me turned and said in Bernese dialect, "*Ein Meischterschuss!*"

We were now in Tell country. The wind soughed through the pines and though the sun was still shining, a storm was rising. I recalled that the lake was known for its storms, for violent winds sweeping down canyons; it was such a storm that rescued Tell from his captors. Albert Kunz was hurrying everyone to the dock to begin the short voyage to Lucerne. The lake was rough and ominously green and the boat seemed to be palpitating with apprehension. Penelope Lars and I found seats in the stern. On the deck below Peppi Rosato was sitting with an English girl who had joined us that morning at Interlaken, and Gretel Dobish was watching disconsolately from the bow. The wind whipped the flags and upset a bowl of flowers on the deck. A waitress brought wine and when I asked her for something nonalcoholic she replied nastily, "A glass of lake water, perhaps?" The skies darkened. Three alphornists began to play and the strange sonorescense echoed across the waters like trumpets of doom.

We followed the shoreline to St. Niklausen, where an antique flat boat was waiting to carry the costumed party the last three knots to Lucerne. Black in color and flying the flag of Canton Uri—a black bull against a yellow background—the unwieldly vessel resembled an Egyptian barge. The English reembarked, and the rest of us chugged into the rising storm. The dark boat followed us, the bull billowing in the wind. Two of the girls tossed bouquets into the churning waters and the effect was eerily like a burial at sea.

Suddenly, with implacable swiftness, the tempest broke. The wind roared; the sky turned dark as night and the gray lake crested with foam. Lightning rent the heavens and thunder exploded like rockets. A wall of rain descended and behind us the barge disappeared and reappeared like the Flying Dutchman. Suddenly it vanished altogether and a rumor spread that it had capsized and some women began wailing like sirens.

With no visibility at all our pilot guided us into the jetty. A crowd was waiting and a band blared. Trees crashed to the ground and panes from a leaded-glass canopy over the pier were loosened and splintered at our feet. The band changed to a dirge and I thought for a moment it was "Nearer My God to Thee." An old lady nudged my elbow and shouted in my ear, "I was in England when the Queen died!" The boat that had brought us disappeared in the darkness and inside the battered boat station we were soaked by rain and spray. An old man standing near me shrugged and said, *A chlies Wetter*, "a small weather."

As suddenly as it broke the storm calmed. Except for a few white clouds the sky was blue. The dark barge carrying The Group had waited out the storm at a pier down the lake and now was sailing serenely into the harbor. The band played a soothing lullabye, "All Through the Night." The Group, pale and subdued, disembarked. The only casualty was a small handbag containing jewelry which a wave had washed into the lake. Two policemen on a launch went to look for it and found it floating in the water.

A caravan of horse carriages took us across the bridge to the Schweizerhof Hotel. By this time my throat was swollen and I had a temperature, and I knew for certain I was ill. I asked the concièrge to recommend a doctor and he sent me to one a square away. The doctor, who had been to America for medical conferences, spoke English. He said I had an acute strep infection and asked me to tell him in detail what I'd done in the week past. I began to laugh, releasing a well of suppressed vexations. I reviewed the week and got as far as my swim in Lake Geneva six days before.

"You swam in a Swiss lake?" he asked incredulously. "Go no further!" He began to scold, "Don't you know better than to go into our lakes which are filled with infections? Are Americans always so careless, so incautious for their health?"

"The Swiss were swimming," I replied in defense.

"Because others are fools, must you be a fool too?" he replied, feigning anger. He injected me with penicillin and ordered me to bed and forbade me under any circumstances to make the scheduled ascent of the Rigi the next day. To make certain I obeyed he ordered me to appear in his office at two o'clock in the afternoon.

I was relieved. Though the Rigi had been heralded as the dramatic climax of our journey I was happy not to have to undertake it, delighted to be liberated for one whole day from the lunatic odyssey.

When I went to my room my baggage had not arrived. I called Peter Suter and he called back in an hour to report it was still in Grindelwald.

JULY 4

At three the next morning we were up, fervent as Persian devotees, to pay our orisons to the sun.

A small American flag mounted on a breakfast roll reminded me that it was the Fourth of July. My temperature was down but I was still fatigued and could not move for soreness. I slept until noon, when my bags arrived from Grindelwald. I bathed, dressed, ordered some lunch and, after eating, went to see the doctor. He took my temperature and looked at my throat.

"You are going to live," he decided. "You are lucky. Before the discovery of penicillin you would probably have been a Swiss funeral." He gave me another shot and charged me forty francs—ten dollars. "Remember to stay out of Swiss lakes," he warned.

The afternoon was warm and bright. I walked up a hill to the city's most famous monument, the wounded Lion of Lucerne. I had seen it before, always in the company of others, and now, viewing it alone, its beauty moved me as if I were seeing it for the first time. Birds sang in the trees and a trickle of water flowed down the canyon wall and splashed into a pool which mirrored the prone form in perfect clarity. The bas-relief was carved into the wall in 1821, after a design by Bertal

Thorvaldsen, to commemorate the 786 Swiss officers and soldiers who died in an unsuccessful defense of Louis XVI and Marie Antoinette against the Tuileries mobs in 1792. I could feel no sympathy for the Swiss tradition of mercenary soldiering. The professional warriors— some of my own ancestors had been among them—sustained wars that might otherwise have been more expeditiously concluded. But art transcends history and politics and the lion exists in itself, a creation of heart-stirring beauty.

As I sat there in that serene and calming place the madnesses of days endured seemed to vanish and my sanity returned. I felt a healing of the spirit, and I knew that for me Miss Jemima's tour was over, that my travel must be a solitary thing, a freedom for experience and reflection, and I realized that Mr. Cook's great idea had no substance for me.

In the evening there was another storm and when it was over I walked on the quay in a pale moonlight which silhouetted Lucerne's mountain sentinels, Pilatus to the southwest and the Bürgenstock and the Rigi to the east. The isolated peaks were believed in the Middle Ages to be the habitats of dragons and in the Lucerne museum there is a "dragon stone," purported to have been dropped accidentally on the town by a dragon transporting it from the Rigi to Pilatus.

Pilatus bears the name of Pontius Pilate whose body, according to local legend, was sunk in an inaccessible lake on the mountain where it is responsible for the catastrophic storms of wind, lightning, and thunder which plague the area. To avoid arousing Pilatus's wrath the medieval government of Lucerne made it a crime to approach the summit; in 1387 six priests who climbed it were imprisoned. The legend was not discredited until 1585, when one Johann Müller surreptitiously ascended the mountain and taunted the ghost of Pilate by throwing stones into its gloomy tarn with no apparent result. Today Pilatus serves Switzerland's inner cantons as a weather vane. A round halo of clouds over the summit is assumed to be a signal of fair weather and a stratified veil hovering over it a warning of bad.

Because of its superior vistas the Rigi is more popular with tourists. In 1863 Miss Jemima's party made the nine-mile climb in three and one-half hours. The travelers went at once to bed and were awakened at 3:00 A.M. to witness the spectacle of sunrise. The vision, Jemima piously wrote, "was more a heavenly than an earthly glory, fair emblem of the

Holy City, the new Jerusalem as seen by the exiled John from the great high mountain, descending out of heaven from God, prepared as a bride adorned for her husband."

Eight years later, in 1871, the first rack-and-pinion railroad was built, but purist travelers still continued to make the ascent on foot. Among them was Mark Twain, whose view of the sun was less transcending than Jemima's. According to his famous account he was aroused by "booming blasts," rushed out "cocooned in red blankets" only to discover that the sun was on the wrong side of the mountain, that he had missed the morning reveille, had slept through the day, and was looking at a sunset.*

JULY 5

The morning was to be one of leisure, the first of the kind in our programme, so a breakfast earlier than eight was not enforced.

At one o'clock in the afternoon those of us who had withdrawn from the Rigi excursion went to the railroad station to meet the returning group and board with them a train for Berne.

The company arriving at the station was no longer familiar. Old faces had dropped away—Peppi Rosato had left in the morning for Rome and Gretel Dobish for Vienna—and new ones had taken their places. The ten days had brought nearly everyone to his limit of endurance. Even Albert Kunz was subdued. "Excuse my saaxy voice," he croaked.

The Rigi trip had turned into a muddle. Disregarding the protocol of retiring early to prepare for an early sunrise, the journalists had caroused most of the night and Peter Suter was in a temper over a drink bill of 400 francs charged to the Tourist Office.

When the signaling alphorn rang out at 3:00 A.M. the sky was dark and gray and the sun was visible only a few seconds through a rift in the clouds. "It was really rather a flop," said Thomasina Thornton. The most exciting episode was Westcott Jones' discovering, in an old

---

*A Tramp Abroad

registry of the hotel, the signature of Miss Jemima inscribed in July 1863. Three Americans had signed it the same day. They were Edward Mills of Georgia, and American Consul-General Warner L. Underwood and Juanna Louis Underwood of Kentucky.

Our train passed through rich and fertile Emmental, the valley of famous cheese. Large brown house-and-barn combinations in which both humans and cows lived were surrounded by heaps of manure, a status symbol of wealth, and red geraniums blazed on every window ledge. I shared a luncheon table in the dining car with some of the costumed English. "Of course, I've loved much of the trip," said Janet Edwards. "But the everlasting moving has been rather a trial and I'm very tired. I suppose the most exciting episode was that boat adventure in Lucerne. It wasn't until it was over that we realized the danger of it and we became quite terrified." In her lap was a bouquet which a stranger had thrust upon her in the station. "And so many flowers which they're always giving to you. At times I quite imagined I *was* Jemima, that it *was* another century. I suppose it is the actress in me. Nothing very special you understand, I'm not really brilliant in anything but then I'm not exactly bad either. Of course Jemima was rather a bluestocking and that I certainly am not . . ."

In Berne we were booked into the wondrously comfortable Bellevue Palace Hotel. Gifts of fruit, flowers, and more chocolates greeted us in our rooms. At three-thirty in the afternoon Albert Kunz rallied everyone to the Berne gas works, a complex of chimneys, pipes and funnels, for a balloon ascent over the Bernese alps. Though ballooning was not included in Jemima's tour, it was added to ours because the tourist office was promoting ballooning as a tourist attraction. Still feeling vertigo-prone, I declined the opportunity and instead watched the embarkation of Janet Edwards and young Thomas Cook. While cameras ground and clicked the balloon was permitted to rise thirty feet, then was drawn back down by twelve brawny youths tugging on ropes. The "ascent" was repeated three times until all the photographers were satisfied. The fourth time it was released. Janet Edwards waved a dainty handkerchief and the balloon floated westward toward snow-peaked alps. An hour later, while having a drink on the hotel terrace, Penelope Lars and I watched it descend gently to a green meadow on a distant hill.

JULY 6

The weariness induced by rapid journeyings came upon us . . .

Bathed in morning sun the city was like a huge toy fair. Penelope Lars and I strolled the streets watching processions of crowing cocks, bears, and knights in the clock tower, taking pictures of fountains including the *Kindlifresser,* "the child gobbler," which chomped on fat naked infants and is the bogeyman evoked by generations of parents to terrify recalcitrant children.

We walked to the bear pit in which the brown symbols of Berne danced, folded paws in prayer, and smiled toothily, performing for handouts of carrots and biscuits dropped by humans from above. A lady told us the bears were not as amiable as they appeared, that they had torn to shreds a drunken student who had fallen into the pit and killed a boy who crashed his bicycle against the wall and was catapulted into the pit. The servile beasts so docilely adapting to human fatuity depressed me. A woman pushed a pram across my foot and to the infant in it she shrilled, "Look down, Dorali! Look at the bears!" With the *Kindlifresser* still in mind I had an almost uncontrollable impulse to push the pram into the pit, and I suggested to Penelope that we leave.

In the afternoon we said goodbye in the station. "They've been quite lovely, these last days," Penelope said. I kissed her. "Haven't they?" she asked. "I mean it's nice that sanity returned before the end, that we didn't miss one another . . ."

I watched my traveling companions depart for Bienne, after which there would still be Neuchatel. They were riding in sunlight on antique open cars under billows of black train smoke. An orchestra in the first car played a gay melody.

Fifteen minutes later I took a Zurich train and on the way I read the conclusion of Miss Jemima's book. "We had acquired," she wrote, "a wider knowledge of human nature, habits of self-reliance, and valuable lessons of our own ignorance that amply repaid us for the fatigue and inevitable annoyance . . ."

20

"E GUETS NÜÜS!"

I was going home to Elm to celebrate the New Year. It had been snowing for a week and when I got off the train at Ziegelbrücke Kap appeared out of the swirling storm like a Cossack. We drank some rum in the station and then started up the valley through canyons of snow. Forty minutes later we were in Elm. The snow lay three feet deep.

Before Kap could stop the motor his son, Hansjörg, ran to the car, the excited bearer of bad news. *Grossmutti*—grandmother—had fallen on the ice and would have to be driven to the hospital in Glarus.

Kap raced the car up through the village to his parents' home. His mother, one arm in a sling, was describing her accident to two daughters.

"I was carrying the baby [an infant grandson] when my heel caught on a step and my other foot slipped on the ice," Frau Rhyner was saying. She was a short, commanding blond woman with a strong chin that jutted up as she spoke.

"Mother, it's too early on New Year's Eve to stand on your head," said Kap, who was relieved to see her as robust as usual.

"Don't you want to hear what happened?" she asked.

"Yes, I want to hear it all." Kap's attachment to his mother was a strong force in his life. He spoke of her affectionately as "the definitive

Swiss matriarch" and called her "a female Napoleon." She resumed the story which she was enjoying more with each telling. "Fortunately I held up the dear baby so he was not hurt," she said. "But my elbow was cut open and the snow was red with blood. Father went for the doctor who sewed up the elbow and said I must go to the hospital for X rays."

Kap bundled his mother into a coat and shawl and assisted her to his car. "I'll be back," she called. "The doctor said I had to stay but I told him that was impossible, that my family was coming for the New Year, and that my husband was elderly and could not be left alone." Kap's father, Fridolin, a slightly built, gentle-spirited man seven years older than his wife, lay on the ledge of a green tile warming stove, listening silently.

He got up from the stove to outfit me with a pair of his boots, and Pia and the children and I started back down to the village. We stopped at the Hotel Elmer for cocktails with Kap's sister, Barbara Bässler, who appeared calmly unperturbed by the incident involving her mother and her baby son. Of the five Rhyner children she was the most serene. She and Kap, the two eldest, were the family achievers. Barbara's cool dignity and logical mind perfectly complemented Kap's hearty extroversion and dynamic energy. Working together, they had moved the family up from a low economic level to one of village affluence. Barbara's German husband, Philip, a professional gardener who helped her manage the hotel, was a quiet, industrious man.

We were joined by Hans Rhyner and his wife, Maria. Hans, eight years younger than Kap and smaller, resembled their father. He had a perpetually happy spirit and a sense of humor which frequently defused family tensions. He worked as an assistant manager in Kap's firm and was not, like his older brother and sister, driven by ambition. The domestic checks and balances in the spirited Rhyner clan were fascinating.

At eight-thirty Kap was back. X rays had shown no broken bones and his mother returned with him. He reported she refused to be wheeled into the hospital in a chair and when attendants insisted on it she accused them of worrying that her high heels would mar the waxed floors.

Three hours later, after a fine meal and many drinks, we walked to The Sun to greet the New Year. At the door we were met by a merry, rheumy-eyed little man named Kap Rhyner who said that with our arrival there were six Kap Rhyners in the cafe. The steaming room was crowded with young dancers thumping stiffly in boots like pairs of dolls on music boxes.

At midnight the clarinet player led a procession of dancers out into the snow. Church bells were ringing. The moon was full and the cold night had the clarity of day. Looking up at the surrounding mountains, Hans said, "I hope it snows tomorrow so I can sleep. Otherwise I have to go skiing." People were shaking hands, shouting, *E guets Nüüs!* wishing one another a Happy New Year! Like a Pied Piper, the clarinetist led the procession up through the village. *Guets* was dropped from the greeting and voices repeating, *Nüüs, nüüs, nüüs,*" sounded like hissing geese.

As the procession approached the Rhyner house Kap suggested we stop to wish his parents a Happy New Year. With her good arm Frau Rhyner poured glasses of Malaga wine, which she called "women's whiskey," to toast the New Year. At the same time she recounted her hospital visit. One doctor had been "a black one."

"Negro?" asked Hans.

"*Ja, ja!* A half Negro at least. He was so beautiful I would have stayed in the hospital but he said he was going home."

"Have you made another appointment with him?" asked Kap.

"That's my secret," Frau Rhyner said. "My sons need not know everything."

"Mother, you have a loud mouth," Kap said. "You talk too much."

"*Ja, ja!* I don't see any nails on your tongue!"

The banter between mother and sons continued. Fridolin, the father, lay on his stove ledge smiling, smoking a pipe. Two daughters also were silent; the scene was one to which they were accustomed.

The small low-ceilinged parlor was stifling hot. The wine was making me sweat. When a glass was empty Frau Rhyner refilled it without interrupting her discourse. "My arm is beginning to wake up," she said, refilling her own glass. "I need more anesthetic." She drank and went on, "A lady in the hospital had two goiters, one large and one small." Her family laughed. Goiters are a frequent affliction of Alpine people and Hans told a story of a little boy staring at a slender-throated woman on a train and the mother reprimanding him, saying, "Stop

staring and be thankful you have all your parts." Frau Rhyner moved
to where Kap was sitting and rubbed his belly. She did the same to
Hans's and she said, "My sons are both pregnant. Tomorrow we call
the midwife." She twitted Kap's ear. "Look, he has four-cornered ears.
He must be a goat with the women." I saw Pia flush. She was no longer
amused.

It was after two o'clock. The father was sound asleep on the stove and
it was time to leave. But the brothers were not ready. More "women's
whiskey" was poured; the New Year was toasted again. At two-thirty
Hans rose and everyone but Kap prepared to leave. "Not ready for the
nest yet?" Frau Rhyner asked. Kap replied he wasn't, that he was
returning to The Sun. Hans and their wives agreed to go with him. I
returned alone to the power station.

In the morning there was a visitor, a carpenter named Jakob
Schneider, who had come to tell me that he was my relative; that his
grandfather, a mountain guide, was the most famous Kubli in Elm
history. The first man to climb the *Zwölfihorn,* Jakob Kubli died in the
mountains in 1904 at the age of twenty-nine crushed by falling rock.
The carpenter invited us to his parents' house to see some mementos of
the grandfather. We trudged through the snow into the oldest quarter
of the village. The four-story house, upon which the date "1557" was
carved, had been an inn and supply station for travelers over the
Panixer Pass.

We entered a long, dark corridor stacked with firewood. Inside I was
almost turned back by the stale smells of a primitive toilet in the hall.
The carpenter's father, convalescing from a broken leg, was sleeping on
a couch. Two little girls were baptizing their Christmas dolls. The
carpenter's mother, a small energetic woman who resembled her father,
the famous guide, directed us to a glass-enclosed shrine bearing the
words, "*Zum Andenken an Jakob Kubli.*" The cabinet contained
pictures of a jaunty, moustachioed little man, a wreath of wax flowers,
a collection of crumbling clippings, and several sentimental poems. The
mother urged us to stay for coffee and some pastries. But I declined,
fearing that if I did not get out into fresh air I would be ill.

The village was white and silent; cemetery tombstones were humps
of snow. Church was letting out, and men in their black tailcoats and

stovepipe hats, and women in long black dresses moving between the snowbanks looked like pictures of American pilgrims.

The second day of January was *Bärtelistag.* Swiss double holidays are intended to provide a phasing-out, and this one, sometimes erroneously referred to as the Feast of St. Berchtold, serves as a day of recovery from the New Year. In the Swiss Lexicon, I found that *Bärtelistag,* deriving from *berchteln,* an old German word meaning to beg in disguise, translates into "masked beggar's day." Like the New Year it is traditionally celebrated by drinking, dancing, and masquerading.

In the evening Kap and I were invited to a stag party in Zurich by architect Jakob Zweifel, a native of Glarus. The invitation mysteriously spoke of "a cannibal feast to eat a roasted general." The party was to celebrate Zweifel's promotion to major in the Swiss army artillery. Kap was eager to go.

The party was held in a theater in the old city, in the basement of a chateau called the *Winkelwiese.* In a walled courtyard two fur-clad butchers, their faces red with the light of glowing coals, stomped in foot-deep snow, turning a large pig on a spit. Drippings from the pig exploded on the coals like tiny rockets.

The theater was filled with young and old army friends enjoying a clamorous reunion. A few in uniform were officers; the others, wearing dark suits, were bankers, lawyers, and businessmen. Zweifel, a good-looking bachelor in his fifties, was pouring wine.

There was a trumpet fanfare and the pig, a general's cap cocked jauntily on its glistening head, was rolled in.

"Isn't that a fine swine?" I heard a voice say in English. I laughed and the speaker introduced himself. He was a young man named Hans who commenced telling me of a ten-week visit to Polo, Illinois, on a Rotary exchange scholarship. The butchers carved massive chunks from the pig and served them on plates with bread and salad. The meat was finely seasoned and superb. "Some of the greatest gourmets in Switzerland are eating it," Hans said. He continued talking of his American journey, saying, "Every week I lived in a different house. Ten weeks, ten different houses. Every family I am with make two or three parties for me and it is ten weeks I am going from party to party, never ending. I made speeches for Rotary and Kiwanis and Lions. I had one speech which is so popular I make it all the time in which I did an imitation of a Swissair stewardess. By my successes in America I have become representative in Switzerland for small computers. But I have decided when I am thirty-five I will move to America to live. Everyone is so open-minded. That is my impression."

I asked Hans if he thought a young American visitor to Switzerland would be as exuberantly celebrated as he had been and he replied, "Oh, yes, I think so if he came as a guest of Rotary."

At eleven o'clock Kap departed on the solitary journey back to Elm. Hans was still detailing his adventures in Illinois. "I seen the monumental to Lincoln in Springfield and the great cornfields by Peoria," he said. I said goodnight and trudged through snow over the hill to my apartment. *Bärtelisnacht,* it turned out, was a "free night" when the midnight curfew was lifted and bars offered one free drink for each guest. In the square below my window a crowd was dancing in the snow to music from an accordion. The yodeling and shouting continued most of the night. In the morning it was quiet. The New Year was launched.

21

JOURNEYS WITH KAP

In January in the National Museum in Zurich I discovered a reconstruction of the ceiling from a parish church in the Graubünden village of Zillis. The medieval paintings, like a rustic Sistine chapel, so excited my imagination that I returned to the museum several times, and then resolved to see the original church.

I spoke of it to Kap who, it turned out, knew the church well. "We'll go see it together," he said. "Graubünden is my favorite canton and I want to show it to you." I wondered if January were a good time for a mountain journey. "The best," he said. "The sun shines in the mountains. We'll start with St. Moritz where there's a *Pferderennen*—horse racing on the ice—on Sunday."

I, also, was ready for a journey. A Zurich doctor had diagnosed my sore throat as a common allergic response to Zurich's damp winter and suggested a trip to the mountains. On a gray Saturday morning I took the train for Ziegelbrücke, where Kap was waiting in the station in booming high spirits.

"I needed a trip," he said. "You gave me the reason. A time comes when I have to get out of Elm, when I have to recycle, like the water that cuts through the glacier and flows into the valleys, that rises in mists and falls in rain and freezes again on the glacier."

We were on the long road to St. Moritz which Kap dreamed of shortening with a tunnel under the Alps. In the Julier Pass there was only snow and dazzling blue skies with blinding sunlight. Kap pointed to a solitary pine at the highest elevation for a tree in Europe, and told the story of a Graubünden lady named Donna Lupa who, during a war with Austria in 1499, was preparing a funeral meal when a group of Austrian soldiers appeared in her kitchen. She told them she was cooking for Swiss troops who were expected any minute. The invaders fled and Donna Lupa ran to the church to call the men from the funeral. The men took the iron crosses from the churchyard graves and pursued the fleeing enemy, killing forty soldiers and winning the battle. Donna Lupa's heroic act is commemorated by a monument in her village of Tschlin.

It was early dusk when we arrived in St. Moritz. The massive multispired Palace Hotel was a myriad of lights sparkling like a gargantuan Christmas tree. "I could not stay there; I would not know how to behave," Kap said. "In any case, it costs four hundred francs a day."

We had reservations in the new glass-and-chrome Crystal Hotel, which was filled with young multilingual skiers. The narrow streets between high banks of snow were crowded with sports cars and skiers dressed in a fantasia of bright costumes. It was time for a drink and we followed some music to the Chesa Veglia, a tumultous *après ski* bistro. On the street floor an accordionist was playing Viennese waltzes for dancers clomping over the floor like robots in boots. We could find no places so we descended into the basement where a shaggily pompadoured Italian rock trio blared and a singer was shouting, "Why, why, Delilah?" Kap put his fingers to his ears to shut out the din. We ordered whiskies and the skimpy shots we were served cost ten francs. The floor was jammed with dancers who, smiling blissfully at the ceiling, leaped and writhed through the motions of copulation. "*A Seggeli Schüttler,*" I said. The phrase, which I learned from my father, translated into "ball shaker." Kap roared; the expression was familiar to him.

Many of the dancers were Italians. St. Moritz was in the grips of racial tension following the trial of two young Swiss for the murder of an Italian in a fight begun when the Swiss addressed the Italian as "*Tschingg,*" an insulting racial epithet. The Italian ambassador had registered a protest with the Berne government over the short jail sentence—two years—given the murderers.

The musicians subsided into a sentimental mood. Conspicuous in the room were groups of beautiful young women in tight stretch pants, smiling brightly, but who did not have the tawny dark skins of skiers. "A commodity of St. Moritz," said Kap. "What a smörgasbord!" The girls put him in a reminiscent mood. "When I went to school in Zurich I had no experience with women," he began. "In Elm all the girls were like sisters; we knew them too well. I was nineteen when I left. In Zurich I worked as a stonemason during the day and went to school at night. I did not have time for friends and no money to spend on girls. Sometimes I would ask a girl to a film, or a walk on the Uetliberg. But they would always want to know what I did and when I told them I was a stonemason they were finished. There is a sickness in Swiss cities—no one wants to do honest labor; everyone wants to wear a white collar. Masons have dirty clothes and hands and the Swiss think that should be only for Italians and Spaniards. They prefer their sons in offices, wearing neckties, even if they earn only one-fourth what a mason earns. For this I think Swiss women are to blame—they want only men with a 'position,' with soft hands. Working clothes are a mark of inferiority, even a disgrace. I used to say to myself, 'show them!' As I see it now, all those girls who didn't want me with dirty hands really helped me. They drove me; they goaded my ambitions, made me work harder.

"Then I met Pia. She knew I was a mason and she stayed with me. She had faith; she worked hard to help; she wrote my letters and she waited until I had the time to see her and she never complained. Though she was a city girl, she came to Elm. Today she is as happy in Elm as if she'd lived there all her life. She understands that Elmers are like trees. You cannot take a palm tree from Lugano and plant it in Zurich. You cannot take an Elmer away from Elm and expect him to thrive."

In the morning we went to a gallery filled with the works of a nineteenth-century landscape painter named Giovanni Segantini. I had seen Segantinis in the museums of Zurich and Basel and I remembered Alpine subjects painted in glowing realism with clear mountain settings. The gallery was open only one hour a week, from eleven to twelve on Sundays, and as Kap kept checking his watch and racing the car over icy pavements I sensed that for him the trip was a pilgrimage. "There has never been another like Segantini," he said. "He was our great painter of the Alps; he understood the mountain soul."

An air of piety pervaded the small museum. We were met at the door by the caretaker-guide who gave us brooms to sweep the snow from our shoes and felt overshoes to put over them so as not to soil the polished floors. Seven persons waited reverently inside and I realized it was the hour for church worship. The guide began, like a priest, with a lecture about the artist, an Italian born in Austria who lived most of his life in Maloggia, west of St. Moritz.

The pictures were meticulously detailed—glistening drops of water cascading from the muzzle of a cow at a trough were clearly delineated. Most of the canvases were large and the three largest, for which the museum was built, were an allegorical triptych of the human cycle. The first, entitled *Werden* ("Becoming"), portrayed a mother and child, an Alp nativity in a springtime of flowers and grazing herds. The second, *Sein* ("Being"), showed a peasant herding cattle and his wife tending a calf. The final, *Vergehen* ("Passing"), was of a winter funeral in the Alps. A horse and sleigh, waiting in the snow before a hut, were surrounded by black-robed, sorrowing figures huddling in a gray, dank winter landscape while a coffin was carried out of the door. The painting, unfinished because of the painter's own death, had a haunting, ghostly quality. A cloud rising into the bleak gray sky symbolized the ascending soul.

Kap asked which of the three I liked best and I said the third, which in its incompletion lacked the over-detail of the other two and had a sweeping transcendental spirit. To my surprise he said he also liked it best. He could not seem to turn from it. "Death in the winter in the mountains," he said. "Everything is included. Segantini understood that without resurrection it would not be endurable. Look again. You will see in it many books."

Before a death portrait of Segantini by his friend Giovanni Giacometti, Kap described Segantini's death at forty-one of appendicitis in a mountain hut during a snow storm when he could not be rescued for an operation. We returned to the haunting third panel, which in the meantime seemed to have become the artist's own funeral, and I seemed to hear music, the "Agnus Dei" from Mozart's requiem mass, which the composer believed in the last month of his life he was writing for himself.

In the afternoon there were the horse races on the ice for which we had come. A track was laid out on St. Moritz Lake and bleachers were set up on the shore. Kap secured two tickets in the press tribune. The morning sun had vanished and the gray afternoon was so cold my pens would not write. In front of us a shivering little man in a fur coat was cursing the typewriter on his lap which had ceased to function. Most of the women and many of the men were bundled in furs and several young women were encased in leather like subaqua divers. In the next section France's Olympic skier, Jean-Claude Killy, was fending off photographers and autograph seekers.

There were only five races but, with time allotted for placing bets, the event took more than two hours. After each race an announcer gave results and favorites in the upcoming race in four languages: German, French, Italian, and English. The horses, wearing knitted masks to protect them from the cold, looked like interplanetary Pegasusses. In the first race, harnessed horses pulled men on skiis; one skier upset and his horse won the race without him. In the second race, jockeys rode horseback and the clods of frozen snow from the horses' hooves pelted the crowds in the tribune. The horses smoked like locomotives and when the race was over the riders trotted them once more around the track to cool them slowly. In the third race, sulky wheels whipped up a blizzard of snow and, in the fourth, elegantly prancing horses pulling cutters were a scene from Currier and Ives. The final race, on horseback over hurdles, ended in high comedy when a horse threw its rider, leaped over the hurdle and, continuing to run inside the track, received the greatest ovation of the afternoon.

The event concluded with a traditional Engadine procession of sleighs, but by this time everyone was so chilled that the crowd dispersed before it could begin. The caravan of beribboned sleighs and riders in costumes, including a sleigh filled with musicians, continued for five minutes before it also succumbed to the cold. "It's all a theater for tourists," Kap said. "Everyone pretends to more than there is. That is St. Moritz's problem. They keep having to invent some silly thing or other to give the impression something is happening. St. Moritz is a victim of its own fantasies."

We needed a drink. Behind us the Palace Hotel spread over the hillside like Crete's Knossos and we decided to assail the citadel of the *très snob* turbo-jetters. Swiss newspapers maintained a running *Almanach de Gotha* of the Palace's numbered-bank-account guests, of foreign royalty, film stars, corporate directors, Greek shipowners, and German playboys.

The great Jugendstil interior had a fairy-tale quality, as if it had been designed by the mad dreamer Ludwig II. Huge windows framed mountain landscapes and halls were separated by wrought-iron gates. An orchestra was playing and guests were drinking tea. Some were playing cards. We found a bar and were intercepted by a doorman who said nonguests were not served. Immediately a soft-voiced man appeared to circumvent a disturbance. He introduced himself as Andreas Badrutt, grandson of Johannes Badrutt who built the hotel in the 1890s. His ejection of us was smoothly tactful, a technique perfected through years of experience. He showed us a large painting, an *Assumption of the Madonna* attributed to Raphael, which he said was once owned by the dukes of Este. He told us Herbert Karajan, Stavros Niarchos, Prince Abdullah of Morocco, and Sadruddin Aga Khan were in residence, a ploy apparently intended to humble our libertarian impulses. While propelling us discreetly toward the exit where, shaking our hands, expressing his delight at meeting us, he gave us the names of several bars in the town which, he said, "serve transients."

I found his performance amusing but Kap was provoked. "We are fallen angels," he muttered as we trudged up the hill. "We've been cast out of Paradise." We found a small and quiet restaurant and settled for wine and a long dinner. Kap went on, likening the Palace and its guests to Nero's Rome. He fumed about sexual morality and the frequent divorces among Palace clientele. Divorce was something to which he was passionately opposed. "In the entire history of Elm there has never been a single divorce," he said. I believed him; there had been no divorces in New Glarus either when I was a child. The sternness of Kap's morality and the quixotic mercurialness of his moods were like those of my father whom Kap was continuing to evoke. "I could not endure in such a society," he said. "Skiing all day and dancing all night would drive me crazy. I cannot bear to be alone; I need human contact. I have it in Elm to a degree but it is not enough; I need to seek it elsewhere. So I have my class in Schwanden; I teach twenty apprentices in masonry and carpentry. I don't do it for the money, which is small. I do it because I need those young people. The class is the last thing in life I would give up."

More snow fell during the night. In the morning our plans to ski on the Piz Corvatsch had to be canceled because the lifts weren't operating. Kap telephoned a friend, the manager of the slopes at Piz Lagalp, above Pontresina; the friend said his runs would be opened by noon and invited us for lunch.

The anticipation of a reunion with his friend Eugenio Rüegger buoyed Kap's spirits. They had met in military service six years before. At the time of their meeting Rüegger was a ski instructor famous for his good looks and his reputation as a Don Juan. Now, at age thirty, he was settled into marriage with a girl as stunning as he. "A good thing," said Kap. "If she weren't beautiful it wouldn't work." The Lagalp slopes were among the highest and most difficult in Switzerland and geared to professionals rather than amateurs. There were three trails, identified as Red, Blue, and Black. The Black was considered the most perilous.

Rüegger was waiting in the restaurant. He was a rather short, black-haired man with a tightly knit athlete's form and the classic good looks of a silent film star. His most striking feature were his green-golden eyes with lashes so thick and long it was hard to believe they were real. The restaurant looked out on the slopes, on a constant rise of cable cars and a swirl of skiers winding down the trails. Through lunch and two bottles of wine the two old friends shared recollections of military life. Next to family ties, army friendships are the most enduring bonds in a Swiss man's life; they are renewed each year during three weeks of reconaissance service and they continue through life.

After lunch we took a cable car to the summit. A high wind was blowing and a cover of clouds was so thick there was almost no visibility. The situation filled me with apprehension. I decided I had drunk too much wine to ski, and Kap set out alone on the difficult Black trail, disappearing at once in clouds.

When he returned in the cable car an hour later Rüegger and I were into our second bottle of Fendant in the summit restaurant. Kap drank a glass and with a lusty whoop set out a second time on the hazardous run. Pleasantly light-headed, Rüegger and I descended in the lift. When we got back to the control station Kap had not yet arrived. Rüegger took me inside to see the automated mechanisms controlling the arrival and departure of cabins. When Kap still did not appear we became anxious and, as more time passed, alarmed.

Suddenly we saw a strange spectacle, a skier swooping down on one ski and swinging his right leg for balance. I sensed at once it was Kap. Like a tightrope artist he was waving his ski poles in one hand and his second ski in the other. The crowds of skiers in the station began to cheer and I wondered if the bizarre performance could be some manic impulse of exhibitionism. When Kap saw us he let out a yell and swerved to a crunching halt, and I saw a broken cable on the unused ski.

The crowds applauded him like a hero. He made some joke but I sensed a tension in him, a kind of shock. Sweat poured from his brow. He did not respond to questions and seemed at a loss for words. He packed his gear into the car, said goodbye to Rüegger, and we started down the mountain.

After ten miles we stopped at a country inn and ordered hot tea and rum. Two cups relaxed him and he began to talk, making light of his adventure. "Better that my cable broke than the one on the lift," he said. He explained what happened. "I jumped over some rocks and when I landed the cable broke. I tried to repair it but after two hundred yards it was wobbling and I could not go on. I had a choice of walking down or trying it on one ski. I was sure I could make it by swinging my right leg for balance. Curves were difficult—I had to throw my weight in the opposite direction. I stopped twice to rest." His buoyant spirits seemed retored. "It's not something I would choose to do every day," he said.

The inn was empty except for two middle-aged couples playing cards, the women paired against their husbands. One of the women accused her husband of misdealing. "You looked at the cards," she shrieked.

"Only at their backs," he replied.

"I saw you," the wife insisted.

The husband sighed. "What did you see?"

"You were holding the deck at an angle so you could see the corners." The man threw his hand down on the table and got up. "Women talk too much for cards," he said.

"It is better to talk than to cheat," his wife scolded. "A player who cheats is as bad as a thief."

The squabble grew louder. Kap threw back his head and laughed. "Now you see how it is if women have the vote. They have no mercy for men." He was opposed to women's suffrage.

We drove past a wintry graveyard in a lonely field, where edelweiss covered the graves in summer, and arrived at twilight in Zuoz, a village of poor families living in grand houses with vaulted entrances, grilled windows, and white stucco walls decorated with ghostlike images of warriors and shields, flowers and Greek motifs. Such Graubünden decorations were not frescoes but graffiti. We stopped to examine one showing a procession of cows and Kap explained the difference. "Frescoes are painted on the surface," he said. "A Bündner house is painted black, red, or green, the primal colors of soot, ox blood, or native plants. Then it is whitewashed and the artist carefully scrapes away the lime to bring forth the design in the original colors." In his restoration of the *Suvarovhaus* in Elm, Kap was discovering similar graffiti made by a Bündner artist more than two hundred years ago.

The fine houses of Zuoz were built in the sixteenth century when the village was a station on the Bernina trade route between Munich and Rome and a commercial center of Graubünden. When the Gotthard pass was opened to the west, the Bernina traffic ceased and Zuoz declined. Except for some small boys playing in the snow and speaking a Romanisch tongue I could not understand, a silence lay over the town. A meter of snow hung out from the roofs and posted on a bulletin board was an avalanche warning.

In the morning we drove back over the Julier Pass as far as Lenzerheide, where we left the highway and, turning southwest on a serpentine country road, entered a steep-walled narrow valley. It was a stunning Eolithic landscape with blue waterfalls colored by sulphur and frozen solid, like Ice Age Gothic towers.

It was an area Kap loved. Each hamlet was familiar to him and he was taking me to one with an extraordinary baroque church unknown to tourists and not recorded in guide books. The village was called Obervaz and Kap pointed it out on a ledge high above, a cluster of dark huts huddled about the towering white church. Soon the single-lane dirt road was too slippery for driving and we parked a distance below the village and continued up the muddy lane on foot. Approaching the church, we could smell the stench of sewage trickling down the center of the path. We passed empty houses with broken panes. "The people are too poor," Kap said. "So they leave. The villages of Graubünden are dying."

Before us the stucco church glittered with bright frescoes of saints. It was built in 1681 by an ambitious priest and, because it was too grand for its poor parish to support, it fell in the passing centuries into decay. Its recent restoration was the triumph of Carlo Casutt, a zealously dedicated priest who solicited funds from federal and canton governments and from private organizations to realize his singular dream.

Father Casutt appeared. He was a small, dark-haired, excitable man whose welcome was an effusion, a pouring forth of gratitude that someone should seek out his church. He was forty-two years old and had been in the valley for seventeen years. "When I came here the church had been damaged by fire," he said. "The cracked walls were crumbling; its beauty was nearly destroyed. I knew at once why I was here, that I'd been called by God to save the church. I could not rest until the money was raised. Then for two years I was in the church every single day, watching the workmen, seeing they did things right. Now it is finished."

Father Casutt unlocked the church doors and urged us inside. The high white walls were frescoed with scenes from the life of St. Luzius, first Bishop of Chur, to whom the church was dedicated.

"He came to Chur to bring the gospel to the pagan heathens living in the alps. They put him into a kettle of boiling oil. But God interceded and by a miracle he was not burned. He spent his life battling the forces of the Devil and in the end, in the year 380, the pagans stoned him to death. His tomb is in the cathedral at Chur."

There was a painting to illustrate each episode and six wall panels were filled with a fantastic bestiary of elephants, unicorns, lions, and dragons. "Everyone who sees them thinks they are modern, that they are surrealist," the priest said rapturously. "They are not at all; they are old as the church."

It was difficult to depart from Father Casutt. He clung to us, beseeching us to stay overnight as his guests, to tarry at least for lunch, and when we said we could not, he implored us to come another time and stay for a week. I felt guilty for going and wondered how long it would be until other visitors would appear. "I love this church," he said, holding to us still. "It is the single joy of my life." I saw tears in his eyes and thought how in another age his fine single-purposed madness might have qualified him for sainthood. As we walked down the road we met a spastic idiot boy emptying a bucket of household excrement in the street. Idiots were not unusual in the villages, a consequence of centuries of inbreeding.

We spiraled down into a deep, wild canyon and stopped at a stone bridge to drop some pebbles and counted the seconds on our watches until we could hear them splash into the churning waters of the Solis River two-hundred and fifty feet below. Continuing through the high-walled Schyn Pass, we drove through tunnels to the broad base of the fertile Domleschg Valley. From the market town of Thusis we followed the Rhine River into the Via Mala, the Evil Way, a link in the historic San Bernardino trade route from Italy to the north. A narrow gorge was cut by the river between limestone cliffs 1,600-feet high and sometimes barely thirty-feet apart and the ingeniously engineered road squeezing through crevices and hanging on shelves made a dark and chilling passage.

"I'm trying to imagine it before the road; the apprehensions and terrors for travelers," I said.

"That's only part of it. The real dangers were the bandits who turned the gorge into a hideout for looting and murder. No wonder we have a mythology of malevolent, acrimonious, supernatural forces preying on human victims," Kap said.

After three and one-half miles we crossed a final bridge and, like Orpheus delivered from the underworld, entered into the open valley of Schams. Ahead we saw the town of Zillis and the tower of the church which was the destination of our journey.

The great monument of medieval art had survived fire, damp, and attacks from worms for eight hundred years. Little known because of its isolation, it was brought to the attention of the world in the 1930s when a federal commission for historical monuments restored and remounted the paintings under a fireproofed ceiling. At the same time the facsimile of the ceiling was painted and installed in the National Museum in Zurich.

The afternoon had turned gray and the church, standing among some cemetery tombstones in a snowy field, had a bleak and melancholy air. Inside, the single-naved Romanesque structure was dark and empty and as we entered the west portal, opposite and facing the altar, the 153 paintings twenty-four feet above us were upside down. The proper place to view them, Kap said, was at the altar, in the place where the priest opens the Holy Book. On a table were some hand mirrors to aid visitors in viewing the paintings without the muscle fatigue and nausea from looking straight up. Even with the mirrors the vividly teeming three-foot-square pictures were almost too overwhelming to assimilate. The designation of "rustic Sistine chapel" suggests their unique grandeur, but there are no actual similarities to Michelangelo's monumental ceiling. The flat primitive style of the draftsmanship, the solid bright colors as heavily outlined as fragments of leaded glass, were more like illuminations of mystery plays or pictorial testaments in a holy comic book. Apocalyptic and visionary beasts in watery scenes suggest Revelations and the story of Jonah who, in the Middle Ages, was regarded as an Old Testament antecedent to Christ; his vomiting forth by the whale as a prefiguration of the Resurrection.

A charming sense of playfulness is present in the miracles, beginning with Jesus, at age twelve, bringing clay birds to life. The Gadarene swine hurtle into the sea like obsessed lemmings; the impotent man cured at the pool of Bethesda seems almost to be dancing with joy, and Lazarus appears slightly apprehensive over his own resurrection. Localized details suggest that the artist was a native of the valley. The mountain in the background of several pictures resembles the Piz Beverin, which hovers over Zillis, and in the Palm Sunday procession crowds are waving the willow branches carried in Graubünden.

The meager afternoon light was fading and the small mirrors were inadequate. The span of pictures would have been too much to absorb on one visit even under perfect conditions, and we finally gave up.

Despite our frustration, the day had a mysterious unity as if the journey through the Evil Way were a necessary ordination to the viewing of the church. When I spoke of this to Kap he said he was certain that the artist had intended this, that in the ceiling passage from unknown terrors to spiritual salvation there was a subtle parallel to the fearsome gorge as a test of faith before deliverance into a valley Eden.

We drove two miles to Andeer, the largest village—six hundred inhabitants—in the valley. It was Kap's habit to reveal places and events in our journey in the moment of their imminence and now he told me that in Andeer I would see the most famous graffiti house in Graubünden. He found it in a narrow street and even in the winter's dusk it was a fantastic sight. Its three-storied walls were covered with gray images of flowers and fruits, comic knights, and animals that might have been designed by Ronald Searle, and a phantasm of abstract designs. In one wall a fragment of the decoration had been destroyed to make space for a window. After that incident the house was declared a national monument and, though it is privately owned, no further alterations will be allowed. The first floor of the house was a blacksmith shop. From an upstairs window an old man, probably the smith, watched us enjoying the animated theater on his walls.

It was Kap's plan to spend the night in Juf, which at an elevation of 7,000 feet was the highest village in Europe and, outside the Himalayas, perhaps the highest in the world. But it was beginning to snow and to my relief he agreed to remain the night in Andeer and set out for Juf the next day.

In the morning a gale had turned the storm into a blizzard. Our trip to Juf seemed a madness but Kap would not be dissuaded. He was wearing his tasseled red cap. He had two—red and black—which he alternated according to his mood. With reckless abandon we set out. We passed a chimney sweep wearing the traditional black stovepipe hat and Kap was jubilant. The chimney sweep, he said, was a good luck omen for our journey.

We were going to need it. A whistling wind swayed the car and snow formed a swirling scrim around us. "*Mir gfallt das,*" he shouted, "I like this!" Whenever he was excited, he commenced to yell as if I were deaf.

With the car in first gear we pushed slowly upward, passing through tunnels in which ceilings were stalactites of ice. Kap was explaining that Juf was one of a score of villages settled in the twelfth century by nomadic Alemanic tribes called Walsers.

"The Walsers were the folk wanderers of Europe, the Vikings of the Alps," he said. "When the Franks pushed them out of Germany in the sixth century they moved south into Helvetia.* They were poor and the free land they sought was the highest and least fertile in the alps. Seeking always more isolated areas, they wandered like gypsies."

It was the first time I'd heard the story. I asked why the wanderers were called Walsers and Kap replied, "Because in their second migration in the ninth century they settled in the mountains of Canton Valais where they stayed for two hundred years. When other tribes encroached on their territory they moved again and this went on for a thousand years. In the fourteenth century some of them crossed the Segnes Pass and they settled on the higher slopes of Elm, places from which your people came and mine. Quite certainly we are of Walser blood."

So that was it! Our extraordinary winter ascent was a search for clues to his own fiercely independent spirit and also to mine. "The Walsers speak the oldest German in the world today," Kap continued. "The language disappeared from Germany in the twelfth century. In Juf and in the valleys above Elm you will hear it still."

We passed above the tree line and through Cresta—a church and a cluster of shuttered huts. Our car fought the wind; the sun was a hazy blur. Of all the Walser settlements in the mountains of Austria, Italy, and Switzerland, Juf was the most isolated, the most remote.

After seven more kilometers we were at the end of the road. Some buried huts and barns were humps in the snow, like igloos from which steam rose like smoke. A bearded old man watched from a hole in the snow, actually a buried barn door. As we got out of the car he disappeared.

"*Grüss Gott!*" Kap shouted. The low-roofed stall was dark as a cave and warm from steaming manure. The stench pouring from the open-

---

*Helvetia was the Roman name for alpine provinces now part of Switzerland.

ing was overpowering. "Hallo!" a voice responded from the darkness but the man did not appear. We trudged through the snow to the *Gasthaus Alpenrose* and were admitted by a small dark man with glittering blue eyes. He was Claudio Luzio, the owner, and he invited us into a tiny public room where three men were drinking hot beer from steaming beer warmers. Sheep dung glowing in the grate filled the room with an acrid odor and snow blowing under the door formed a small drift at my feet.

After a long silence one man took a swallow and sighed. "*Ja, ja.*" A second did the same. The three men were snow removers from Gröt, a hamlet several kilometers below.

"*Ja, ja,*" the third man said, and after a silence another replied. The single two-lettered expletive means "yes"; it was a sigh of sorrowing resignation I knew well. I had heard it often in my childhood but never had I heard it repeated with such measured and pregnant poignancy. The men might have been three Siberian peasants engaged in a meaningful one-word dialogue written by Samuel Beckett.

"*Ja, ja . . .*" Sigh and silence.

"*Ja . . .*"

Luzio brought us rum and tea and we drank and I heard Kap sigh also. He broke the melancholy fugue by recalling the death of a skier on a peak above Juf.

The men remembered the incident. A youth had lost his pole in a crevice. An accomplished skier named Jakob Oertle went in search of the pole. When Oertle did not return three others, Kap among them, went to search for him. They discovered that Oertle had loosened an avalanche and was buried beneath it. The body was found next day by dogs trained for locating bodies in snow.

"*Ja, ja,*" one of the men sighed at the end of the story. "*So ischt es,* so it is."

"*Ja, ja,*" the second of the men sighed, a reminder to his companions of snow to be plowed.

"*Ja, ja,*" said the third, standing up. The three men shook our hands and departed through a blast of snow. Luzio invited us for still another hot rum and made one for himself. We were surrounded by hunting trophies, including an eagle with wings spread across the width of the room. The most curious was a marmot with four berserk incisor teeth, the top ones coiled like tusks and the bottom ones jutting out like white moustaches. Luzio said he had seen the strange beast alive on the mountain and had shot it for his collection. It stood there grinning ludicrously at us.

"Marmots are good to eat if you remove the fat," he said. "The rendered fat cures toothache, bellyache, stiff joints, bloating in cows, many things. But when it's cooking it makes a great stink and it is necessary to leave the house." The hot liquor was making him convivial. The inn, he said, was also the Juf post office and he was the driver of the mail. "Until seven years ago when the road was built I was the last horseback mail carrier in Switzerland," he boasted. "I covered the sixteen-mile route twice a day. German hitch-hikers are always asking how soon their postcards will be delivered. I tell them we empty the post box once a year on New Year's Day. Everyone who comes up here thinks we're behind the moon."

Luzio's father-in-law, the old man in the barn, was sixty-nine years old and the richest man in Juf. He owned eighteen hectares of land, a tractor and hay-mower, nine cows and calves, a dozen sheep, and some chickens. The old man had two daughters, one of whom was Luzio's wife. "I call my marriage the fifteen-years war," Luzio said dourly. There were two children and the family, including the old man and his unmarried daughter, all lived in the inn. Six families, totaling twenty people, were the total population of Juf. "The young people leave and those that stay are lazy and won't work," Luzio said. "My ten-year-old likes cows. I hope he will remain in Juf."

As we were leaving we met Luzio's wife carrying a load of hay on her back. She was handsome and gracious and permitted us to take a photograph. I shook Luzio's hand. "*Ja, ja,*" he said.

"*Ja, ja,*" I replied.

As we rolled down the mountain, Kap said, "I have an idea for a novel. It's about the last man or woman in Juf slowly going crazy, yet unable to leave." He was dwelling on a favorite theme, the migration of young village Swiss to the cities. "But I believe Juf will go on. These men cannot live anywhere else. If Juf dies out it will be only because there are no more girls and the men cannot find wives."

The blizzard seemed to have strengthened. Along the way picks and shovels were attached to stakes, left there for the use of motorists in trouble. In the Schams valley snow fell so thickly we could barely see the road. "It is time for some sun," Kap said. He turned south and after a half hour we entered the eight-mile-long San Bernardino tunnel. On the south side we emerged into warm, bright sunlight. In the village of San Bernardino we found a restaurant and ordered a bottle of rich red Italian Barbera and a hearty meal. It was to be our last together, as Kap was returning to Elm and I was going to Zurich. Kap offered a toast. "To a fine companion," he said. "I've never had one better. We see things through the same eyes." I was thinking, but did not say, that the success of our companionship was due in part to my submission to his overpowering will. I began to speak of something that had been constantly on my mind, the dreams of my father which had recurred each of the four nights of our journey. After my father's death twelve years ago I had dreamed of him every night for a year. Now the dreams had commenced again, troublesome dreams of my boyhood nearly forty years ago. Tears filled my eyes. "I've had too much wine," I said.

"No, not too much wine," Kap said. "It is feeling of which you have too much. The Elmer heart is a tempest of feeling. We try to contain it, but sometimes we cannot help ourselves and it overflows."

Perhaps he was right. I was glad our journey was at its end; I needed a rest from him. The waitress brought our check and there was the usual argument over payment. It was a matter of honor to Kap that I not be permitted to pay for anything.

"No, Herbert," he said firmly, pronouncing my name "HERR-bert," giving it a noble ring. "You cannot be allowed to pay. You have brought great good fortune to me and to Elm. A man like you coming back to his native village is something we never would have expected; we never believed could happen. Men go away and some become famous and they do not come back. You have returned to us; we are beholden to you." I asked for a cigar and a girl came with a tray from which I selected a modestly priced one. Kap took it from my hand and returned it. He picked the most expensive cigar on the tray. "This one is worthy of you," he said.

We drove back through the tunnel, back into winter. We stopped for a moment in the square in Andeer where a schoolteacher was herding a class of children wearing carnival masks and costumes, small demons who besieged our car and recalled the monsters on the church ceiling.

We returned through the terrifying Passage of Evil and a valley of castles. After Chur sunlight lit up the cliffs on the left side of the Rhine. To our right, dark, menacing clouds lay on the mountains. The wind howled; it was a Wagnerian afternoon. As we raced toward Ziegel-brücke to catch my train for Zurich snow began to fall.

22

SEXUAL BALANCES

In 1971 the men of Switzerland voted almost two to one to give women the right to vote in federal elections and to hold federal office. The German-speaking double cantons of Appenzell—Innerrhoden and Ausserrhoden—opposed the constitutional amendment and in these and in isolated communities in three other cantons women were still not permitted to vote in cantonal and municipal elections.

Why had it taken so long? Why should a country which took pride in its model democracy and its advanced social legislation be the last European state to withhold suffrage from women? Why should it have persisted, along with Saudi Arabia, Kuwait, and Yemen, in the long outdated discrimination against half the human race?

In the opinion of dramatist Friedrich Dürrenmatt, the women themselves shared responsibility for the curious dichotomy. In 1963 he said, "The women who want the vote are mild, timid workers' wives and working women without influence. Those women who oppose it are devastatingly powerful matriarchs who run the country without the vote, who feel that politics is an amusement for men and a waste of their time."

I told an editor of the *Neue Zürcher Zeitung,* that I would like to meet these formidable ladies and he offered to put me in touch with

Frau Marta Klauss,* a secretary of the *Bund der Schweizerinnen Gegen das Frauenstimmrecht,* the Society of Swiss Women Against Women's Suffrage.

Before I had the opportunity to contact Frau Klauss, she telephoned to invite me to dinner at her home in the Sihl Valley south of Zurich Lake. She suggested I take a train at 6:30 and said, "My husband, a country lawyer, will meet you at the station." Her warm cordiality disarmed me since, from conversations with journalists, I had conceived an image of her as fractious and eccentric.

When I arrived at the station on a hot summer afternoon, a storm was gathering. It broke with a sheet of rain just as the train was leaving. We ascended slowly through a blinding deluge, passing through Gontenbach and Langnau, and after a half hour arrived at Sihlwald where I stepped out into the rain. The wet coolness was a pleasure and I felt better.

I was greeted by a jovial man with a Benedictine's round laughing face and gray curly hair. "I am Bruno Klauss," he said in English.

He led me to a small sedan and as he sped us through a rustic Arcadia he described friends living in the houses we passed. He laughed a great deal and I had the impression of an utterly happy man, an anomaly in a land known for its male anxieties. On the slope of a mountain, the Albishorn, we turned into a bower of roses, to a large old house which was situated among farmer's meadows in which cows were grazing. Herr Klauss opened the front door and called out, "Here we are, honey." It was the first time I'd heard a Swiss use that English endearment and speak so intimately to his wife before a stranger. We entered a large handsome room filled with books and musical instruments and were met by a slim dark-haired woman.

"I am happy to meet you, Frau Klauss," I said. The lawyer and the lady burst into laughter, for it was not the lawyer's wife to whom I was speaking but Frau Johanna Gersten, a vice president of the Society Against the Right to Vote, who had come from Bern for the dinner. I

---

*The names of Marta Klauss and Johanna Gersten are pseudonyms.

asked the lawyer how many women he called "Honey," and this brought forth a second explosion of laughter.

At that moment Frau Klauss burst into the room and with girlish exuberance embraced and kissed her husband as if she hadn't seen him for a month. This also was something I'd never seen happen in Switzerland. Though she was not tall, her straight leanness, the severe styling of her dark hair, and the simple striped dress she was wearing made Frau Klauss seem taller. "I hope you have not come expecting to find us rather odd," she said. The Oxonian English she spoke reminded me of the actress Joyce Grenfell, whom Frau Klauss remarkably resembled. Indicating Frau Gersten, she said, "We want you to see us as we are, very average, happy Swiss women." As she bounded about the room, setting things in order, continuing to speak, Joyce Grenfell's comic characterization of an English club woman persisted in my mind. I noticed that both the Klausses and Frau Gersten had brown eyes. Frau Klauss' were a flashing bronze; her husband's were darker, softer and merry. I heard the lawyer call his wife "*Glugg*" which I interpreted as "luck," but which she explained with a ripple of laughter was short for "*Gluggere,*" which means a brooding hen. The name, she said, had been given her by her children.

She urged us to sit down. The room was walled with books, had nineteenth-century Swiss landscapes and a piano. Cellos, violins, and flutes were scattered about.

Suddenly a large damp butterfly fluttered into the room from the storm and settled on my wrist.

"Lovely!" Frau Klauss trilled. "What an omen of good luck! See how content he is. He knows you are not a nervous man." I began to speak softly to the butterfly. "He understands you," Frau Gersten said excitedly. "He is astonished to hear an American speak such perfect Swiss!" The butterfly fluttered away and landed on the arm of a cello. "He is drawn to beautiful things," said Frau Klauss. "Of course he loves music."

I was hoping desperately for a drink but the Klausses, it turned out, were *alkoholfrei*. Frau Gersten apologized that her husband, a broker, could not be present; then a very young couple appeared, a serious youth in white shorts and a sweetly demure girl. "This is my son Hugo and his bride," said Frau Klauss. "Hugo studies law and supports himself by driving a taxi in Zurich. Taxi-driving is a very broadening education for a young man." Hugo smiled, somewhat wisely I thought; perhaps the education was broader than his mother realized. It turned out that the young people were not married but engaged. The girl was completing her studies in music and was a church organist. The Klausses had four more children. "Like their father three of the children have chosen law," Frau Klauss said. "All the young people love music." The joyful vivacity with which she offered the information was apparently unsubsiding. She went on, saying, "At Lilly's wedding the bridal music was played by an orchestra of eleven musicians, all members of the groom's and bride's families." An image of Joyce Grenfell conducting the orchestra flashed through my mind.

Outside the storm was clearing and the air was cool and fresh. "Of what are you a professor?" Frau Klauss asked, and when I replied it was English she said excitedly, "Of course, I should have guessed." In a gush of enthusiasm she told me that her area of learning was English, that she had taken her degree in literature at the University of Zurich and then gone to England to continue her studies at Queen's College where she had written a dissertation on a nineteenth-century author named Percival Longman. "Of course, you haven't heard of him," she said. "He was unknown until I rediscovered him. His *Phoenix Flight* is one of the great novels in the English language. Longman had an amazing talent for adapting the style and subjects of other writers and building an unforgettable result of his own. His theme was a singleness of mind and purpose. It was stolen *from him* by Charles Morgan for his trio of singleness novels, *The Fountain, The Voyage,* and *Sparkenbroke.* When I published this discovery Morgan was annoyed, of course, and was forced to admit his ideas came from Longman. I didn't criticize him; after all Longman stole his ideas so he deserved to have them stolen. But Mr. Morgan thought he could get away with it because the Longman novel was forgotten. And he did until I came along."

Frau Klauss leaped up and ran from the room to fetch a copy of her dissertation. The interlude gave me time to sort over a flood of impressions. I felt a surge of sympathy for poor Charles Morgan, running afoul of this indomitable woman. Certainly Longman's "singleness of purpose" theme for which Frau Klauss had such a high regard revealed a great deal about her own character. She was unique, a Swiss woman intellectual of which I'd met few, and none who seemed so zealously to have combined learning with homemaking. In a complete Swiss sense she fulfilled the roles of wife and mother but unlike other Swiss women she had moved beyond them into a life of the mind. I found myself admiring her and I understood the fear with which Swiss men regarded her. She was, as Dürrenmatt had warned, "formidable."

She was back with the book and I asked her to tell me more about herself. She was fifty-two years old, which surprised me—misled by her youthful enthusiasm, I had judged her to be younger. She was born Marta Fahrni, the daughter of a professor of history and a leader in the Swiss cooperative movement. In the first ten years of her marriage to Herr Klauss, a native of Bern, she taught English in a private high school.

Herr Klauss smiled proudly at his wife, quite content to let her lead the conversation. I found this extraordinary. While the matriarchal household was common in Switzerland such an overt one certainly was not. Swiss women ruled their husbands and children by subtle indirection, by intuitively permitting men the outward signs of power, by supporting their image of household heads. Here no such game-playing was apparent. The enigma I could not resolve was how Frau Klauss' queenship could possibly include a determined resistance to women's suffrage.

The telephone kept ringing and though each call was for the lawyer, it was his wife who leaped up to answer. One of the calls was from a young Italian worker in the local chemical factory. "I have many calls from Italians inquiring about their visas and immigration problems," Herr Klauss said. "It usually turns out they have no real problems. They are merely homesick and after I talk with them in a friendly manner they feel better."

Frau Klauss urged us into the dining room. A Spanish maid served a vegetarian meal of open, toasted cheese sandwiches, two salads, both with an excellent dressing of herbs which Frau Klauss said were from her own garden, and bowls of raspberries, gooseberries large as plums, and wine-dark cherries. To drink there was bouillon, good but salty, which only increased my thirst and I ate a lot of fruit. During the meal Frau Klauss conducted the conversation like a symposium, directing questions to me, refuting my answers, allowing her husband and son to speak now and then but never the son's fiancée. "You will find us a very typical Swiss family," she said.

"I doubt that," I said, and she asked why.

"For one thing," I said, moving cautiously, "I don't believe that such a sympathetic rapport between husband and wife is common. Marriage in Switzerland seems more likely to be controlled formality."

"But you are wrong," Frau Klauss said. "A warm communication between the sexes is exactly what the Swiss have."

It went on like that. Every observation I made—the Swiss mothers' bondage of their sons and hostility to husbands, the preoccupation with possessions, the moral self-righteousness—Frau Klauss vigorously argued away. "Your impressions are completely wrong," she said. "You have been meeting all the wrong people. I will see that you meet some *right* people."

At this point Frau Gersten entered the conversation with her impressions, gathered from Swiss friends who had lived in America, and from Americans visiting in Bern, of life in "materialist America." "No sensitive person can possibly be happy in America," she said. "In Switzerland we are well-adjusted; our life is civilized and pleasant."

This dialogue was abruptly interrupted by a burst of spontaneous merriment at the expense of myself and the Spanish maid when I accidentally put my foot on a bell button under the rug near my chair, and the maid ran into the room. I thought the mirth rather exaggerated and determined to keep my foot from the bell. But a few minutes later I forgot and the maid returned at a gallop and the family and Frau Gersten collapsed a second time into laughter.

When the meal was finished the lawyer and the young couple excused themselves and Frau Klauss invited me and Frau Gersten into the library for coffee. Quite clearly the time for our discussion of women's suffrage was at hand. The conversation was slow in developing, as if no one were quite sure how to begin.

"Perhaps you have noticed," Frau Klauss commenced, "that Swiss women have no interest in politics."

"The women of Switzerland are not political," Frau Gersten continued. "In the old valleys they don't want to be drawn in."

"In all the houses in the Sihl Valley, I know of only one where the women want to vote," Frau Klauss said. "If we wanted the vote we would get it."

Why, I asked, did they not want to vote? My question excited the two women and opened a rapid dialogue including both.

"It is our clear and strong wish to preserve the natural sexual balances," Frau Klauss said. "Swiss women like strong men. As wives and mothers we are queens in our families."

"We are not an organization; we are a movement. A spontaneous rising of the women of Switzerland," Frau Gersten explained.

"Our dignity would be destroyed if we served in politics with our husbands, our sons, and brothers. Of course, they ask our opinions and we help them with their decisions. By giving them political responsibility we preserve their manhood."

"Only a few over-intellectualized Swiss women want to vote," Frau Gersten said.

"My sons would not marry intellectual women," Frau Klauss said firmly. "They can't bear them."

I said that I was astonished, that my impression was that she, Frau Klauss, was an intellectual. She reacted to this with alarm.

"No, no! Our feminine ideal is intelligence in women but never intellectualism. A proper Swiss woman would be insulted to be described as an intellectual."

"Intellectual women are against our national life," Frau Gersten said. "We have suffragettes—a hundred or so—who are always going about passionately talking, and they are not truly Swiss."

"We want to cooperate, not compete, with our husbands and sons," Frau Klauss said.

"We are a happy country because our women are not intellectual," Frau Gersten said simply.

"We have a very deep conviction that intellectuality in women leads a country down, not up, that if we gave women this right to destroy we would lose our national soul," Frau Klauss continued.

"Politics in Switzerland are very demanding. Our men go to meetings and elections every few weeks. It all takes a great deal of time. Can you imagine what would happen if we had to do this?" Frau Gersten asked.

"Women and men who want women to vote don't have the natural contact with the opposite sex that we have with our husbands," Frau Klauss explained.

At this point Herr Klauss entered the room with a tray of coffee and cups and a platter of wafflelike cookies called *Brätzeli*. He put down the tray, kissed his wife warmly, served the coffee and cookies, and quietly left the room. It was a performance such as I had never seen in Switzerland and I was stunned. The dialogue resumed.

"The intellectual suffragettes are revolutionaries who wish to change the body of the vote and destroy our sexual balances," Frau Klauss said.

"Our Swiss constitution is male. Switzerland is a male institution," Frau Gersten said.

"The Swiss spirit of freedom comes not from the French revolution, but from the Ruetli which was a male event," Frau Klauss said passionately. Her reference was to a meadow on the shores of the Lake of Lucerne where men of the cantons Uri, Schwyz, and Unterwalden, in the year 1291, took an oath of allegiance which is considered to be the cornerstone of the Swiss Confederation.

"In the cantons of Appenzell and Glarus where the old traditions continue you will not find a single woman who wants to vote. It would mean the end of the *Landsgemeinde* which is sacred." Frau Gersten said, referring to the traditional annual outdoor congress at which legislation is passed and officials are elected by a popular show-of-hands vote. "In Vaud only a few women voted and the men who felt their privileges being taken from them stayed away. The election was a disaster." Vaud was the first canton where, in 1959, women were permitted to vote on local but not national issues.

"Men are traditionalists in politics and can be trusted. Wherever women vote politics become corrupt," Frau Klauss said earnestly.

"In Sweden when women voted, all parties swung to the left. In Italy, the Communists have been strengthened by women. The revolutionary women in Switzerland would move us toward the welfare state; they would demand more schools and hospitals and free medicines. Who would pay for it? Taxes would have to be raised," Frau Gersten said excitedly.

At last I was able to detect a logic in the ladies' views, the logic of the conservative privileged. Prosuffrage "revolutionaries" and their concerns for human welfare were looked upon as threats to wealth and position.

"The natural rights of women have nothing to do with equality. Equality would not improve women's position, but degrade it. Swiss women are fortunate because parliament does not force upon them this power which they do not want," Frau Klauss said, biting into a cookie.

"We believe that the problems of our times are due to the disturbance of the sexual balances. In America the role of the father is disappearing. American men are suffering because they have lost their sexual roles," Frau Gersten said.

"The influence of women covers everything in America," Frau Klauss said. "You can read it all in Tocqueville, and it grows worse."

"Feminine women are rare in America. In Switzerland we feel privileged to be feminine. We preserve a happy family life," Frau Gersten said.

"We are feminine little Eves who understand that a man must rule," said Frau Klauss. "We are the happiest women in the world."

"They call us antifeminine when instead we are really profeminine. We are occupied with our womanly role as heart of the family," Frau Gersten said.

"We have strong men whose strength is our gift. They do not realize that we are their masters, that if we want a law passed in parliament they pass it for us." Frau Klauss smiled.

"The unmarried working women, the divorcees, and spinsters, are with us. They have enough of competing with men; they don't want equality," said Frau Gersten, taking a sip of coffee.

"Men's logic is more precise; their ideas of justice are seen in black and white. Women think with their instincts," Frau Klauss said.

"I don't like the word 'equality.' I don't like it at all. It's a social pressure word. All my American friends are unhappy with it and its terrible conformism which does not exist in Switzerland. We are proud to be individuals," Frau Gersten said.

At this point Frau Klauss began to speak mysteriously of the "single-mindedness" of Percival Longman's and Charles Morgan's novels which she said was the guiding force of her life. I asked her to explain this and she said, "Not to be influenced from here and there, but living always your own character."

"We are proud to be sound males and sound females," Frau Gersten said.

"Those countries which have gone too far over the sexual frontier will all come back; they will retrench," Frau Klauss said.

I pointed out that Switzerland had many distinguished professional women, including doctors, pastors, an atomic physicist.

"Precisely!" Frau Klauss said. "We want women to enter every field, so long as they stay out of politics. Our deeply rooted instinct rejects that. We have a more realistic view of life."

"Our movement is growing," Frau Gersten said.

"Votes for women will never be approved in Switzerland," Frau Klauss said.

I said that the issue would be settled by men, that they would be voting on the suffrage issue.

"Of course," Frau Klauss said. "Our suffragettes don't want women to decide. They know quite well what would happen. We are not afraid. The men will listen to us and vote against it."

Herr Klauss then entered the room and kissed his wife. I asked his opinion of women's suffrage and his reply might have been spoken by his wife. "It's a woman's question," he said. "If women want the vote they can naturally have it. But they do not want it and so the men are not going to force it upon them."

"It will never happen!" said his wife, her voice a ringing bell. "Never! Never! It is not possible!"

It did happen in 1970. In December 1980 I received a letter from my friend Midi Schuler of Zurich, a former activist in the fight for women's suffrage. She wrote:

"We have just celebrated our ten-year jubilee of the passing of the suffrage amendment. These ten years have seen a steady upward movement during which women gained more and more ground in Swiss politics.

"We now have three women, of a total of forty-six members, in the *Ständerät,* equivalent of your U.S. Senate. Of a total of 200 members of the *Nationalrat,* comparable to your House of Representatives, twenty-one are women. Of the 180 members in the legislative body of the Canton of Zurich, nineteen are women. Women serve in the governments of practically all Swiss cantons and in most legislative bodies of Swiss Communities.

"The moment women won suffrage the opposing organizations died. One of the most prominent leaders against suffrage has undergone a Saul-to-Paul conversion and, according to her own words, now realizes 'that women must help one another' On the whole women seem to make the same uses of the right to vote as do men.

"Not surprisingly, women have had to prove their qualifications for public service more than men. An important result of suffrage has been the eligibility of women to serve on school boards, commissions, juries, and other positions previously closed to them. Such innovations have proven beneficial to the community since women in public service are very conscientious and, as a rule, have more time to devote to their responsibilities than men who are busy with professional careers and earning money."

23

MORE NOTES FROM A LOW VILLAGE

February 4: The grotesque, blood-chilling "devil exorcism" trial in the Zurich court house is over; an excommunicated priest and his mistress have been found guilty of flogging to death seventeen-year-old Bernadette Hasler for *Teufelshuhlschaft,* for "coupling with the devil," and are sentenced to prison. The self-styled "Holy Couple," leaders of a religious cult, are believed to have held hypnotic powers over a congregation of lower-middle-class farmers and laborers who were sending their daughters to the couple's chalet outside Zurich to be educated. Jurists described the case as one of the most shocking ever to come before a Swiss court of law, and psychiatrists are studying the case as the manifestation of a medieval mentality still existing in alpine valleys and gorges.

The moral fury aroused by the trial was as demonic as the crime itself. Demonstrating mobs outside the courthouse shouted, "String them up!" and police had to guard the defendants against would-be lynchers. The court received threats of bombing if the punishment were less than the maximum. One letter-writer suggested tying the couple to a telegraph pole and delivering them to public anger; another proposed sealing them in a barrel filled with spikes and setting them afire. A journalist remembered Dr. Jung's observation that "mountains are not only geographical barriers; they also limit the horizons of the human spirit." Another writer recalled that the last execution of a witch in Switzerland occurred in Glarus in 1782.

When I enter the university class in American studies about twenty-five students, seated around a conference table, rise and clap their palms on the table. The greeting is traditional for a professor; no student would presume to enter the classroom after him. Students are polite and neatly dressed; the men wear neckties. They ask questions about women's liberation and equal rights, racism and black writers, national elections and the power of the president. When the class is over the students stand quietly in their places until I have left the room. Exhilarated by such attention and respect, I am a better teacher.

My apartment neighbor Pius Göntli, son of a rural Catholic family from the Toggenburg and a bank economist, is reading *Portnoy's Complaint*. "The book is about me," he said. "It is my father and mother who are portrayed. Portnoy's problems are exactly mine. It is fantastic! I tell myself, this man is a Jew of another culture and another language half way around the world. Yet he and I live on the same plane; we have everything in common." Dr. Göntli goes to his bank to work evenings and Sundays and holidays. He is overcome with guilt when he is not working. "To get ahead in a bank you have to be absolutely single-minded," he said. "Everything else must be sacrificed." He looks forward to living in a time when "machines will surpass men in intelligence. Only then will there be an orderly utopia, because machines are not given to caprice and have none of the evil impulses of men." I wonder if he is mad.

With Max and Midi Schuler, on one of Max's intricate railroad itineraries, via three trains, to Romainmôtier in the Jura region of Canton Vaud. The village, in a narrow valley, is seen first from above, its rooftops huddled about a fifth-century Roman church. Cattle stalls, farm machinery, and piles of manure surround the church, permeating it with stench. Inside, sandstone columns are carved with birds, trees, and grain representing the natural forces of sun, water, earth, and air.

Christian symbols have faded away—what remains is a pantheistic temple.

Across the single road is the Hôtel St. Romain and we went there for lunch. A gesticulating idiot greeted us at the door. A high incidence of retardation and cretinism in the Jura is attributed to the consumption of absinthe, called *fee verte,* or green fairy. Though sale of absinthe is prohibited by the government, it is privately distilled by peasants. The dining room was a scene from a Buñuel film. Some cardplayers at a table had faces like gargoyles. A huge, long-haired man, who the waitress said was the local poet, sulked in a corner. The waitress, a lanky, dark girl, dropped a half-franc coin on the floor and refused to bring our wine until she had found it. As she bent to retrieve the coin, four more coins rolled from her pocket and soon all of us were on the floor, under the table, searching for coins. Midi burst into laughter and the poet rose from his seat and stalked from the room. The girl broke into tears and Midi apologized.

I went to a theater in an Italian quarter to see a Swiss documentary film, *Siamo Italiani,* about Italian workers. The amateurishly made film was heartbreaking in its eloquent portrayal of an endless Kafkan bureaucracy with which the confused Italians are confronted, and the squalid hovels in which they must live, because Swiss landlords will not rent them decent quarters. Stony-faced Swiss women, their faces ugly with hatred, spoke in dialectic Swiss, saying, "The Italians are ignorant, dirty, noisy, and immoral. One is not safe on the streets . . ." Young Italians, their anxiety, eagerness, and puzzlement coalescing into a soft radiance in their faces, spoke in their own language, "The Swiss are different from us; they are not well-bred; they do not have good manners. When we are not working, that is the worst time . . ." Bands of lonely men, most of them temporary bachelors with wives and children in Naples, Lucania, or Calabria, were shown striving to fill empty Sundays by wandering the streets or gathering at the railroad station— which they have made their clubhouse—for the poignant diversion of watching trains leave for the south. In this matter of foreign workers Switzerland resembles the Roman Empire with its first-class proprietor citizens and its second-class slave citizens.

The polarized antipathies go beyond politics and economics and are rooted in the ideological foundations of two cultures. Swiss, whether Protestant or Catholic, cling to their notion—either conscious or subliminal or both—of Calvin's Holy Commonwealth, of being in a Biblical sense a chosen people, burdened as God's proxies with His responsibilities. Living with a commitment to Calvin's *Materialismus* and its terrifying option of damnation, they are affronted by the seemingly pragmatic and self-indulgent Italian Catholic spirit. If the Italians have not quite accepted doom, they have at least learned to live comfortably with its possibility. With their voluptuous smiles, their warm tactile glow, they let you know that they seek to enjoy the very best that is possible for them in their hard lives; if they're going to burn in hell in any case why depress themselves worrying about it? It is this easy Italian acceptance of sin and corporeal commitment, of a pursuit of small worldly pleasures and open carnality, that so passionately infuriates the self-denying Swiss. They have turned the Italian's *mea culpa* into *nostra culpa.*

The popular Swiss canard of Italian uncleanliness is an injust irony. The Swiss, whom a psychiatrist defined as an anal people with a *Putzfrau* mentality, are preoccupied with image cleanliness. Forever cleaning their houses and doorsteps with angry vengeance, they are less concerned with personal cleanliness. Italians, being an oral and extroverted people and strongly narcissistic, are less concerned with cleaning things than they are in keeping themselves clean and are frequent bathers. Banker Hans Baer made the point that Italians are actually much cleaner than the Swiss. Swiss employers, he said, complain of Italian maids who bathe daily, using expensive hot water. Swiss students rent rooms without bathing facilities and are expected to return to their parental home for weekend baths.

I addressed the Lucerne Society for Swiss-American Friendship; the fee agreed upon for my appearance was 200 francs. After the talk the Society's president presented me with a carved wooden carnival mask as a "token." Since I collect such masks I was pleased. Today I received the check in payment for 150 francs, fifty francs having been subtracted as the price of the mask.

There is a great flap in the newspapers about the Bührle Company's sale of munitions to warring African nations. Dr. Dieter Bührle, president of the company and son of the art collector, is quoted as saying, "Without the foreign sales of arms, the Swiss munitions industry could not survive; nine hundred technicians would be out of work." I discussed this with Banker Hans Halbheer who said, "Arms is always a dirty business. The Swiss government needs arms and it cannot alone maintain Bührle's production. The government has urged Dr. Bührle to stay in munitions as a patriotic duty. So, of course, the company must sell to Biafra, Kenya, and Israel."

Good Friday in the Niederdorf. Shops are closed; for workers it is a holiday. In spite of an unceasing ringing of bells, a pagan spirit is in the air. Bands of Italian workers are out in chartreuse, purple, and orange velveteen suits like human Easter eggs, pursuing the whores for whom it is a day of booming commerce. Never have so many girls been out at one time; Gräbligasse and Zähringer Street are filled with them. They scream insults at the Italians who have come to ogle rather than negotiate and are cluttering up the marketplace. Urged on by his friends, a bantam Italian, hardly five-feet-tall with long curly hair, swaggers up to a band of girls and they draw away from him, shouting ribald insults on his stature. He tries a second cluster of miniskirted girls and they strut away like haughty hens. A recording of "When the Saints Go Marching In" reverberates from the open door of a bar.

A taxi moves slowly through the crowd. It stops and the girls crowd around. Two business types, wearing dark glasses, lower a window and negotiate. Two girls leap into the cab and it speeds away.

Kap Rhyner's uncle Fridolin Zentner arrived in Elm unexpectedly from San Francisco. It was his first visit since he left Switzerland forty-three years ago. He stepped off the bus and walked to the house of his birth, now the home of a nephew. A niece, who did not know him, met him on the path. "The apple tree is gone," he said to her.

"You must be Fridolin," she said, and invited him to her house next door.

"No, thank you," he replied. "The house from which I left will be the first to which I return."

He had come for a long visit but after four days he is already making plans to return. "Everyone works too hard," he said. "In America life is easier."

Since I have been in Switzerland "anarchists" (a catch-all epithet which the Swiss use for all categories of rebels and protestors) have bombed the police station and City Hall, and Arab terrorists shot up an Israeli plane in the Zurich airport. In February a disgruntled employee set fire to the Zurich central telephone office and a third of the city was without phone service for a month. Last night—June 11—university students, protesting inequities in the Swiss courts, demonstrated outside the Palace of Justice. The courthouse entrance and the street outside were spattered with bloodlike red paint. Two Red China flags, one on each side of the door, framed a banner, reading *Zurich's erste Bordell-Justitia!* (Zürich's first brothel—justice!) Officials have done nothing to obliterate the display, shrewdly leaving it for shocked crowds to view. As a result, public indignation against the students is high. "How is it possible that something like this could happen in Switzerland?" a banker asked.

A Swiss saying: "In America paupers appear to be millionaires; in Switzerland millionaires appear to be paupers."

Jim McCracken was mowing his lawn on Sunday. A policeman arrived. "You are mowing the lawn," he said dourly. "Yes," Jim replied. "You are not allowed to mow on Sunday," the officer said. Jim thought he was joking and laughed. "I just got in from London yesterday and I'm going to Vienna tomorrow and as you can see the lawn needs it."
"It is against the law to mow on Sundays," said the officer menacingly. "You are not even allowed to pick a flower in your garden." Realizing the officer was in earnest, Jim stopped. A neighbor living across the street, to whom Jim had never spoken, had telephoned the police station.

"I have a headache," said a student yesterday. "Tomorrow will be a bright day." His prediction was accurate; today is shimmering. The sky is blue and clear and beyond the lake the Glarner mountains are clearly detailed and appear extremely close. It is the *Föhn,* a warm dry wind that rolls down mountain slopes into the valleys and causes a variety of extraordinary symptoms and alters human behavior. The affects are similar to those of the menacing French mistral, the Italian sirocco, and the southern California Santa Ana. According to my Swiss doctor, the *Föhn* shrinks arteries, reduces the flow of blood to the brain, and causes everyone to "spin" or turn crazy. The two or three days of a *Föhn* are a time of allergies, nervousness, and depression. Suicides increase, patients in mental hospitals become uncontrollable, schoolchildren are obstreperous, and surgeons postpone operations because blood does not clot normally. Crime increases and in some courts the wind is accepted as an extenuating circumstance in establishing innocence of intent. Even animals are believed affected. Dogs become vicious, horses unruly, cows give less milk. Once the fact of a *Föhn* is established, a communal psychosomatism takes hold; everything is attributed to it. Because I am not so preoriented my responses are not pernicious. I feel a light-headed euphoric larkishness, a heightened erotic sensibility, a sharpening of perception. If I spin it is rapturously.

24

SECHSELÄUTEN

Zurich's most exuberant festival is its springtime *Sechseläuten*. The word, which translates to "six o'clock ringing," refers to a pealing of church bells to celebrate the lengthening daylight and the public burning of the winter *Böögg*, or bogeyman.

The pagan celebration has its origin in a socialist revolt in the fourteenth century when a group of dissident aristocrats joined with tradespeople and organized eleven trade guilds to wrest control of the Zurich government from a small clique of nobility and rich merchants. The ousted ruling class then formed their own opposing *Constaffel*, or "Society of Knights." The guilds were closed shops and tradespeople who were not members could not sell their products in the city markets; nonguild tailors were unable to buy wool from guild weavers. The guilds governed the city until the French Revolution when political control was turned over to the entire citizenry and the 12 guilds changed from political organizations into affluent bourgeois men's clubs.

In the late nineteenth and early twentieth centuries, as the growing city incorporated outlying suburbs and border villages, thirteen new regional societies were organized. They took their names—Fluntern, Hottingen, Wollishofen, etc.—from the geographic areas in which their members lived and they adopted the rites and customs of the traditional guilds. Today's guild members are the social aristocrats of the city, its bankers, professors, and business and professional leaders. Guild houses are palaces containing some of the best restaurants in Switzerland. There is a story, which seems credible, that the haughty *Constaffel* has for more than a century accepted only sons of members into its brotherhood and that a newly rich industrialist offered a contribution of a million francs in exchange for membership and was refused.

Though the exorcising of winter is the climax of *Sechseläuten,* most of this annual gathering of the guilds is a chauvinist celebration of maleness and is a temporary cease-fire in Switzerland's battle of the sexes.

So that I might participate in the festival I was invited to be an "honored guest" of the *Schneidern,* the tailors' guild, which had a clubhouse and fine restaurant called *Der Königstuhl* (the King's Chair) conveniently around the corner from my apartment. My sponsoring godfather was Dr. Emil Hirt, whom I had known almost exclusively in the solemn halls of the private bank where he was a vice-president. A lean, handsome man about forty years of age, he struck me as an earnest and slightly snobbish aristocrat. He wore dark banker-style suits and spoke with a soft, deep voice.

It was Emil's duty to prepare me for the event. When he arrived at my apartment a week before to instruct me in the *Schneidern* rites and to measure me for a tailor's uniform, his personality was so astonishingly transformed I could hardly believe it was the same man. Talking rapidly, his eyes blazing with excitement, he gave the impression of a man fifteen years younger. He began by telling me of a feud between the tailors and the shoemakers over which might be the original craftsmen. The shoemakers, he said, "insist that Adam wore sandals in the Garden of Eden before his fig leaf and that this proves shoemakers preceded tailors. Of course that is an erroneous supposition, since quite certainly Adam wore his stitched fig leaves before he wore sandals and the Eden tailor who designed the fig leaf loin covering used buttons made from tortoise shells, which proves indisputably that tailors came before shoemakers." Tailors, Emil went on, included in their ranks also glovers and truss-makers, known as *Secklers* (literally "baggers"), but glovers were not allowed to line gloves with fur, that being reserved for the furriers' guild.

Up to this point I had looked upon my inclusion by the tailors as a harmlessly diverting lark, like a college fraternity initiation. Now, subjected to Emil's zealous thrall, I began to feel a certain apprehension. "A brother in the *Schneidern* is a brother forever," he said. I was not certain I was ready for that. Still, such youthful enthusiasm in an adult was ingratiating; the fine madness of him was utterly un-Swiss and so irresistible I felt myself caught up in it. The family of Hirt, he said, had the longest uninterrupted membership in tailor history. In one of his books he pointed out the record of the first Hirt induction in 1522. His voice suddenly somber, he said that he and his father were the last living Hirts in the tailors' guild and since his own three children were girls the long continuum would end with his death.

Emil listed distinguished tailors I would meet, including bankers, an official of Swissair, and a rancher who was coming from South America where he owned an area "larger than Switzerland." I asked if there were any real tailors in the tailors, and Emil said there was one, a fashionable society tailor who was president of the Master Tailors' Association. He was Adolph Schmid, whose name meant "blacksmith"; the name, also, of another guild. I suggested jokingly that the inclusion of a peasant like myself must certainly involve a liberalizing of tailor standards. "Not so," said Emil. "On the contrary, sometimes clever young men from villages who advance in business and marry daughters of tailors are made members."

The day was Monday, April 21. It had been snowing damply for a week. Winter was putting up a valiant resistance and the fires of spring were surely overdue.

At eleven o'clock, when I was still making notes for the speech I had been told I was expected to make, my sponsor came to fetch me. He was a fantasy to behold, a nineteenth-century dandy dressed like the Mad Hatter in tightly fitting pearl-gray trousers, sky-blue swallowtail coat, a bright vest embroidered with flowers, a huge wing collar that flapped like a nun's hat, pastel pink flowing sash necktie, and a high gray cylinder hat. "Naturally, we tailors are the most elegantly dressed of all guilds," he said. He was carrying a gigantic pair of scissors which tailors used "to cut things."

"What things?" I asked uneasily.

"Men's neckties and ladies' belts and aprons." Seeming suddenly to have gone mad he began to leap about the apartment, snapping the scissors open and shut, pantomiming the cutting of aprons. "In the old days we even cut ladies dresses and hair," he said, winking suggestively. "We tailors are regular devils."

From the square below we could hear the skirling voices of women and Emil said, "The ladies will get very excited when they see all the men and they will throw flowers at us. You will be covered with flowers."

As we left the apartment he whispered something in confidence to Anna Guler, the apartment manager, and she responded with laughter. Later I would find out that he had asked her to fetch me in a taxi should I pass out during the ensuing twenty-four hours. The gathering up of incapacitated celebrants was, along with the throwing of flowers, a *Sechseläuten* commitment of women.

The King's Chair was roaring. Outside crowds of women waited with arms full of flowers, and Emil's wife and two of his daughters rushed up to present me with a bouquet of red carnations. I was hustled upstairs into a dressing room to put on my costume (borrowed from a tailor who was holidaying in Spain, a musician named Willy Hardmeyer who was organist at the Zurich crematorium). The costume was being unpacked by Willy's son, René, a droll, orange-haired medical student wearing a red version of the same costume worn by *Zünferssöhne,* the sons of guild members. He and Emil assisted me into his father's suit and it fit quite well.

"Now we are a Biedermeyer fantasy," Emil cried out and pursed his lips into a cupid's bow before a mirror. The description was appropriate to his trim elegance but my own image was closer to Mr. Pickwick's.

A booming welcome greeted us on the top floor. Tables were set with a glittering array of silver urns, tankards, and bowls, and golden goblets (hidden during the French Revolution to prevent their being stolen, Emil explained). Most of the men wore trimly barbered beards, moustaches, and mutton chops, and the artificial ones were so perfectly fashioned it was difficult to tell them from the real. In the company of such male splendor I had a feeling that I was participating in a profane production of *Parsifal* designed by Charles Dickens.

At each place setting there was a menu, on the cover of which was embossed the stern profile of Ulrich Zwingli. I was seated at the head table, across from the "Guild Master," Dr. Hans Zehnder, a slender,

cultivated schoolteacher about fifty years of age. Around his neck was
an enormous silver chain supporting medallions of authority which
appeared extremely heavy. Between us stood a great gold chalice, the
guild's "holy grail," which Emil said had belonged to Charlemagne.
Next to me was a portly red-cheeked man called Toni, an officer of
"Swissre," short for Swiss Reinsurance, which he unhesitatingly
informed me was the "most important firm in Switzerland."

He pointed to his son, born in the United States where once Toni had
been a banker. "I returned to Switzerland for his education," Toni said.
"In your country education is very bad; there is no elitism to it; nothing
but least common denominator and the privileged classes are penal-
ized." Toni asked me why I had not been at the guild ball the night
before and I replied that I had little enthusiasm for balls. "What a pity!"
he said. "You would have met all your peers, everyone you should
know. The entire establishment was there." Establishment! It was a
word I was to hear over and over, spoken very earnestly, and not
ironically as I was accustomed to hearing it in America. It was used to
indicate aristocracy, some mysterious Platonic elitism. "It is important
to maintain the establishment," Toni said.

Waitresses brought plates of food: veal in wine, asparagus, roasted
potatoes and salad. All of it was excellent. Lusty eating was accompanied by spirited toasts, and waitresses with silver beakers kept glasses
filled. Whenever my eyes met the eyes of a brother, either at my table or
another, he would raise his glass and drink, indicating for me to do the
same. Aware of the hazard in this I tried avoiding glances by staring
straight ahead. "You must drink!" Emil said as he nudged me and
raised his glass.

In a corner of the hall a red-jacketed band began to play. I asked
Toni if the musicians were tailors. "Oh, no," he replied. "Musicians are
socialists and of course socialists are not accepted in the guilds."
Remembering my godfather's history lesson, I pointed out that guilds
had begun as the trade union socialists of their time. Ignoring this, Toni
continued, "The fine thing about the *Sechseläuten* is that the establishment can take over the town for a day with no opposition from the
socialists. Musicians and police, of course, are all socialists. But they
cooperate with us. There is nothing hidden, no secrecy. It's a very
happy demonstration of real democracy and this is the unique thing

about Zurich; it couldn't happen any other place in the world." His logic was addling me. "But of course we could not accept them as members," he said. Two brothers arrived late and were clamorously welcomed. "Swissair and National Cash Register," Toni said.

The spirit commenced to turn boisterous. The band was oompahing so vigorously conversation became impossible; the tubas were rattling the leaded windows. There seemed nothing to do but accept the signals of raised glasses across the room. I tried to keep my eyes lowered and I barely touched my lips with my glass, sipping only a drop or two, as in church communion. The Last Supper, indeed! Beside me Emil's artificial beard was jutting like John Calvin's; the stern face of Zwingli looked up at me from the table. A new ritual was spreading through the hall, an interlocking of arms with one's neighbors, a kind of embrace while drinking together. Emil linked an arm through mine and we drank; wine spilled on both of us. I was thinking how in the halls of carpenters, boatwrights, butchers, spice merchants, and hat makers, hordes of men were acting in the same strange way, preparing for their occupation of the city.

Emil was shouting in my ear, telling me of a tailor who shunned the *Sechseläuten* because he could not tolerate, in such unrestrained conviviality, being addressed in the familiar "*du.*" "Of course when we drink we say *du* quite a lot," he said. "So he does not come."

At a signal from the Master the band stopped. He offered me a cigar and, bowing and clicking his heels, made a ceremony of lighting it for me. He told me he had read one of my books to prepare himself for our meeting and he apologized that most of his remarks would be made in Swiss because "some of our members would not understand English."

He began, saying, "We have commenced our jovial hours and I hope we will endure until tomorrow." There was loud applause. The oldest brother was introduced; he was eighty-eight and appeared drunk. The Master read a poem by an absent member, Emil Hirt, Sr., father of my friend, a retired professor in Berne. The poem was applauded and then the Master began his introduction of me in English.

It was time for my speech. I'd written it in the morning with the help of Anna Guler who had laughed over its bawdy humor. Now I worried that I might be too raffish. I told of some problems incurred by speaking the New Glarus nineteenth-century peasant patois in the polite society of Zurich: How a lady had slapped my face when I referred to my jacket pocket as a *Schlitz,* which in Switzerland is sometimes used as a vulgar connotation for vagina; and how a New Glarus cousin referred to his wife as a *Wiib,* which in Swiss denotes a woman of ill-repute. I told stories of my father, a third-generation American who never visited Switzerland, who was distressed when his children married non-Swiss Americans, how he'd spoken of his son-in-law as "though not Swiss a good fellow all the same."

I was applauded like Tannhäuser. It was not, I realized, what I said that delighted the tailors so much as the language in which I said it. There were shouts of *"Hoch!"* Glasses were raised and as soon as they were emptied serving girls filled them.

It was time to assemble for the parade. We clattered down two flights of stairs to the street where women again pelted us with flowers. I was carrying a bright red umbrella from the Tessin, using it as a cane. All the tailors had them; they blended very well with our costumes. We followed the blaring band across the Urania bridge to Löwenstrasse, where we joined a dazzling medieval panoply. Each of the twenty-five guilds had fifty or more men bearing flowers, a band, and a float, and many had a cavalry of mounted horses and a children's cortège. The *Constaffel* were Renaissance princes, the *Saffran*—spice merchants— were dark Bedouins, the *Widder*—butchers—wore aprons and carried cleavers. When the time arrived to fall into line the sun burst forth and this, after two weeks of miserable weather, was hailed as a heavenly benefaction.

The dazzling procession backtracked on Bahnhofstrasse so that it appeared to be going two ways at once. Sidewalks were jammed with women bearing baskets of flowers, which they ran out to present to the men with a kiss. The marchers slyly gauged one another's popularity by the quantity of flowers each carried. There was an air of heart-touching absurdity about the solemn men, some old, others fat, laden with flowers, treading like walking wreaths.

Each guild had its identifying emblem. The carpenters' was a wooden bridge mounted on a lorry almost a block long; the boatsmen carried baskets of fish, which they threw at screeching ladies. The most unruffling symbols were our own five-foot-long gleaming scissors with which our "sons," weaving in and out of the crowd, cut neckties and beards and ladies' scarves and ribbons. Their leader was my godfather who, leaping about like a goat, measuring with his tape the busts of shrieking ladies, seemed demented by a pagan ecstacy. One popular ploy was a scene from *commedia dell'arte*. A youth approached a gentleman in the crowd with his opened scissors and the gentleman, backing away, had his hat seized from behind by the scissors of another youth, who running across the street, placed the hat on the head of a screaming woman.

We marched four kilometers. Several of the brothers carried canisters of wine with which faltering members, drinking from a spout, were restored. Twice ladies ran out from the crowd to bring me a stein of beer. The well-timed procession ended a few minutes before six o'clock on Bellevue Square where the *Böögg* was mounted on a great pyre of logs that men were soaking with gasoline. The square was a sea of people; on the lake boats were filled with viewers and choppers circled overhead.

The crowd silenced to wait for the striking of the clock in the tower of St. Peter's Church. On the sixth knell a torch was put to the pyre and the flames swooshed up. Firecrackers in the pyre exploded like an artillery charge. A black column of smoke rose into the skies.

As the flames leaped, cavalrymen shouting like Cossacks raced their horses around the conflagration. Watching the robed horsemen whirling about the fire, I felt a strange and inexplicable thrall, and I tried to understand what it all signified. Bells were ringing over the town and bands blared everywhere. The exploding firecrackers scared the horses, which leaped like crazed Pegasuses in and out of the smoke. Two riders were thrown and one had to be taken away in an ambulance, its siren adding to the clamor. A brother explained that the way the *Böögg* burned and the manner with which its head exploded would indicate the summer's weather and fruitfulness. The *Böögg* took fourteen minutes to burn and its leaping flames, reflecting in the glass vestibule of the opera house, made the theater glow as if it also were burning. Cecil B. De Mille could not have staged a more ostentatious Apocalypse.

Quite suddenly it was over. The multitudes dispersed and we marched behind our band back to the King's Chair. Another banquet had been prepared and because everyone was exhausted its mood was subdued. Sitting across from me was the famous brother from Brazil whose name was Hans August Schweizer. He was a tall, lean man who spoke of his coffee plantation and cattle farm. His two sons were doctors in Brazil. "But only in the afternoons. In the forenoons they are ranchers," the old man said. He added that he needed periodically to return to his Zurich townhouse to experience Switzerland's northern climate. "I'm sick of sunshine," he said. "I long for clouds, for rain and snow."

It was time for the Master's annual message. He began by reviewing with rhetorical flourishes the glories of the tailors. In what seemed a curious nonsequitur he moved into an attack on protesting students in Paris, Germany, America, and Switzerland. He called the students "mentally disturbed anarchists, a discredit to human society, who would destroy everything you saw today, everything in which we believe." He concluded on a cheering note, "Today you saw youth of Zurich participating in traditions which glorify our history, perpetuate our ideals, and preserve our bourgoise society."

After the meal the tailors, like every other guild in the city, split into two groups. Senior brothers remained in the King's Chair to hold court for visiting bands of young guildsmen, and the younger tailors set out to visit other guilds. Since my godfather was a leader of the rovers I chose to accompany them.

The evening was mild and the city was like a Medician fête, with spotlights glowing on churches and public buildings. Instead of one great parade there were now twenty-five small ones moving through the streets, each choosing its own spontaneous course. Flowers were abandoned for lanterns with flickering candles and the covert movements of lanterned groups through the old city were strange and wondrously mysterious. Bands played everywhere and streets were filled with dark clusters of witnessing women.

We commenced our night journey by boat, making our first visit to the Riesbach Guild, which had its headquarters on the shore of the lake. Chugging softly up the Limmat and onto the lake, we met other flotillas of lantern-lit boats. At the Riesbach dock we disembarked in the same moment as young visiting wine merchants emerged and reembarked in their own water procession. A herald went inside to announce us and returned in a moment with a summons to enter. Like young knights visiting a foreign court we stalked in and were met by girls bearing trays of wine-filled goblets. There were toasts of "*Hoch! Hoch!*" and glasses were refilled. The hall was resplendent with banners and tapestries; the Riesbach seigneurs wore red, gold, and black robes, and gold chains about their necks.

My godfather gave an account of our journeys that turned into a paraphrasing of Homer's *Odyssey* with imaginary perils and sirens repulsed en route. Odysseus had remained in the court of Nestor for a year, he said, but we, unfortunately, did not have the time to stay as long.

The Riesbach Master responded jocularly, saying that he hoped we hadn't too much difficulty embarking—a reference to our drinking—and he congratulated us "for getting your billygoats around the fire" in the afternoon. Polite insults were delivered in Biblical-sounding rhetoric and gifts were exchanged.

It was four guilds later and after 2 A.M. when we marched around Grossmünster Cathedral to prove to ourselves we were still mobile, and like errant knights returned to our home castle. When we arrived we were required to give a detailed account of our night's journey to our stay-at-home brothers. Emil, our spokesman, began, "We return refreshed in spirit and joyful at being reunited with our fathers and brothers . . ." Shouting with excitement, the veins throbbing on his forehead, he summarized our wanderings, naming all the streets through which we had passed, abstracting all speeches made and heard. He enumerated the glasses of wine we drank and the girls whose clothing we assailed with scissors and he embellished his report with fantastic details of pursuing sirens and evil witches and "a Spanish lady with a fabulous measurement" whom we had rescued in a sea battle with pirates.

Our elders invited us to be seated and listen to their account of everything that had occurred in our absence in the King's Chair. When that was finished there was a communal partaking of *Mehlsuppe*, the sobering creamed soup of scorched flour, served at the conclusion of drinking orgies.

At 3:30 A.M. some of the older men began to totter away and I slipped out with them. The Niederdorf was still roaring. I met two women supporting a tottering drunk and one of them was sing-songing baby talk like a lullaby, saying, "The poor little Rudi, so bad in the stomach, so dizzy in the head."

My manhood, so manifestly celebrated, was completely spent. Creeping wearily home, I continued to wonder what it all meant.

25

LANDSGEMEINDE

There are countries in which the people and the government exist as separate entities, appearing to have little to do with one another. In Italy there are frequent lapses without government and both the people and the nation continue to function without interruption. In the United States a growing disenchantment with government is blamed for the diminishing participation of voters in elections.

In the Swiss political structure the people *are*, by definition, the government. The governing of "communes"—villages and cities—and cantons and the federation of cantons is the constantly preoccupying responsibility of voters. There are local, cantonal, and federal elections and referendums, usually held on Sundays and as frequently as once a month.

Cynical critics of the system maintain that all this activity is a delusive screen to distract the public while the country itself is really being commandeered by powerful bankers and industrialists. There is no doubt that these two well-organized and sophisticated power groups exert great influence on matters of national policy in Berne. But Switzerland is a true federation of autonomous, self-governing states and it is on this level that most of the country's domestic housekeeping is administered. Many Swiss women were opposed to suffrage simply because of the demands that governing makes on a citizen's time. Caring for home and family, they argued, left no time for politics.

The most striking demonstration of Swiss government by the governed is an annual outdoor legislative assembly of all qualified voters called the *Landsgemeinde.* This historical tradition of open and oral democracy, going back to the Middle Ages, continues to be observed in three cantons: Appenzell, Unterwalden, and Glarus. In Appenzell participation is compulsory for all men over twenty years of age. This small canton in northeastern Switzerland, completely surrounded by the larger canton of St. Gall, is divided into two half-cantons, Roman Catholic *Innerrhoden* and Protestant *Ausserrhoden,* names that literally mean inner and outer clearances in a forest. Each conducts its own *Landsgemeinde.* On the last Sunday in April I attended the Catholic assembly in the town of Appenzell and a week later, on the first Sunday in May, I was invited to the congress in Glarus.

In Appenzell I was the guest of the *Bauernmaler,* Albert Manser. Then only thirty-two years old, Manser was known as the "Grandpa Moses of Switzerland" and his primitive paintings sold for up to 5,000 francs on the Zurich art market. Manser had developed his style of minutely detailed and glossily bright landscapes during ten years employment as a pastry cook, the profession by which he was still listed in the telephone directory. One of my purposes in Appenzell was to buy one of his paintings but he had none for sale and was six months behind with commissions. We discussed subject matter, size, and price as if I were ordering a suit of clothes and I placed an order for a picture measuring fourteen by twenty-four inches, of a springtime procession of garlanded cows departing for the alps.

Albert was a short, cherubic man with a jolly disposition. His wife was his business manager and there were two small golden-haired boys. The Mansers were a pious family—their house was decorated with crucifixes and madonnas and a vial of holy water was used to exorcise evil forces and spray the house during electrical storms. From the studio window we watched a toylike red-and-yellow two-coach train rattle over the bridge below the house. In every direction the views of rolling mountains, great barns, and tiny fields seemed compressed and reduced in scale, as in the bright child world of Albert's paintings. In the prevailing sweetness there was one alien element, a strong smell of manure. "I could not stand that as a boy. It made me sick," Albert said. "That's why I was a failure as a farmer's son. I chose to work in a pastry shop where the smells were sweet."

We had an early lunch of cheese fondue and white wine and at eleven-thirty Albert and I walked down into the town. It was a dazzling spring day and the streets were filled with tourists, most of whom carried cameras. Rows of pastry shops offered local cakes such as *Biberfladen* and *Kräpfli*. Television cameras and sound trucks surrounded the official platform. The entire country was expected to watch for a special reason—the men of Appenzell were going to vote on the controversial question of women's suffrage. The proposed amendment was concerned only with the right of women to vote in local politics, in matters of community housekeeping such as schools and churches and taxation. The question of suffrage in federal elections was resolved in 1971 when a referendum won for women the right to vote in national issues.

Promptly at noon a band pealed out a fanfare and the "flag march" commenced. Boys costumed as medieval heralds carried the flags of the canton and its counties. Each man qualified to vote carried a sword, the symbol of his franchise. The procession moved at a funereal pace but its course was short and the square filled quickly. Though women were forbidden in the square, their faces appeared in the windows of a hotel and the houses around the square. The retiring *Landammann*—governor—opened with a paean to the Swiss "*idealismus* of freedom" which he contrasted to Communism, "the most dangerous element in the European politick." As he talked, my attention fastened on a large flag furling and unfurling over the heads of a seated bishop and two priests, displaying the Appenzell symbol of an upright black bear against a white background with the only color on the banner the bear's bright red tongue and dagger-honed penis; I wondered how it happened that a horny bear on a sexual rampage should be the patriotic symbol of pious, puritanical Appenzellers.

Youths not old enough to vote listened from red-tiled roofs and boys were perched like monkeys in the branches of trees. The new governor was sworn in. Members were elected to the cantonal council. The governor determined results from a show of hands. In one case two candidates received a nearly equal show of hands and several votes had to be taken until the governor came to a decision and announced, "I declare Josef Hirsch elected."

After the disposition of some small matters of finance the assembly arrived at the controversial amendment for women's suffrage. The first speaker, an old man named Josef Keller, supported the proposal. Speaking in the old-fashioned up-and-down singing style of Appenzell, which is known to cover four octaves, he spoke of his shame in explaining to an American lady why the women of Appenzell could not vote. "The eyes of the world are on us, on what we call democracy, a democracy which does not recognize half of its citizens," he said. Disapproving murmurs rose from the square. Aware no doubt of television cameras focused upon him, the white-haired speaker continued to describe a caucus of party leaders (in Appenzell there is only one political party, the Catholic Conservatives) at which eleven men had voted against the amendment and nine for it. "I am proud of the young men who stood up for our women," the old man said. In the square men booed.

A youthful blond man, nattily dressed in stylish sports clothes, rose up in the square and said he would speak for "the young men of Appenzell." I assumed he would support the amendment but I was mistaken. With oratorical bombast he spoke of "women's place in the home, her God-assigned role of homemaker and mother." He was interrupted by a roar of applause that fired his ardor. His voice husky with emotion, he cried out, "*Was gits mit de arme Göfeli wen d'Fraue immer gu wähle müend?*" ("What will happen to our poor little kids if our women are always having to go and vote?"). His voice almost cracking, he repeated two more times the heart-catching phrase, *die arme, arme Göfeli* ("the poor, poor little kids"). From the thunder of applause it was obvious he was voicing the attitude and emotion of the majority. Men stood up and shouted, "We want our women at home with the kids; our kids need their mothers. We don't want politicians in our houses . . ." A middle-aged man, taking a moderate position, said, "We should first slowly acquaint our women with political problems and be sure they understand them before we make such a dangerous move." The old man Josef Keller returned to his feet, shouting, "If we don't pass it this year I promise with God's willingness to be here to urge it next year." From a cluster of young men came loud whistling and the governor rapped for order, shouting, "If you do not stop then I must ask you to leave. In Appenzell whistling is not a custom."

As the speakers continued it became increasingly apparent that the men in the square were acting out the familiar drama which they had played before and would be repeating in years to come. After an hour the governor himself addressed the assembly on the issue and voiced the position of the council, a row of old men on the platform. "I believe," he said, "that the men of Appenzell prefer that women take care of their houses and their children and that they do not waste their time with involvement in politics.

"However, we will ask the women what they want. The issue is not whether women are the equal of men in this matter, but what they themselves want." Speaking now to the TV cameras focused from trucks and rooftops and to the microphones in front of him, the governor proposed that the women of Appenzell be canvassed during the next year and, if enough of them supported the proposal with signatures, then the matter be reconsidered at the next year's Landsgemeinde.

The delaying action he was suggesting seemed little more than a diversion for television, for it was obvious that the governor and the men seated behind him were convinced that the women of Appenzell would not take up the fight, that the issue would languish for another year. I looked at the docile, submissive women's faces in the windows and on the outlying benches and I guessed that the men were probably right.

The vote was taken. A fair-size raising of hands for the amendment was jeered and booed. A huge show of hands against it was greeted with tumultuous and joyful shouting. The governor raised his hand for order and when he had succeeded in silencing the men of Appenzell, he said to them, "I wish to say how happy I am that this correct and proper majority has voted and I thank you."*

One item remained on the agenda, the electing of applicants into Appenzell citizenship. This was not a formality but a matter in which

---

*Appenzell remains the single canton in which women may not vote in cantonal elections. In the canton of Graubunden, where women may vote in federal and state elections, some thirty small and isolated mountain communities continue to deny women participation in local elections.

each case was seriously and carefully weighed. The seven candidates included two Italians, a Czechoslovakian political refugee, one Austrian, and three Swiss from other cantons, each of whom had agreed to pay a citizenship fee ranging from 500 to 5,000 francs, amounts determined by the size of the candidate's family and whether he was a foreigner or a Swiss. A group of voters, opposed to granting citizenship to anyone, voted against all the applicants and each candidate had his own enemies. In the case of one of the Swiss, two showings of hands were necessary before the governor judged the decision in his favor. But eventually all were admitted into citizenship.

By two o'clock it was over. The band led the procession from the square and I watched the bishop shuffle away under the sign of the rutting bear. The electorate of Appenzell quickly dispersed to their homes or to restaurants for holiday dinners.

Albert came to fetch me and said that he had of course voted against the amendment. "It is an illogical idea that women should want to vote. They would have to carry swords and that would be ridiculous."

The Glarus *Landsgemeinde,* dating back to 1387, is known throughout the Western world. Photographs of more than 5,000 voters filling the Glarus marketplace have appeared in American school civic books for as long as I can remember.

Early in April I was informed by Kap Rhyner, a member from Elm of the *Landrat,* the canton legislature, that I would be invited to the event as an *Ehrengäst,* a guest of honor. To be so chosen was a distinction, comparable to a government decoration.

The formal invitation from the governor did not come until a few days before the event on May 4. This, I later learned, was because of a factional dispute over whether I qualified for the honor. It was traditional that *Ehrengäste* be men of either military or political prominence and, since I was neither, certain bureaucratic traditionalists had opposed my nomination. Perhaps an even stronger reason for the resistance was the fact that I had been nominated for the honor by Kap Rhyner and that I was a hereditary citizen of Elm, a village that the status-conscious Glarner patricians considered a rustic enclave of uncultivated peasants. In the end the dispute was resolved by the governor himself, Dr. Fritz Stucki, who ordered the invitation sent. It included a dinner, given by the governor for guests of honor on Saturday evening in the Hotel Glarnerhof.

During the week before I had the opportunity to discuss the *Landsgemeinde* institution with a young liberal journalist in Zurich. He spoke of a growing resistance to the tradition, especially among young people. "They no longer see it as active democracy," he said. "They consider it a carefully planned theater, a script to demonstrate democracy on TV and the radio."

He also spoke of charges of an occasional expedient miscalculating of raised hands which are not actually counted. If a vote is close the *Landammann,* assisted by the councilmen on the platform, decides whether *Yes* or *No* has the majority.

"To all this the people no longer know how to react. A proposal for a new twenty-five million-franc cantonal hospital is passed in three minutes because it is too complex to discuss and understand, and an issue of whether a midwife should receive a retirement pension of six thousand francs may be argued for an hour. The art of talking is important. Certain exhibitionists will get up and spout on anything. Professional talkers, paid to make speeches to promote causes, will talk for or against anything. On the other hand, voters with valid opinions are too shy or frightened to speak. For all these reasons, the people lose interest and stay away. In Glarus there are probably eleven thousand qualified voters but at the most five thousand attend, depending on the issues and the weather.

"The *Landsgemeinde* is very much a male institution and it is well known that the strongest opposition to women's suffrage was in cantons which maintain the tradition. The men were opposed to women voting because they believed it would mean the end of the *Landsgemeinde.*

"The only real democracy, of course, is the secret ballot. But the *Landsgemeinde* makes a nice television and tourist show."

When I arrived on Saturday afternoon Glarus was filled with soldiers and tourists. I had taken a room in the Glarnerhof and when I went downstairs for the evening reception, a handsome lady crossed the lobby. "You must be Professor Kubly," she said in English. "I am Mrs. Stucki. Everyone is looking forward to meeting you."

Mrs. Stucki introduced me to several members of the federal parliament. Governor Stucki entered and greeted me in *Schweizerdeutsch.* He was a tall, rangy man with a strong earnest face and warm twinkling eyes. He was by profession a scholar, a historian. He introduced me to the other guests of honor: Roger Bonvin, a former president of Switzerland and now a federal councillor, a position comparable to an American cabinet post; and two majors who commanded an infantry battalion assigned to Glarus to participate in the Sunday parade. Minister Bonvin was an exuberant, high-spirited little man and the officers were stiff and pompous. One was accompanied by his wife, a tense woman wearing a black dress and pearls. She and Mrs. Stucki were the only women present. Wives are not ordinarily included in the social life of Swiss officials.

The governor himself arranged the seating, placing me between Minister Bonvin and an American-educated senator named Peter Hefti. My two dinner companions could hardly have been more dissimilar. Bonvin had an irrepressible curiosity and spontaneous humor. A native of the Valais, his first language was French; with me he spoke *Schweizerdeutsch.* "Do they have professors of *Schweizerdeutsch* in New Glarus, teaching people how to speak?" he asked. "You have the intonations of a mountain Swiss. Are there mountains in Wisconsin?"

"There's a high hill which separates my farm from the village," I replied. "I climbed it up and down every day to school and I dreamed of building a tunnel under it . . ."

"Yes, that is thinking like a Swiss." Roger Bonvin, a professional engineer, was at this time minister of transportation and energy and an enthusiastic proponent of tunnels. He told me he was an alpinist. "At sixty-eight I still make four thousand meters," he said. He invited me to a convention of mountain guides in his native Valais in two weeks. I told him I was not a mountain climber. "No matter, you must come and let them hear you speak."

Our conversation did not interest Senator Hefti, a fastidiously groomed man wearing a turquoise ring. Speaking precise English very softly, he discussed a proposal before the United States Congress to change the processes of presidential elections from electoral to popular vote. I said I approved the change, that in the electoral system the results were not necessarily the will of the majority of voters.

"Ah, but they are the will of the state, the establishment." I pondered what he meant. At the end of the table the major's wife was addressing me in English, saying, "I hope you write poetry because it is the only English I read."

"But there is a danger in the will of the people," Senator Hefti was saying. "The will of the state is more important. Government must represent the authority of the establishment. Fortunately for you, President Nixon understood that very well."

"But the people are the state," I said.

"There is a big difference. I will illustrate by telling you a story. A Swiss man was taking a seat on a train when the conductor came to inform him that he could not have the seat, that it was reserved for someone else. The passenger protested loudly, saying, 'All men are equal.' The conductor replied, 'Perhaps in heaven men are equal, but in Switzerland we have order.'

"In America the establishment understands this, that it is necessary to have order," the senator concluded, and his words seemed a curious prologue to the next day's demonstration of democracy.

In the morning the sky was dark and threatening and everyone speculated on the weather. At nine o'clock Kap arrived from Elm to escort me to the assembly. "It's going to be a wet one," he said. "But there are advantages. It will keep everyone from talking too long. On a sunny day you can't turn them off."

At ten o'clock church bells began to peal. A military band played a march and the procession started forward, soldiers following the band. In the square the voters of Glarus were already settled on benches. It began to rain. Faces of women and tourists filled the windows of five-storyed gabled houses surrounding the plaza. Kap pointed to a slight, ruddy-faced man who, he said, was the "*Landsgemeinderedner*," the "*Landsgemeinde* orator" who appeared every year to make a speech on a subject chosen by him, and whose right to speak was honored by the governor. He told me the man's name and hearing it I guessed—correctly—that he was another of my relatives.

Governor Stucki declared the assembly convened and then, without ceremony, began a long introduction of me, speaking of my ancestry and my Elm citizenship, my familiarity with the local language and, with hyperbolic flourishes, of my occupation as professor and writer.

As I listened, water was running down the inside of my collar and the dampness was soaking through the newspaper on which I was sitting. At the end of the introduction I was applauded.

The governor then introduced the majors from the United States, Spain, and Czechoslovakia, and when that was finished he administered the oath of citizenship to 4,000 voters in the square.

Unlike one-party Appenzell, Glarus has four major parties, none with a majority. They are the Center Democrats, to which Governor Stucki belonged; the Social Democrats, a left party of industrial workers; the Catholic Conservatives; and the Liberals, to which Kap belonged, and which, despite its name, was of rightist persuasion. Holding his right hand on the sword, the governor declared the *Landsgemeinde* in session. As if on signal the rain stopped. Patches of blue sky appeared over the snow-covered peaks which contained the valley like a shell. Birds swooped over the square.

A financial report was approved and prevailing tax rates were extended for another year. Two judges were elected and sworn in and a law to control the bag limit of fish taken from streams and lakes was passed. The first business on the agenda to arouse discussion was a proposal to increase the salaries of government employees, including teachers. Governor Stucki read a recommendation from the Board of Councillors for a sliding salary increase beginning at eight percent for government employees and rising to ten percent for teachers. Speakers of the Center Democrats supported the recommendation. A Social Democrat argued that the sliding scale was inequitable and asked for an across-the-board eight percent increase. A Liberal Party member wanted the increase for teachers to be twelve percent. "Teachers' salaries in Glarus are among the lowest in Switzerland," he said. "It becomes increasingly difficult to hire good teachers." A Center speaker leaped up to say that Glarus had the lowest paid police chief in Switzerland. "I beg for Professor Kubly to make a note of that," he said, and he was loudly applauded.

The vote rejected a salary raise for the police chief. For other employees the Center proposal for a ten percent increase for teachers and eight percent increase for other employees was unanimously passed.

A new law to control water pollution was unopposed. The perils of contaminated streams and lakes were dramatically described by several speakers. "In this matter," one said, "Glarus is at the very bottom of the Swiss waterfall." Kap pointed to the bleachers where the *Landsgemeinde* orator was seated. "Now he's beginning to stir," Kap said. "It won't be long."

Within moments the fellow was on his feet. The governor beckoned him to the platform and introduced him as a "civic minded citizen." His face was flushed and he was wearing a red necktie. He spoke of streams turning into sewers, of poor gasping fish, and of children infected by bathing. He accompanied his torrent of words with gestures, as if his hands were weaving the web of words he was speaking. "God sent us pure water and we foul it," he shouted. "He sent us fish and we do not let them live. Our beautiful little land is a cess pool ... We are bringing our own Apocalypse," he cried, his voice beginning to crack. He stopped for breath. Before he could begin again the governor stepped forward, saying, "We thank you for your sympathetic views." The crowd applauded wildly and the speaker acknowledged the ovation by raising a hand as he descended from the platform. Because there was no opposition the governor declared the law passed without a vote.

A final and controversial proposal was for an amendment to increase automobile taxes by fifteen percent to provide revenue for road building. The suggested tax hike was supported by the governor and opposed by the president of the Glarus Touring Club, a large, corpulent man named Peter Schlittler. "One day the increase may have to come," Schlittler admitted. "But let's not hurry. Let's think of the burden to the poor auto owner and put the matter aside for further study." The president of the village of Betschwanden responded in favor of the increase. "By his size it is apparent that the touring club president is not in want ..." There was muffled laughter and then loud disapproving whistles that continued until the governor called for order. Kap said, "There is an inviolate rule that issues only are attacked and never personalities. The governor must be shocked. That stupid remark will create sympathy for Schlittler and defeat the proposal."

The vote was close, so close that the show of hands had to be repeated before the governor decided that the tax increase was defeated and its opponents had won. During the debate hardly anyone seemed to notice the dark clouds returning. It started to rain and umbrellas burgeoned like mushrooms.

At twelve-thirty the governor declared the *Landsgemeinde* adjourned. The procession re-formed behind the band and moved slowly through a downpour back to the State House. I heard someone calling my name and a dark-haired woman ran into the street to introduce herself. She was Frau Zogg-Kubli, another relative, and the daughter of the founder of Elm Mineral Springs, Ltd., now managed by her husband, Heinz Zogg. Frau Zogg asked me to dinner on Tuesday and invited Kap also, specifying that he should bring his wife.

We drove through the rain up to Elm for a *Landsgemeinde* meal of veal sausage, mashed potatoes, and stewed prunes, the traditional menu being eaten at the same time in homes and hotels throughout the canton.

26

IN FRONT OF THE MOON

The next morning Kap drove me to Glarus on a mysterious mission. He took me to the courthouse, into the offices of the cantonal archives where the lineage of every family in the canton is documented back through the sixteenth and fifteenth centuries and in certain distin- guished families to the fourteenth and thirteenth centuries. The aston- ishing genealogical studies were begun early in this century by a histo- rian named Johann Kubli, a distant relative, and my own family was one of the most carefully researched.

The archivist, Dr. Josef Müller, and a colleague, Dr. Heinrich Rellstab, a white-haired seventy-five-year-old, were waiting.

"*Herrgott!* What a morning!" said Dr. Müller, an irrepressibly en- thusiastic man. "Eight people named Kubli have been here to ask if they are related to you. One was Frau Zogg. I told her the relationship would take several days to trace, and she said, 'But I can't wait several days. Professor Kubly is coming to dinner and I have to know at once.'"

He handed me a large book bound in brown covers and I opened it and read, "*Stammbaum von Herbert Kubli.*" The book was a meticu- lously documented chronicle of my ancestors and my relationship to several thousand Kublis in the archives. Included were Kublis in

France, Hungary, Holland, South America, Australia, and Cuba. "The blood was always restless," Dr. Rellstab said. The idea for this gift of a family tree had been Kap's. Many persons were involved in its preparation, including Governor Stucki, a historian. Dr. Müller and his staff had worked on it for three months. "Some of the recent New Glarus records are not completed," Dr. Müller said. "My dream is to come to America to finish them."*

I was taken into an empty courtroom and there, unfurled on the floor like a Torah, was an 18-foot-long chart that diagrammed my ancestry with lines descending through the generations to myself.

There was still more. A smaller chart, a caprice of Kap's, documented his own and my own relationship. It revealed that we were kin not once but twice. Through a Kubli-Rhyner alliance a century and a half ago we were sixth cousins and through an Elmer-Zentner alliance of the families of my grandmother and his mother we were seventh cousins. "You see, I always knew it," Kap said. "We are related by incest."

Dr. Rellstab was overcome with laughter. Incest, it turned out, was his research specialty. For forty years he had served as medical recorder in the cantonal hospital and when a child with physical or psychological aberrations was born it had been his duty to trace its genealogy. Since his retirement he had continued a study of "chromosome defects" resulting from village inbreeding and he was preparing a book on the subject. Among deviations he credited to chromosome defects were retardation, insanity, suicide, albinism, night blindness, crossed eyes, and a biological reversion known as "monkey children." "If I see someone in the street with a defect I know at once what family he is from; what his last name is," Dr. Rellstab said. As he spoke I took out a pad and made notes. The old man began to dance with excitement. "Are there others in your family who write with the left hand?" he asked. The two genealogists and Kap were laughing. "You have a chromosome defect! I am not surprised. Your parents had a common ancestor seven generations ago!"

I stopped writing and put away my pad. Assuming he had offended

---

*He did, the next year.

me, Dr. Rellstab said, "It's not necessarily all bad. If you go back far enough in Elm everyone is related several times. Seven generations is rather a long time for Elm. You must understand that good incest produces gifted people, sometimes geniuses."

I tried to feel reassured. I was aware that in the asylums of Glarus and other cantons there were physical and, more frequently, mental cripples whose afflictions were said "to run in families." I knew of Glarus families, some of them affluent, whose eccentricities were spoken of in hushed voices, families with high incidences of retardation, suicide, alcoholism, and schizophrenia, and I knew that such afflictions were stoically accepted as unavoidable conditions of life. In villages like Elm the unfortunate victims were tolerated, accepted, even protected by the community until such time as they might become unmanageable, when they were committed and forgotten. I remembered a cousin who had disappeared in this way and had become a ward of the state.

My three friends were finding a grotesque comedy in such realities. To me this nether limbo of life seemed sprung from the imagination of Hieronymous Bosch. I recalled being frightened as a child by "monkey children," wizened anthropoidic little creatures with baleful eyes who played in the streets because they could not go to school. Perhaps it was true, as Dr. Rellstab was insisting, that there was good and bad incest, that one was an involuntary issue of either and that I was one of the fortunate ones. Who could say by what caprice nature had opted in my favor and how many blighted existences there were to balance the scales? In this new book created for me, what lay hidden between the lines; how many tragedies were contained in the chronology of births and deaths? The unusual gift became in that moment threatening, an ominous Pandora's almanac.

At noon Governor Stucki arrived, driving his own car, to take me to his home in the village of Netstal for lunch. A fine meal of lamb chops, new asparagus, and a salad prepared by Mrs. Stucki was served with a chilled white Neuchatel. During our lively conversation I was astonished to discover that Mrs. Stucki, whom I admired and whose bright sophisticated humor I enjoyed, was against women's suffrage. I should not have been surprised. The men of Glarus were against women's suffrage because they considered it a threat to the *Landsgemeinde*. Even though he was an intellectual, Dr. Stucki could not, as governor, support suffrage. As the governor's wife, Mrs. Stucki would be expected to uphold his position. Nothing else would have been possible.

On the other hand, Mrs. Stucki complained jokingly of a tradition among Glarus men to exclude wives from their social life. "We are always at home," she said. "The canton should buy every wife a television as a public service." She would like, she continued, to attend a party scheduled later in the month to mark the last journey of the little red train from Schwanden to Elm before it was replaced by a bus line. But, as usual, women were not invited. I said that since I was invited and, since Americans were expected to be unorthodox in their social conduct, I would take her as my guest. She thought the idea very funny but the governor did not.

Later in the afternoon the governor took me to the Netstal archives in the basement of the Town Hall and brought out the Kubli files. They contained some interesting items.

According to the records, most Kublis lived, until 1758, in the village of Matt, the first village below Elm. On January 25 of that year a fire destroyed six Matt houses, one of which belonged to Hans Rudolf Kubli, who then moved to Elm and became the progenitor of Elm Kublis. One of the more fascinating chronicles told of a Dutch branch of the family founded by Rudolf Kubli, a first cousin to my grandfather who at age fifteen, in 1814, left Elm to become a foreign mercenary soldier in Germany and in Holland. An apparently prepossessive youth, he caught the attention of Crown Prince Wilhelm, who made Rudolf his personal adjutant. When the prince became King Wilhelm III, Rudolf moved with him to the Royal Palace in The Hague. Rudolf had four sons of whom one, Hendrik, became Royal Housekeeper and another, Wilhelm, Palace Concierge. I remembered that in 1925 the daughter of Wilhelm III, Queen Wilhelmina, made a visit to Elm, ancestral home of the family closely bound to her own for a century.

In the evening I returned to Elm where I was invited to supper at the home of my cousin Jakob. The repast, at eight o'clock after the evening dairy chores, was an entirely male affair. The mother and the grandmother remained in the kitchen and Jakob, his three sons, and I were served in the parlor by a niece named Maria Elmer, a professional waitress from Schaffhausen who was on a holiday visit to her family in

Elm. The entrée was raw smoked bacon for which I had no enthusiasm. There were also potatoes and a green salad. Jakob and his hardworking sons consumed vast quantities of the fat raw meat. Every time I managed to dispose of a piece the waitress was on hand to refill my plate.

The conversation turned to Jacqueline Onassis, whose life continued to be of absorbing interest to the people of Elm. A magazine had reported that Aristotle Onassis had spent a weekend with Maria Callas in Paris.

"Poor Jackie," said Rudi, the eldest son. "He's gone and left her to go back to that singer."

"Well, he is rich enough," said his father. "He can afford two houses and two women."

"Even more," said young Jakob. "He is probably a Mormon."

"A money Mormon," said his father. "With plenty of green cabbage any man can be a Mormon."

The waitress brought a third bottle of wine and Jakob and his sons were growing mildly tipsy. For dessert there was the traditional *Nidelschwung,* great mounds of sweetened whipped cream in meringue shells. When the meal was finished, Maria, preparing to leave, confessed that she was afraid to walk the hundred yards to her parents' house in the dark. It did not, apparently, occur to any one of the Kubli boys to offer to accompany her and with great trepidations she set out alone.

Why, I asked, should Maria be frightened since there was no crime in Elm?

Young Jakob shrugged. "Women," he said contemptuously, "see things at night that are not there."

A few minutes later the telephone rang. No one answered and it continued to ring and finally stopped. Jakob explained it was Maria who had called to let them know she had arrived safely home. By letting it ring three times without answering, the message was conveyed with no charge for the call.

What, I asked, would Maria have done if one or the other of the two households had no phone?

"She would have to come back to tell us she got home all right," Heiri said.

The next day I walked through the village with Kap's six-year-old daughter, Madelene. She and her brother, Hansjörg, who was eight, were fair-haired, handsome children who separately provided exquisitely mannered and ingratiating company. Together they frequently created an eruptive chemistry due, I believed, to jealousy created by Kap's pride in Madelene, who was the more aggressive. On our walk Madelene was a sweetly earnest, informative guide.

A light spring mist was falling and farmers were manuring the fields. Some were spraying it through hoses, filling the air with overpowering fumes. "They have to cook it a little and stir it." Madelene said. We stopped to call on an old Widow Kubli who, whenever I was in Elm, sat at her window watching my movements, observing whom I visited, and fretting when I passed her by. The old woman was working in her garden over which she had spread aged goat manure. She was planting leaf vegetables under the sign of Pisces, the fish, to assure their abundance, she explained. Her root vegetables were already planted under Aries when the moon was upside-down.

At the end of a lane in the old part of the village we came to a well-kept chalet decorated with copper mobiles hanging from the eaves and surrounded by dazzling flower beds. It was the home of Jakob Schneider, an artist whose paintings I had seen in the Hotel Elmer. One especially had impressed me, a large panoramic canvas of Russian soldiers roasting one of their horses in Elm in 1799 when they were escaping from Napoleon's army. I knew that Schneider was supported in part by his wife who worked as a community crafts teacher. Because he did not hold a job the people of Elm considered him indolent. His only advocates in the village were Kap and his sister, Barbara Bässler, who hung his paintings in the hotel where they were for sale.

We knocked on the door and Schneider opened it. He was a small, nervously shy man who stammered after I introduced myself. He called his wife, a strong handsome woman with a slight limp as a result of childhood polio. I remembered Kap saying that the Schneiders always paid their bills promptly, that if they had not, their position in the community would be untenable. Schneider showed us his pictures in a variety of styles. There were sunlit impressionist landscapes and bright floral still lifes. One picture caught my attention. It showed a pink horse and a pink colt flying like two Pegasuses through a wintery landscape. I asked why he had painted the horses in that color and he replied, "Because that is as I saw them in my mind."

"Ah, yes, the pink horses," Kap said at lunch. "The people say he paints horses pink so he must be foolish. In our village pictures have no value and serve no practical purpose; they are a childish preoccupation. So walls are decorated with ribbons won by cows at fairs, with shooting festival medals, portraits of grandmothers, and religious pictures. Of course, if Schneider became rich and famous everyone would buy a picture." Quoting Schiller, Kap said, "The night passes slowly out of the valleys."

The event for which I'd remained in Elm was dinner that evening in the home of Heinz Zogg to celebrate the discovery by his wife of her kinship to me. Though the Zoggs lived in the town of Glarus, Herr Zogg's position in Elm as manager of its factory was similar to that of a medieval duke, and the invitation was like a summons to court.

Herr Zogg was a lean, sun-tanned man with gray hair and bright blue eyes. His wife, slender with dark eyes and hair, had a youthful vivacity that was subdued in the presence of her husband. Their patrician house was elegantly furnished with French furniture and alpine landscapes. Three bachelor sons were present. None, the father complained, was interested in the family business, and one was studying to be a clergyman.

The future pastor mixed drinks. Herr Zogg turned the conversation to the consuming passion of his life, the Rotary Club. He was Rotary district governor for Switzerland and Lichtenstein and boasted of devoting 75 percent of his time to the organization. He addressed clubs in Austria, Germany, and Sweden; was leaving in a few days for a Rotary congress in Australia; and in October would chair a governors' meeting at international headquarters in Evanston, Illinois. "We have six hundred thousand members in one hundred and ninety-two countries," he said excitedly. "Rotary is Number One in quality! Only the most distinguished, the best men of the world are admitted. There are a hundred clubs in Switzerland. Of course, here in Glarus we are always facing problems in membership, to keep up the high quality. We accept only men of the best society . . ."

As he went on, something became clear to me. His preoccupation with Rotary was his escape from loneliness. Membership gave him the illusion of 600,000 brother friends, a purpose for fleeing from the strictures of life in Glarus as frequently as possible. Rotary was a fulfillment, an identity, an alliance with a world outside the confining valley.

Dinner was the *Landsgemeinde* menu of *Kalberwurst,* mashed potatoes and stewed prunes served with fine French wines. When it was over and we said Goodnight, Herr Zogg said, "We're glad you came. We wanted you to know that here in Glarus we are not behind the moon."

27

FURTHER JOURNEYS
WITH KAP

THE VALAIS

At the Glarus *Landsgemeinde* Roger Bonvin invited me to a festival of mountain guides in Fiesch, a village in his native canton of Valais.

Kap suggested we combine the festival with a spring journey through Valais. Arrangements were made for the children to stay with relatives so Pia could come with us. "You're going to see things you'll never forget," Kap promised. Our route to Canton Valais crossed three other cantons and each border crossing included a snow-banked mountain pass.

The Oberalp Pass took us into Uri, where Kap pointed out doors in the mountain walls behind which were military installations with munition depots, hospitals, and offices. The Susten Pass brought us into Berne, where we descended through a spiral of tunnels into the Haslital, a fertile green valley surrounded by mountains 12,000 feet high. We made our first stop in the valley's main town, Meiringen.

In the late nineteenth and early twentieth centuries, when travelers pursued the leisurely pleasures of mountain climbing, alpine botany and—peculiar to this valley—butterfly collecting, Meiringen was a popular resort. Now the moribund hotels were filled with military officers on mountain maneuvers. The hotel in which we had reservations was called the Victoria and had been modernized.

Meiringen's historic attraction is a church described in guidebooks as "the Swiss Pompeii." As Pompeii was covered by cinders and ash, so the Meiringen church, dating from the eleventh century, was frequently inundated by floods and stone and mud avalanches catapulting down the Hasliberg. After each inundation the town was rebuilt. Archeologists have traced seven different architectural styles mounted, like Babel's tower, one upon another. The present late-Gothic church was built in the seventeenth century.

Kap guided us up through the architectural *mélange,* beginning in a dank deep cave. After our eyes had adjusted to the darkness we saw that we were in a crypt carved from stone with broken arches, an altar and a lectern, a place like the catacombs of early Christians. We climbed to the level above, a Romanesque stone church with a high altar facing the east and an oriental feeling of a synagogue or a mosque. Fragments of frescoes from the Old Testament remained on the walls.

At the top of the tower of churches, soaring as if buoyed by angels, was a vast sanctuary made of wood. The Bernese are builders in wood and the master of the Meiringen church, Melker Gehren, is one of the most renown. Slightly elliptical Grecian columns of wood, painted with ox blood to a deep Siena red, stood more than 30-feet high. A canopied ceiling was decorated in oriental motifs. Kap strode over the floor and found it measured forty-six by eighteen paces. A hidden organist commenced to play, filling the vast space with the lordly measures of Bach's *D Minor Canzona,* and Kap said the church was popular for music festivals because "wood is best for sound; it softens and magnifies the tones instead of smashing them." The celestial music filling the church might have been celebrating the triumph of human faith. "They never gave up," Kap said, his voice awed. "Each generation triumphed over its own catastrophe. The people believed God was testing their faith and they would not be defeated."

When we left the church, the valley was covered with black clouds. The wind whistled and claps of thunder reverberated through the mountains. A waterfall leaped out from a cliff and appeared to be pouring over the roofs of the town. The moisture spattering our faces might have been rain.

Next morning we crossed the Grimsel Pass in a raging blizzard. Kap stopped to take some headache pills and promised that the weather would be sunny in the Valais. "I can tell by the pressures," he said. "My head is an infallible weather bureau."

Driving into the blinding swirl, I was able to make out the ghostlike surface of a lake on which floated islands of green ice. "Dammit!" Kap cursed. "One of the great engineering feats of Europe and we can't see a thing." He described Grimsel Lake, formed by two hydroelectric dams. "The dams hold back one hundred million cubic meters of water which is conducted in pipes to turbines down in the valley. One of the dams is curved like the theater at Epidaurus. The other has a causeway auto road to the Grimsel Hospice which replaces an old inn covered by the lake."

We waited for a traffic light at the entrance to a one-lane tunnel and when it turned green we passed under a glacier and emerged into the Valais, where the storm was as violent as in Berne. We descended cautiously through the invisibility until, suddenly, we drove into sunlight. Kap let out a bellow—his built-in weather antenna had proven infallible.

We faced a stunning panorama. A cornice of white peaks encircled us. Below, the road coiled back and forth across the slopes. To our left was the glittering Rhone Glacier. Its slowly moving ice descended into the valley like a soiled white apron. A creek of melting water trickling from its base was the beginning of the Rhone River.

We rolled down into the narrows of the valley and into the village of Gletsch—the name means glacier—crossroads of two famous passes, the Grimsel and the Furka. It was a barren treeless place where snow still lay in shaded places. There was a railway station and a hotel and a small English church, all boarded up. An attendant at a gas station was the only visible inhabitant.

We stopped and walked up through a meadow of flowers along the gurgling creek, so narrow we could leap over it. Clumps of cowslip were mirrored like narcissi in cobalt waters where dark trout lazily swam. Looking up into the mountains, Kap said, "Here it is! The geographic heart of Europe." The river springing forth at our feet flowed west and south to Geneva and into France and the Mediterranean. Behind us, fifteen miles to the east, another trickle turned into the headwaters of the Rhine flowing east and north. Over the Furka Pass cascaded the waters of the Reuss, joining the Rhine before flowing through Germany and Holland into the North Sea. To the southeast glacial waters began their descent to the Ticino River which, emptying into the Po in Italy, flowed into the Adriatic. Sixty miles to the east were the headwaters of the Inn, the main tributary of the Danube which flows into the Black Sea. "This is the beginning, the parting of the waters," Kap said. "All of Europe is watered by these glaciers."

We coasted down the valley beside the rippling brook. After an hour we arrived at Visp, turn-off point for Zermatt, and decided to go there.

I had been in Zermatt eighteen years before when the only transportation into the valley was by train. Now a road of sorts had been built but it was said to be perilously narrow and without guardrails, so we decided to leave the car in Visp and go by railroad. The narrow-gauge combination adhesion and rack train creaked past roaring waterfalls up through a valley so narrow the sun had already set inside.

The twenty-two mile journey took ninety minutes. The train rolled through pine forests and into green meadows. It crossed a stream and curved to the left and, suddenly, before us, jutting into clear blue skies, was the slightly askew snow-streaked pyramid of the Matterhorn, the most majestic mountain in Switzerland.

In the 1950s Zermatt was a single street of 1,200 inhabitants; a disorderly ghetto of Victorian hotels and brown chalets mounted on mice-inhibiting slate discs, surrounded by manure piles. Now it was changed. There was an auto parking lot at the lower end of the town and, as a result of a typhoid scare in 1963, there were fewer manure piles; those that remained were covered with disinfecting lime and ludicrously resembled great chocolate cakes sprinkled with powdered sugar. A river, fed by three glaciers, gushed through the town in a straight concrete chute. The shaded eastern slope, which I remembered as meadows of grazing cows, was an overbuilt suburb. The town boomed with the cacophony of construction, with reverberating hammers, creaking derricks, and roaring steam shovels and concrete mixers raising new hotels. They seemed to be everywhere. We found rooms in one of them, a jerry-built catacomb with sagging floors, a malfunctioning elevator, and walls so thin we could hear conversations in adjoining rooms.

We called at the government tourist office where a herd of black-and-white goats, bells tinkling, passed a window. "My goats," said the director, Constant Cachin. "In the old days goat-keepers drove their herds up the street to pastures in the morning and back down in the evening. The goat procession became part of our tradition, a daily event. So when farmers sold their land for building sites and ceased keeping goats, I rented a herd which is driven through the town twice a day. You see how things change. Those fifty-four goats are on government payroll."

Zermatt's 3,000 citizens pay no taxes. Revenues come from a tourist surtax of a franc a day and from the railroad and mountain cable cars which are municipally owned and controlled. "Some years," said Mr. Cachin, "revenues exceed government costs and property owners are paid dividends."

The magnet which lures travelers to Zermatt is the Matterhorn. For more than a century the lordly pyramid has been as ominously irresistible to mountain climbers as sirens' songs to Odysseus, and many who have responded to its call have been destroyed by it. Four of the first seven conquerors of the solitary peak never descended to enjoy their fame.

The year was 1865, a time when Switzerland's most zealous mountaineers were Britons. Though most of the surrounding peaks had been scaled, no one had climbed the Matterhorn. A young English climber, Edward Whymper, resolved to be the first. Jean Carrel, a Zermatt guide frequently employed by Whymper, decided he did not want to share the conquest with an Englishman and arranged to climb the Matterhorn's south wall with another guide, Jean Baptiste Bich. Angered by Carrel's betrayal, Whymper collected three other Englishmen, Douglas Hadow, Lord Francis Douglas, and the Rev. Charles Hudson, a climber famous for having made the first ascent of Mont Rosa in 1855. The four Englishmen engaged one of Zermatt's other guides, Peter Taugwalder, who believed an ascent could be made on the mountain's north wall, facing Zermatt. Taugwalder brought along his young son Peter, and the Rev. Hudson brought his personal guide, Michel Croz.

The race was on. The party of seven, divided into rope-bound groups of three and four, set out on July 13. That night the climbers camped at an elevation of 11,020 feet and the next day in excellent weather they reached the Matterhorn's peak at 1:40 P.M. They turned back almost at once. On the way down Hadow slipped, knocked over Croz and, dragging Hudson and Douglas with him, plunged over a precipice. The rope tore and the three Englishmen and Croz hurtled down the 4,000-foot north wall to their deaths. Three days later, on July 17, Carrel and Bich reached the summit and safely descended. An uneasy superstition spread that the violated mountain, like an enraged Olympian deity, had taken its revenge on the lives of the first trespassers. The organizer and only English survivor, Edward Whymper, lived until 1911, a haunted man.

To comprehend the premonitory allure of the Matterhorn, a visit to Zermatt's cemeteries is necessary. In the morning we walked through the cemetery by the river below Bahnhofstrasse. Graves were being decorated for the feast of Corpus Christi and the cemetery was crowded with townspeople and curious visitors. The day was wet and gray; the Matterhorn was hidden behind a wall of dark clouds. The cemetery was divided into two areas, one for Zermatt's dead and the other for the *Ausländer.* Most decorated were the graves of mountain guides and among them the most frequent name was Taugwalder. On one stone were sculptured profiles of the two Peter Taugwalders, father and son, and the epitaph said, *Erstersteiger des Matterhorns 1865.*

The section for "strangers" was an international pantheon of catastrophic dead. Epitaphs in a variety of languages, in German, French, English, and Norwegian told the tragic stories:

Passed into the fuller life from the Matterhorn at dawn.

Abgestürzt am Matterhorn.

An unknown climber found on the Matterhorn 1948.

Gefallen am Matterhorn.

Vernon Allen Crawford, Jr. Denver, Colorado, killed on the Matterhorn. I will lift up my eyes into the mountains.

André Rosenberger, 21. A mon Dede! Mon fils, suite d'un accident, son inconsolable Papa.

William Andrew Bell, James Ian McKean, James William Ogilvie, friends from Oxford killed together on the Matterhorn.

Geoffrey Christopher Gregson, 22. In the sight of the universe they seem to die.

On and on it went and there seemed no end. Carved into the stones were the outlines of picks and axes and coils of rope and in some cases the actual rusted iron tools were fastened to the stones or laid on the graves like warrior's shields.

We climbed a slope above the town to an English church inside which the Rev. Charles Hudson, Vicar of Skillington, was entombed and in a small cemetery outside all the interred were English. The stones bore the symbolic picks and rope coils and they said:

In memory of Frederick Borckhardt who perished on the Matterhorn during a terrible snow storm.

Edward Backhouse, to his fatherland translated unaware.

Griselda Carr, killed in a crevice.

Ellen Emma Sampson, Middlesex, killed by falling stones.

Looking down on the stones, I wondered what it was that forfeited the young lives, whether it was the mountain or the death-seeking climbers themselves. I spoke of this to Kap, who was an accomplished climber, and he said, "A climber is testing. The mountain is a challenge to his strength and his judgment and there can be no rest until he has conquered."

There can be no rest. The phrase haunted me. Like every climber to whom I have tried to speak of this, Kap was being mystically obscure.

"They are striving for the ultimate in the universe and within themselves," he said. Perhaps that was it. The "ultimate" was death and rest from a consuming and extraordinary passion.

Next to the English church is an alpine museum and here a collection of grisly memorabilia details the grim chronicles. Preserved under glass are battered shoes, torn ropes with shattered strands, blood-spattered neck cloths and tatters of clothing, pipe stems, brandy casks, petrified loaves of bread, picks and axes, all possessions of the victims and each one telling a separate story. Here is the rope that snapped in 1865 and beside it a boot worn by Douglas Hadow; Michel Croz's hat and rosary; and Edward Whymper's pick on which is inscribed, *Quand j'ai employé ce piolet, j'ai toujours réussi.*

There is a sketch of the fatal party's arrival on the Matterhorn summit by Gustave Doré and a composite photograph put together later of the seven climbers against a background of the snow-covered peak. Hudson, Douglas, and Hadow are elegant young Englishmen dressed in cutaways for a garden tea party. Whymper and the three guides wear rough climbing togs and carry picks and axes and the guides are smoking pipes.

There are haunting photos of other climbers. A Fräulein Irmgard Schiess, who died on the Matterhorn in 1929 has a lovely wistful face with dreaming eyes and is shown wearing a man's shirt and a foulard properly turned. Other pictures show royal climbers, King Albert and Queen Elisabeth of Belgium and Queen Marguerite of Italy who, judging from their large and fashionable entourages could not have gone very far up the mountain. There is also a photograph of a priest-climber, the Abbé Carrel who planted an iron cross on the Matterhorn's peak in 1902, possessing it for Jesus Christ. As a metaphor his act becomes the most chilling detail of all, transforming as it does the climber's goal to a symbolic impalement on the cross, a dual pursuit of death and of God. It is a small irony that the pious Catholics of Zermatt do not tolerate climbing on the sabbath. Since no guide will hire himself out on a Sunday undaunted climbers set out by themselves.

There are pictures of famous guides, including three from a family named Perrin, who died in the mountains in 1930, 1933, and 1936; and the two Peter Taugwalders, father and son, and two more Taugwalders, Franziskus, who died on the Dent Blanche in 1929, and

Rudolf, who lost his feet and fingers by frostbite on a mountain in Peru in 1908. Mountain guiding is a traditional profession of Zermatt's able-bodied men and the Taugwalders were among the most famous. Looking at a portrait of Rudolf, an old man with stumped legs and fingerless hands, I remembered that I had met him, that in my first visit to Zermatt my companion and I lived in the house of his son Alfons, also a guide. I remembered the grandfather as a handsome, deaf, eighty-five-year-old man who wore gloves and walked stiffly on feet carved from wood, who nodded whenever we met, and greeted me in English. There were stories that he had scaled peaks in North and South America and in Hawaii, that he had had a love affair with an English lady who climbed mountains to be alone with her dashing guide.

28

THE TAUGWALDERS

In 1951 my companion was a student known as Sandy. We arrived in Zermatt on a clear and cold July afternoon. Tourists filled the streets and at the station we were told there were no rooms in the town.

I had a letter from a friend in New Glarus to the keeper of a pension where we hoped to find lodging. We found the pension, a large chalet called *Die Sonne,* at the upper end of the town. The owner, Stanislav Kronig, was a tall and handsome old patriarch who was wearing several layers of sweaters. He poured *Kirschwasser* to warm us and with regret told us his fourteen rooms were filled, that there was space only in an unheated loft for students where a bed cost two francs. I said it was too cold to sleep in a loft and that, in any case, I was not partial to dormitory accommodations. The old man was sympathetic and said he would seek a room for us. He telephoned some hotels and all were filled. Even the Zermatt hospital had rented its empty beds to tourists.

He spoke to his cook, a plump little woman who asked how long we planned to stay. I replied four days. She said she had a room for three in her house, which she preferred not to let for less than a week because she was too busy cooking to change linens. Herr Kronig urged her to give it to us and, as a favor to him, she agreed.

She led us to the house. Her son, Paulus, aged four, plump and wearing an embroidered blouse, trotted along. We climbed some high and rickety outside stairs to a large room with three huge beds covered with feather ticking that looked like baby blimps. Little Paulus started to giggle and so did his mother, who suggested that if we explored the town we might find a *Fräulein* for the extra bed. I said if that came to pass and the weather did not warm up I might persuade the *Fräulein* not to use the empty bed, and Paulus whooped with laughter and so did his mother.

We had barely settled on terms when an excited neighbor lady came running up the stairs, announcing that she had a French couple with children who wished to stay two weeks. The intruder, introduced as Madame Taugwalder, explained in French that she had only one free room and it was too small to accommodate the French family. I could see our new landlady turning downcast at the thought of losing a rental with no linens to change for two weeks. Without consulting us the two ladies agreed on an exchange. The French family, waiting outside, would have the room that had been ours for a moment and we would be given Madame Taugwalder's. On the way out Madame Taugwalder explained that her house was almost filled by fourteen mountain-climbing French girls and we would be the only men. The two ladies whooped bawdily. Wouldn't we like that? I expressed some apprehension and the two ladies and Paulus were so convulsed with merriment that I was afraid the trembling stairs would collapse on the French family waiting below.

Sandy, who spoke French, offered to go with Madame Taugwalder to look at the room. He returned in minutes to report it was a good exchange, that the room was small and clean, and that there was a bathroom, which was not the case in the house of Paulus's mother. By this time word had spread through the crowded *quartière* that two young Americans were moving in with fourteen French girls and as we walked the narrow alley to the Taugwalder house, women's heads popped out of windows and voices cried, "*Très drôle!*"

The Taugwalder house, called the Chalet Diane, was new and ingeniously built over a waterfall. A foaming mountain torrent channeled into a metal tube turned a waterwheel which drove a generator which powered a shop on the first floor where, Madame Taugwalder explained, her husband, a mountain guide, and their oldest son made climbers' shoes and other mountaineering equipment. I lay on my bed to rest while Sandy returned to the station to get our bags. Suddenly I was aroused by a shattering roar, a clap of thunder that shook the house. I ran out. No one seemed to have heard the Olympian peal. Some youths carrying pails, on their way to a milk station, said it was not thunder that I had heard but an avalanche on the Matterhorn, a frequent occurrence in summer when the sun loosened high snow.

It was dark and beginning to rain when Sandy, harried and flushed, returned with our baggage on a hired cart, pulling it against a descending stream of cows and goats that not only refused to make way for him but twice butted the cart upside down. Madame Taugwalder called me to the telephone. It was Stanislav Kronig, saying that even though he had not been able to give us a room in his house, he was expecting us to take our meals with him.

We walked in the rain to the Pension Sonne. The small dining room, which looked out on its own waterfall, was crowded and, next to the kitchen, steaming warm. We had a table near the door which, whenever someone entered, banged in the wind and let the storm lash through. The food was cheap and, as it turned out, good. Most of the climbers were Swiss and all appeared young. They arrived wearing heavy clothes and carrying ice axes, ropes, and backpacks.

The door blew open and a young man entered, a bloody bandage about his head like a character in a school play about Valley Forge. He was followed by a companion who boasted how he had rescued his friend from a 50-foot crevice. "He had good luck," said Stanislav of the wounded one. "He only split his head." The old man hovered over our table, shaking his head, proclaiming to the guests, "Isn't it wonderful? His first time in Switzerland and listen to him speak." Cheese fondue was the house specialty. Almost everyone was eating it and the room smelled like a combination cheese factory and distillery. "I will personally make you a fondue you will never forget," Stanislav promised.

He set a carafe of white wine on the table and disappeared. In a half-hour he returned, bearing a great bowl of Kirsch-laced bubbling cheese and a second bowl of small cubes of dry bread. He set the fondue on a lamp and stood proudly by, watching us eat.

It was more alcoholic than any fondue I could remember and delicious. Our host kept pouring Kirsch, urging us to drink to aid our digestions. Digestion was giving me some concern—the melted cheese stuck to the roof of my mouth and I imagined it glued to the walls of my stomach. Not wanting to hurt the old man's feelings I persevered, aware of my increasing drunkenness. Finally I gave up and asked for something "nonalcoholic" to eat. The old man laughed all the way to the kitchen and returned with a plate of veal and potatoes. The fondue bowl was still half-filled and Sandy kept with it, making it his entire meal.

The room had grown unbearably hot and when we finished eating we left. On the way out I saw Paulus licking the fondue bowl in the kitchen and I wondered how drunk he was.

At the Chalet Diane we were unable to get to our room because the stairway was blocked by a mule being shod. Nailing on the iron shoes was Roland Taugwalder, a short and finely built young man, the eldest of the five Taugwalder children. We turned back for a walk through the village and passed crowded cafes and bars displaying signs that read, "*Hier gibts Fondue.*" The odor of melting cheese hung in the air.

We entered a bar where a German woman was playing a piano and singing. After a quarter-hour Roland Taugwalder appeared in the doorway looking for us, eager to apologize for the mule in the doorway. He joined us for beer and, speaking a halting English which he said he had learned from his grandfather, he told us that his father, Alfons, was not at the moment in Zermatt but up on a mountain installing a cookstove in a youth camp. The stove was forged in the shop and he had taken it up on donkeyback. It was a six-hour climb and he would return the next day.

Roland was anxious to tell us of himself, of what he called "the dilemma in my life." He was twenty-one years old and had to decide whether to leave the valley and become an artist or remain in Zermatt and be a mountain guide. He had studied art for three years in Berne and had come home to work in his father's shop to make money to continue his education. "My mother is a strong woman," he said. "She wants me to leave, to be an artist, and my father expects me to follow the family tradition and be a guide. So I have become a controversy between them." A brother, Sylvester, seventeen, had already made his break from Zermatt and was studying pharmacy in Berne. There were also two sisters and a younger brother, Roger, who would celebrate his thirteenth birthday the next day. "I have a dream to go to America," Roland confided. "In America I believe it is better for artists than in Switzerland. I have invented a new type cleat for mountain shoes which I hope to patent. But a patent costs two thousand francs! Perhaps I could sell it in America. Do you know the cost of a patent in the United States?" I did not, but I said I would find out. The girl at the piano was singing the Marlene Dietrich ballad, "Ja, so bin ich" and Roland began singing the lines along with her in a strong tenor voice and people came in from the street to listen.

The next morning Sandy and I took the rack and pinion railway up the Gornergrat. The car climbed up through flower-carpeted slopes like heavenly meadows painted by Fra Angelico. Over them hovered clouds of insects mating the blooms, fulfilling their brief role in the natural cycle. As we moved higher the varieties changed, the blossoms were smaller and more delicately hued and, when we entered into the snowy upper slopes, clusters of furry edelweiss appeared in crevices.

From the 10,000-foot summit we looked across a sweeping crescent of even higher peaks and, towering over them like their king, the dark symmetrical shape of the Matterhorn. Looking at it face to face, the thrust of its challenge became clear and I felt its thrall on my imagination and in my spirit.

But I am a vertigo-prone nonclimber and I tried to dispel the perilous allure by occupying myself with trivialities, by concentrating on young people skiing over the slopes, on furry marmots standing upright on ledges watching me watching them, on some black ravens gliding smoothly with the wind currents, on two black-robed nuns who, supporting one another in the slippery snow, appeared to be dancing. Yet my eyes were drawn back to the mountain and its irrevocable spell.

We lunched in a mountain-top inn and when we were finished the sun had vanished. Fog covered everything and even the Matterhorn had disappeared. I was relieved, and happy to board the descending train.

We arrived to a great excitement in the Chalet Diane. Alfons, called "Pasha" by his children, had returned in the afternoon with his donkey.

Spent by his journey he had gone at once to bed and ordered his supper served there. When he was told we were back he summoned us into his bedroom.

As in a painting by Rembrandt, the light illuminating the room seemed to come from the radiant figure in the center of the huge bed. Pasha was all technicolor—ruddy-cheeked, brown-skinned, blue-eyed, black moustachioed—a glowing, vigorously handsome man. The dark-paneled walls around him were decorated with chamois heads and deer antlers, with guns and shooting trophies, and religious pictures. There was a clutter of books and journals, of pipe racks and tobacco jars and a radio.

The family was gathered about the bed, participating in a court as if Pasha were a Greek warrior triumphantly returned from Troy. His voice seemed to subdue even the waterfall beneath the house. He told us he had made over a hundred trips up the Matterhorn and more trips up other mountains than he was able to count. He had guided climbers from twenty-five countries and his favorites were Americans because, he said, "They are so casual about climbing. No fuss, no excitement, no long preparation. Just let's get on with it. An American student came to me and said, 'I want to climb that stone.'" Pasha laughed. "That stone," he bellowed, "was the Matterhorn. An American lady asked me, 'What's the name of that mountain?' I told her it was the Jungfrau. 'But the Jungfrau is in the canton of Berne,' the lady said. 'True,' I said. 'But she's here on a fortnight's holiday like everyone else.'" Pasha laughed so hard the bed rattled and his children, who must have heard the stories many times, laughed with him.

The laughter ran down and Pasha assumed a magisterial tone. "The first professional guide in Zermatt was a Taugwalder and there have been Taugwalders on the mountains since the thirteenth century," he said. "Peter, who guided the first Matterhorn ascent, was my father's cousin. Of my father's four sons I am the only one who remained in Zermatt. During the war I was commissioned by the army to teach mountain climbing to Alpine troops. After the war I had an illness and I opened the forge downstairs. Many of my picks are shipped to America."

He paused and his eyes moved over the room and rested on Roger. "I have three sons," Pasha resumed with renewed vigor. "One is already gone from Zermatt and another"—he was looking at Roland—"talks of leaving." I observed Madame Taugwalder listening silently and I tried to comprehend her thoughts. She was a stranger to the valley, having come from another part of the canton, and mountaineering was not in her blood. Moved by a mother's apprehension, she was doing what she could to turn her sons toward other professions. Pasha's eyes turned to the golden-haired Roger, obviously his favorite, and he said, "There will always be a Taugwalder on the Matterhorn."

There was a silence, which I broke to speak of the guns and shooting trophies. "Tell about the rabbits," Roger begged and Pasha, chuckling slyly, began, "You mean the time I saw two rabbits together and had only one bullet? Well, what I did was aim between them. The frightened rabbits turned and they ran in opposite directions around a rock and behind the rock they ran into each other and were stunned and I got them both." Everyone, including the mother, was laughing.

The next morning we said goodbye to the Taugwalders. Madame asked us to sign her guest book and in it she proudly pointed out the signatures of the Prince and Princess Hohenzolleren of Prussia who had stayed in the Chalet Diane during a skiing holiday. I wondered if they had our room over the waterwheel and how they fared in the bathroom.

Roger accompanied us to the station, pulling our bags in a cart. We met a band of scouts, small boys and girls in uniforms carrying backpacks, marching brusquely behind adult leaders toward the Matterhorn. They carried flags and they were singing. I overheard a little girl, whose eyes were raised to the mountain, interrupt her song and say to her companion, "Just look! How beautiful it is!"

When we said goodbye at the station, Roger said, "Next time you come to Zermatt I will guide you."

Now, two decades later, I was confident I could lead Kap and Pia to the Chalet Diane. I was mistaken. The *quartière* where I thought it should be had, like all of Zermatt, grown larger and crowded. The Pension Sonne was shuttered. Old Stanislav Kronig, a neighbor said, had died a very rich man. We explored a maze of paths and when I could not locate the stream and the waterwheel I began to think the Chalet Diane had disappeared. I went to a public phone and called

Constant Cachin at the tourist office, and he assured me it was still there, in the same place, that we simply hadn't found the right path. He gave directions, beginning at a public fountain on Bahnhofstrasse, and he told me Alfons was retired from mountain guiding and was a judge.

We found the house over the waterfall almost at once and I knocked on the door. Madame Taugwalder answered. She had changed little in appearance. I explained who I was and she invited us into the parlor. and I recognized the chamois heads, the religious shrines, and the shooting trophies. Pasha entered and greeted us. He was heavier and somewhat ponderous but still handsome and lustily loquacious. It was obvious neither of the Taugwalders remembered me. Madame got out her guest book and verified my claim by finding my name. They appeared delighted by our visit and Pasha poured glasses of homemade "pernod" which tasted like absinthe and was pungently sweet. I remembered that in several Swiss cantons, Valais among them, absinthe was blamed for a high incidence of mental retardation; that its sale had been illegal since 1910; that the people made and consumed the illicit brew themselves and called it "pernod" after a French trade name. It was also known as "goat milk" because of its white color when mixed with water.

I asked about the children. All were married, Madame replied. She went on to tell us that Roland, with whom I had kept up a desultory correspondence for several years, was a locksmith in Boudry, near Neuchatel. Sylvester, the son I'd never met, was a pharmacist in Basel, and Roger, the handsome youth who promised to guide me up a mountain, was a lawyer in Sion and the father of two children. Pasha's boast that there would always be a Taugwalder on the Matterhorn had not been fulfilled.

Reading my thoughts, he said, "Today I would not permit a son to be a guide. In the old days a *Führer* was the most respected man in the community. Now he is nothing, only a *garcon* for carrying picks." His voice rose; he seemed angry. "Today ski instructors are the admired ones and most of them are foreigners."

Madame brought photographs of her sons and daughters and their children. Roger, thirty-one years old, was bald and his features were set in an earnest mien of ambition and success; his two babies were as radiantly golden-haired and blue-eyed as he himself once had been.

The merry twinkle I remembered was gone from Roland's eyes and a look of resignation had taken its place.

Pasha poured more pernod. "The old days are over," he said. "We have new times and new people. It is another generation. I'm sure you have noticed all the Japanese in our streets. They are not interested in climbing. They like to ski and they ride up the slopes."

We said goodbye and he apologized for not having recognized me. "After you are sixty," he said, "you remember clearly only the good days of your youth."

29

A HUNDRED YEARS
LATER THAN THE WORLD

The next day was the feast of Corpus Christi and we were on our way to the *Lötschental,* a high valley in the northeastern Valais where the holy day is observed with a procession of soldiers known as "Grenadiers of God."

On the way we stopped at Raron, a rustic village in the churchyard of which the poet Maria Rainer Rilke is buried. The church stands on a rocky pinnacle above the village. We climbed on foot up the steep path past dark chalets covered with red roses, breathing in deeply the meld of roses, new hay, and fermenting manure. It began to rain slightly and when we arrived, breathless, in the churchyard, we saw a woman and her young son planting begonias on the poet's grave which lay against the church wall. She was preparing it, she told us, for a commemoration on Sunday when many poets would arrive on a pilgrimage. She was not familiar with the poet whose grave she was hired to tend by a rich countess from Sass-Fee, fifteen miles to the south. Carved on the stone covering the grave was an epitaph that Rilke himself had written:

Rose, o reiner Widerspruch, Lust
Niemandes Schlaf zu sein unter soviel Lidern*

---

*Rose, oh pure contradictions, yearn to be nobody's sleep under so many lids.

303

The poetically ambiguous lines, difficult to translate, seem to speak of the immortality of a poet's songs. What they appear to say is, "Behind the bloom of his poems, the poet disappears, becomes nothing, sleeps a sleep that no one sleeps."

Inside the old church we discovered a Gothic Last Judgment fresco crowded with bodies popping out of graves and shepherded by celestial praetorians toward either a smoking hell or a jubilating paradise. It reminded me irreverently of reveille in a nudist camp and Kap, observing that none of the resurrected had genitals, said it depressed him to think they would probably have no use for them in either place. We heard a roaring clatter which seemed to come down from the heavens and, rushing outside, we saw a train a thousand feet above emerge from one of the tunnels of the Lötschberg and curve around a ledge toward Brig and the Simplon.

We followed the Lonza River up five steep miles to the Lötschen Valley. I remembered that in an earlier journey the road ended and that my companion and I entered the valley on foot through a short tunnel inside of which, bowered in fresh flowers, was a madonna and above her, carved in stone, the words, "Wanderer, greet me. I bless you."

The year was 1957 and I had been drawn to the valley by some wooden masks in a Zurich museum. The terrifyingly demonic faces were carved, painted, and fitted with horse's hair and teeth by the people of the valley to exorcise winter's evil spirits at their carnival preceding Lent. I remembered that in winter the valley's 1,500 pious Catholics were cut off from the world by avalanches of snow which destroyed telephone lines, that the snow fell so deeply it was necessary to tunnel from house to house.

That summer of my visit I had the sense of entering into a pastoral Elysium inhabited by a race of vigorous men and women, of lean, noble old people and bonnie pink children all working together in sunlit fields. Lean, angular, and short of stature with brown lined faces, the people moved with swift loping steps, their shoulders bent forward as if each were unaccustomed to walking without a burden on his back. Even the children walked in this way, beasts of burden conditioned from their first steps. I remembered that there were few young women in the valley, that most of the valley's maidens were in high pastures caring for cattle from July into September while the men remained below to work in the fields.

In my week there I found that in a predominantly French-speaking canton the valley was a German-speaking island that disdained commerce with outsiders; that the people mistrusted other Valaisans and called them scoundrels, and that they themselves were looked upon by their French-speaking neighbors as naive simpletons and made the butts of jokes.

Though there were no doctors or dentists in the valley, everyone appeared to be in vigorous health. Back in Zurich a professor of genetics told me that despite centuries of inbreeding and an unvaried diet of bread and cheese with a few vegetables in summer, the Lötschentalers were the healthiest people in Switzerland. Dental caries and the killing diseases of tuberculosis, pneumonia, and cancer were almost unknown. Unlike the rest of Switzerland, which has a high incidence of mental illness, the Lötschentalers seemed never to have heard of nervous breakdowns. Famous for their longevity, they usually died in their eighties of "water," the local designation for dropsy, a circulatory failing of aged hearts worn out finally by hard labor. This terminal affliction was probably abetted by alcohol. In heavy-drinking Switzerland the Lötschentalers were known for their consumption of wine and beer.

One question above all others interested me. Were the Lötschentalers a happy people? "The word does not exist in their vocabulary," the professor said. "In their masks happy expressions are almost nonexistent. If you found one it would be extremely valuable. Because the people do not understand the concept of happiness and do not pursue it they are, in discontented Switzerland, an oasis of contentment."

A resplendent image remained vivid in my memory. One windy afternoon in a hayfield I saw a tall reedlike old man with long arms, his white hair flying and his robes flapping like a black sail, swinging a scythe like a dark angel of death harvesting souls.

The possessed reaper was the valley Prior, helping his parishioners make hay. I remembered him passionately defending the old ways; of saying, with a ringing voice, "When modern civilization enters our valley we will be finished. We will lose our identity and become like everyone else."

His name was John Siegen and he would now be eighty-four years old. I wondered if he still lived and if he would remember me.

We drove up the sixteen-mile valley over a new road. In the town of Kippel, where one-fourth of the valley population lives, I saw a new school and a modern food market. Away from the center there were clusters of new summer houses built in an alien Bernese style. The streets were filled with strangers and tour buses stood in a parking zone. The old Hotel Lötschberg, where on my first visit my companion and I were the only guests, was filled with groups from France, Holland, and England.

On Sunday we waited outside the church for the Mass to end. A ruffle of drums inside signalled that it was over and in a moment the old Prior appeared, supported on the arms of two priests. I was shocked at how frail he seemed. His white hair and black robes billowing in the wind and his face, red from the cold, were an El Greco image of a feverish St. Jerome. Marching behind him with military precision were thirty-five "Grenadiers of God," also known as "Red Soldiers." They were wearing white trousers, scarlet swallowtail coats edged in gold, black fur hats with red and white plumes, and white gloves. Each bore a gold sword and carried a bayonet. The lustrous costumes were a historical mélange of uniforms from the courts of Catelonia, Savoy, Bavaria, Naples, and France which the men of the valley had served through centuries of mercenary soldiering.

Under a gold canopy supported by four acolytes the Prior led the Red Soldiers and the people of his parish southward to the first of four madonnas set outside the town on altars facing the four directions of the compass. There he prayed for blessings on newly sown fields and on cattle and for an abundant harvest; and he implored the encircling mountains for protection from disasters, from avalanches and floods and drought. In the driving snow the madonna, placed in a bower of fir branches and decorated with lighted candles, might have been a celebration of Christmas.

Seeming to levitate on the supporting arms of the priests, the Prior encircled the town, stopping at altars to the west and the north and the east and before each madonna he repeated the prayers to God and the elements. The procession ended with a benediction in the church and when it was over I introduced myself to the Prior and recalled my earlier visit. He took my hand in his trembling cold one and asked me to repeat my name. Recognition came into his eyes. Yes, he remembered. A visitor had shown him a book in which I had written about him. "I think you understood us very well. It was . . . how many years?"

"Twelve, Your Reverence."

"Yes, a long time." He sighed. "You will see many changes. You must visit me. I will have my rest and then . . . can you come at three?"

He excused himself and, aided by the priests, climbed the steps into the parish house.

Kap suggested a drink. He opened an unmarked door just off the churchyard and inside was a basement room crowded with men, drinking wine. I asked Kap how he knew the house was a cafe. "There is always one near a church," he said. "A place for men to drink while women are praying."

A spare youthful man greeted us. He was Pierman Rieder, the owner, and he invited us to a table and sat with us. A daughter brought coffee and brandy. Two Red Soldiers who were tending bar were a son and a son-in-law. On the table was a newspaper with a headline saying, "Winter in June!" "Some years it's so hot the Grenadiers sweat," Pierman said. "The festival began two hundred years ago so the retired soldiers could show off their French and Spanish uniforms. It has little to do with Corpus Christi. We call it Herrgottstag—God's Day—and we choose this time because it is usually the beginning of warm weather, the fields are green and the trees in blossom. Easter is too cold and by June 15 many of our people are in the Alps. After the long winter we are happy to welcome summer. The prayers to the mountains and the four winds are that they do us no harm and bring a fruitful summer. We're also saying farewell to relatives and cows that go up into the Alps."

God's Day! What I had seen and what Pierman was describing was a baffling fusion of Christian piety and pagan fertility rites in which so many religious ceremonies are rooted. In beseeching the mountains and the winds, the valley people were actually praying to the same elemental gods who controlled the destinies of Homer's Greeks. With their comingling of the antipodal rites, the Prior and his parish were building a bridge between the corporeal and spiritual intuitions of their human natures. It was a tantalizing idea that the people would, in their piety, not comprehend. Still I sensed some secret in it, an explanation for their serenity, their contentment with arduous lives.

At three o'clock we walked to the parish house. The Prior seemed relaxed and restored in strength. His softly lit study was cold and he was wearing a long black overcoat. He rang for his housekeeper to bring wine, and then he showed us his books. There was a collection of African sculpture, including an ebony figure of Christ being flagellated by soldiers with leather thongs and the faces on the Christ and His tormentors were African faces.

I recalled to the Prior our first introduction while he was scything hay and he said, "Come back in two weeks and you will see it again. Our season is short and when the hay is ready everyone works." I asked him how he found the strength for it, and he replied, "We are the strongest people in Switzerland. We eat hand-milled wheat, cheese, milk, and potatoes and, in summer, some vegetables and meat perhaps once a week. It is the good sturdy bread and no chocolate that keeps our teeth strong." He sighed softly and said, "I have made hay every summer since I arrived in the valley fifty-three years ago. But I am not as strong as I was. There was a time when I worked for ten hours and now five is enough."

I remembered a vanity in him, how he had boasted of his reputation as a mountaineer, how as a young priest he had held masses on the Matterhorn and several other high peaks, and I asked if he still climbed each Sunday to Alpine pastures to offer communion to the herdsmen and herdswomen. "Of course," he replied. "But I do not walk anymore. I am driven in a jeep." I recalled how he had boasted that the valley had no need for policemen and I spoke of the two uniformed officers I had seen that morning mingling in the crowds. "They were here on a holiday like everyone else," the Prior said and, with a flash of arrogance, added, "They had no official purpose. I am the only policeman in the valley." He was thoughtful for a moment and then, his voice sharp, he said, "Drinking! That is my problem." He sensed our astonishment at this and he smiled. "Not *my* problem," he said. "Alcoholism is the burden of my people. It is the cross I must bear.

"You have observed the changes," he said fiercely, his blue eyes flashing. "Ten years ago we had only a path for mules. Now there are thousands of autos each year. The world is invading us too swiftly; the change is too sudden. We are a hundred years later than the world and we have to find our own way." His voice grew vehement. "The English are buying plots for vacation houses. Land costs 150 francs a square meter. Our own people can no longer afford to build homes. Our occupation of agriculture is being forced out. Men go out of the valley each day to work in an aluminum factory. Yet most of them keep a cow and some sheep and goats; they are still bound to the earth. Young men go away to study and many become teachers. Lötschental teachers are famous throughout Switzerland."

His voice faltered and his eyes filled with tears. "I have traveled," he said. "I have found no other place in the world where people are as content as we have been. It is why I chose to spend my life here, why I have never been impelled to leave. I did not believe the great changes would come. But now they have. We go out! Others come in!"

He was expected, he said, at a Grenadiers' party in the community hall and he invited us to accompany him. He would see that an exception was made in the all-male affair for Pia. Passing the cemetery he nodded toward the graves and said, "Here you will meet all my contemporaries." He climbed the hill with long strides. In the hall a band of tubas, trumpets, and bass horns was playing a doleful melody and, echoing between concrete floor and plaster ceiling, it assaulted the ears. Men of all ages were sitting at tables drinking wine, eating bread and cheese, and smoking pipes.

The town president made room for us at the councilmen's table and the Prior raised his hands and the room silenced. While he prayed I looked about the room at the fresh young faces of the Red Soldiers and the gaunt Gothic faces of the old men. Lined by weather and age, some were handsome. Others seemed fitted together of mismatched parts like the masks of the valley which parodied them.

A Grenadier introduced himself and drew up a chair. His name was Antonius Obwald and he was a teacher of English in Sion. He told me that many of the older men in the room had been Vatican guards, and he complained that the high honor of parade flag bearers was retained by a few powerful families, that one Grenadier carried the flag borne by his father for thirty-six years.

The president began a speech, describing a future of ski lifts and new hotels. Beside me Antonius Obwald murmured in my ear, "Yes, the president would have us take tickets for chair lifts and clean hotel rooms. He has forgotten we are proud, that we would be ashamed to do such things."

"Tourism will bring prosperity to all our people," the president was saying. "It will give our sons and daughters reasons to stay in the valley. . . ."

Some of the men applauded. The Prior rose to his full height and when the room had silenced he excused himself. The men about the tables struggled to their feet and bowed their heads as the Prior moved toward the door. He stopped and with a rueful little laugh, he said, "I know! You just want to see if I can still walk." Then he left.*

"You saw that?" Antonius whispered. "What is in his heart, what he is really saying is, 'You are all from the Devil!' He realizes his time is finished, that what he has fought his entire life to preserve will soon be out of his hands. He knows that with his death that for which he labored will also die." Antonius's eyes glistened. "If you understand the Prior," he said, "then you understand our valley."

A kind of desperation settled over the men, a reluctance to bring an end to the party which had finished with the Prior's departure. Men gathered around to shake my hand and some of the Grenadiers, swaying unsteadily, seemed to draw support from my grasp. Antonius accompanied me from the hall. The descending sun had broken through clouds and the snow-covered mountains were radiant with mauve and cerise lights as in a painting by Hodler. The cold air cleared our heads and we started walking out of the town. We spoke, not very coherently, of whatever came to our minds. Antonius talked of American books he had read—John Steinbeck and Pearl Buck were his favorite writers—and of his life outside the valley as a bachelor teacher. Being a young man, his thoughts dwelt on women. He said, "A woman

---

*In 1981 Prior Siegen was living in the St. Anna Home in Steg near Zurich. He was ninety-five years old.

who is good both in bed and in the kitchen, and is deep in spirit and mind does not exist in Switzerland. Swiss women are trained for the kitchen, but not for bed. I would as soon forget about the kitchen, for I can always go to a restaurant. But I could never forget about bed or the spirit. I am sure in America it is not like this, that American women are capable of being satisfactory in several ways."

It was a strange discourse from a Grenadier of God. Such urbane thoughts seemed alien to the valley and I thought that he had traveled farther from the Lötschental than he was aware and would find it hard to return.

We were walking in open country. There was something he wished me to see, Antonius said, something old people and children called a miracle.

We arrived at a wayside shrine, a crucifix planted by the road many years ago. Into a crack in the right arm of the wooden Christ a seed had been dropped by a bird, and it had germinated and a young tree was growing out of the old wood. "The people wonder what it means," Antonius said. "They see death and resurrection, new life rising out of the old."

There were tears in his eyes. "It's the way we look at things," he said.

The next morning the snow still swirled and it continued until we passed through the tunnel out of the valley. Kap drove in silence and I attributed his mood to my disagreement with the Lötschental president's speech on modernization; Kap had applauded.

"Catholic Swiss," said Kap, breaking the silence, "are backward and not ambitious." The Lötschental which we were leaving was German-speaking and the Rhone valley which we were entering was French. Both were Catholic.

"But ambition can be a neurosis," I replied. "If Catholic Swiss are less striving and less competitive than Protestants, they are probably happier. Or perhaps I have it wrong. It may be a chicken-and-egg situation. Perhaps Catholics are less driven toward achievement because they are happier." It was a theory I evolved in Italy where I learned to respect the humanism of parochical, or village, Catholicism.

"It is Protestants who move the world," said Kap. "Protestants brought industry and commerce to our country. They settled America. If your people had been Catholics in the Valais instead of Protestants from Glarus, you'd still be here hoeing grapes."

I laughed. "Climate has more to do with it," I said. "German Catholics are as enterprising as German Protestants."

"It's the same all over the world," Kap insisted. "Protestant countries—America, Sweden, Denmark—are progressive and modern. Catholic countries—Spain, Italy, and Austria—are backward and unenlightened. Unfortunately, in Switzerland we have both. And Protestants bear the burden. . . ."

". . . of a Calvinistic deification of property and money," I said. "Isn't that the root of the frustration and unhappiness?"

It was an argument in which both of us were in error and to which we could find no resolution. I, who had grown up in American affluence and with American anxieties, was romanticising the elemental life of the agrarian peasant. In doing so I was forgetting the frustrations of rural poverty out of which Kap had risen and from which my own ancestors had escaped. I was maligning the "progress" which Kap worshipped above all else and with which he was building his own successful life.

We passed through Sion, capital and market of the Valais, a place of gathering-in of succulent strawberries, and cherries, and dewy vegetables that were flown to Les Halles in Paris and Covent Garden in London. We turned into the wild, sparsely populated Val d'Hérem-énce, and climbed fifteen miles up through clouds to the Dixence Dam. The prospect of showing me another hydroelectric plant restored Kap's good humor. Dams, he said, were responsible for the Valais economic development. "The Valaisans were always Switzerland's poor," he said. "They were so poor that army recruits appeared for induction without shoes. Then came the Second World War and its demand for electric power. The deep and narrow tributaries of the Rhone were perfect dam sites."

We hurtled above the tree line into a desolate wintry landscape and entered a dense cloud bank. Still we hurtled on through a nowhere of invisibility and came to a halt suddenly before the looming wall of a dam, the top of which was lost in fog. The place had a chilling unreality, as if we had left the earth and entered a science-fiction complex on a lunar satellite.

"Valais is the greatest exporter of power in Europe," Kap said exultantly. "Eighty percent of the energy goes to France. Villages collect water royalties, some a million francs a year. With the money they develop tourism and their prosperity grows."

We spiraled down through a Stygian landscape, entered the Val d'Herens and arrived in the village of Les Haudères where we found rooms for the night.

The next day was Pia's birthday and Kap announced he was taking us to Saas-Fee for lunch. We followed the Rhone to Visp where we entered the Saastal, another German-speaking valley. Until the road was built with water power royalties in 1951, Saas-Fee had been a small agricultural village accessible only on foot or by horseback. Lying inside a circle of 12,000-foot-high snow-capped mountains, it was called "the pearl of the Alps."

"See!" Kap said triumphantly, waving his hand like an Old Testament prophet over a promised land. "See what is possible?"

Looking over the small metropolis of new hotels and condominiums, of shops and boutiques in which a few rustic old houses seemed misplaced, I understood why he had brought us there. The panorama before us was his vision for Elm. The booming ski and summer resort which Saas-Fee had become in less than two decades was a model for the conversion which he was planning to impose on the village that was his home and also mine.

I did not share Kap's enthusiasm then and my apprehensions continue. Since the visit to Saas-Fee I have met Dr. Gottlieb Guntern, a Swiss psychiatrist who had written a book* on the metamorphosis of Saas-Fee from a rustic agrarian village to a prosperous tourist center. Dr. Guntern spent eighteen months as a practicing physician in Saas-Fee from 1968 to 1970; during this time he studied changes in the physical and mental health of its people. There are, he pointed out, conspicuous parallels between Saas-Fee and Elm. Saas-Fee was in 1951 an agricultural village of fewer than 600 people. Elm, before the development of its ski slopes, had 900 people, 80 percent of whom were engaged in agriculture.

Social Changes in the Pearl of the Alps. New York: Springer-Verlag, 1979.

The result in Saas-Fee, Dr. Guntern said, "has been devastating." Today one percent of its population is engaged in agriculture and ninety-nine percent work in tourist commerce and services. On a typical winter day in Saas-Fee there is a Swiss population of just under 900 and a foreign population of 10,000 tourists and 700 workers, mostly Italian and Spanish. In his book Dr. Guntern says that 15 percent of Saas-Fee natives are chronically addicted to tranquilizing drugs which are sold illegally without prescriptions. Six percent are chronic alcoholics, which is three times the national ratio. Psychosomatic disorders in the local population include chronic sleeplessness (40 percent), chronic headaches (30 percent), cardiovascular stress symptoms (34 percent), and chromic disabilities (more than 40 percent). The introverted alpine character of Swiss farmers, Dr. Guntern concludes, is simply not able to cope with the swift and cataclysmic changes involved in transformation to a tourist culture.

We followed the Rhone toward its headwaters and arrived late in the afternoon in Fiesch; mountain guides of all ages from Switzerland, France, Italy, and Austria were congregated in a government-owned "holiday village" at the foot of a glacier. They were uniformly dressed in brown or gray knickers, belted tweed jackets with suede lapels, knitted stockings, and mountain boots. Many were middle-aged and most were smoking pipes. Five of the Swiss guides invited us to a table to share some wine. They were lamenting the downgrading of their once noble profession. "Guiding is dying out," said a guide who also owned a sporting goods store. "In Saas-Fee we have only forty guides. I am thirty-eight years old and the fourth youngest."

The following morning, a Sunday, we accompanied Roger Bonvin and the guides to an outdoor altar upon which a massive cross, festooned with a coiled rope and a pick, stood silhouetted against snowy peaks in a cloudless sky. A young priest, also a climber, read from the parable of lost sheep in St. Luke: "What man of you, having a hundred sheep, if he lose one, doth not leave the ninety and nine and go after that which is lost?"

When he finished his sermon, the guides took up their ropes and their picks, which they had decorated with edelweiss and alp roses, and formed a single-file procession to the altar where they offered them to the priest for blessing and knelt for communion.

Moving slowly, solemnly, the men might have been warriors presenting their weapons to the gods on the eve of a battle. A thought came to me, as it had in the Lötschental and wherever I have been present at such anomalous mergings of ritual, that in my intellectualized Protestantism something elemental and basic was denied, that a pantheistic union with natural forces, such as was now taking place, was at the center of all religion and that the negation of it was a negation of life.

30

NEW TIMES MOVE IN

Early in the summer, before I left Switzerland, I returned to Elm for two extraordinary events. The first might have been the subject of a children's story: The railway that had served the valley for sixty-five years had come to the end of its life and the people of the valley were assembling for a *Bähnli-Abschied,* a "farewell to the little train."

It was not exactly for a train that they were mourning but for two electric-powered red trolleys which alternated eight times a day on the round trip from Schwanden, up the course of the Sernf River to Elm, a distance of eight and one-half miles, and back again. For the people of Engi, Matt, and Elm, the cars had been since 1905 a lifeline to the world. Before there were autos in the valley the people were entirely dependent upon the red railway. It took them to factory jobs down the valley, to doctors and hospitals and to shop for necessities not available in their villages. It brought medicines, and visitors, and on Sundays it took them on outings. They loved it like a family friend and in referring to it as "our little train" they imbued it with an almost human personality.

Now it was being taken from them and the villain of the perfidy was progress. The gorge of the Sernf was so narrow in places that the single track—which at a half-way point widened into two tracks to allow the

ascending and descending cars to pass—served also as the auto road
and this made traffic hazardous, especially in winter. For five years a
proposal to widen the road and replace the train with motor buses had
been the subject of a referendum battle between traditionalists and
progressives and the progressives had finally won. For Kap Rhyner,
who dreamed of extending the auto highway via a tunnel to Davos and
St. Moritz, the passing of the train was a political triumph. Still he
shared in the nostalgia of its passing and helped arrange its public
mourning. He urged me to attend and ride on the final sentimental ride.

It took place on a Saturday in late May. A soft *Föhn* wind warmed
the valley and the sun shone on the mountains in blinding effusion. I
arrived in Schwanden on the train from Zurich with Peter Studer of the
Tages Anzeiger. Kap met us in the station where three cars—the two
red trolleys and an open freight car—were decorated with wreaths of
gladioli and carnations. Flags and banners displayed the image of the
canton patron, St. Fridolin, and the first car bore a placard tombstone.

The two red cars were filled with distinguished guests. Governor
Fridolin Stucki was there and, seated like a cluster of Biblical patri-
archs, twelve old men who as boys had ridden on the train's first trip
sixty-four years ago. The only women on the train were six members of
a costumed choir in the rear car. There were many women on the
platform.

Our places were in the second car. The train whistle shrilled out its
familiar signal and a band on the platform commenced a dirge. Men's
eyes filled with tears and each seemed also to be weeping for himself, for
his own symbolic death. Peter Studer, who understood this, said, "It's
going to be a rough ride."

The cortège jerked into motion. Wheels rattled and clicked; banners
snapped in the breeze. In the open car behind us a band played and
costumed men and women danced a lively *Ländler*. Their gaiety, like
revelries at a wake, seemed even sadder than the weeping. The conductor on our car continued to pull the whistle cord, filling the valley with
plaintive wails, like the cries of distressed birds. He was a small man
with a humped back. "I'm sixty-one years old," he said, wiping his eyes
with his sleeve, "I've worked the train for twenty-five years and I'd only
four years to go for my pension."

After four miles we were in the station of Engi where villagers were gathered. Fluttering his arms, a schoolmaster conducted his pupils in a sad song about little churches on little mountains and old men and women tugged on handkerchiefs. A band began to play and would not stop.

The whistle blew and we rolled away. Boys on the platform rang cowbells and in the last car a jug of wine was being passed; the dancing resumed and the women's white skirts billowed like laundry. At the two-tracked half-way point the descending trolley was waiting and the two cars, halting a moment, seemed to be bowing to one another.

In the village of Matt funeral bells tolled. Men wore their *Anglais* funeral coats and Abraham Lincoln hats. Old women sat on benches in the cemetery and behind them some red cows watched curiously. Muscular youths in white tights performed gymnastics. A caravan of autos and bicycles joined in and preceded the train up the valley with a wild jangle of horns and bells. Old men leaning on canes saluted the cars as if they were fallen comrades.

In Elm, the end of the line, a salvo of rifles heralded the arrival. The crowd was so large it took ten minutes to clear the tracks so the train could pull into the station. To accommodate TV cameramen the cars reversed and repeated the arrival three times. Old women dressed in mourning crowded around the cars to stroke the red sides and admire the flowers.

We alighted and joined a cortège moving up through the village to an assembly hall in the *Gasthaus Hausstock* where tables were set for a feast. The room was hot and the men crowding the tables drank quantities of chilled white wine and chomped on a hearty meal of cold meats, cheeses, sturdy bread, salads and cakes. The only women were some costumed singers and serving girls. A men's chorus sang a sad song about an immigrant in a foreign land who was homesick for "the little homeland" and then a *Töchterchor,*" a young women's choir, sang of a goat boy dreaming among alpine flowers. "Why must they sing this melancholy rubbish?" Peter Studer muttered. "You'll be surprised to know we also have happy songs in Switzerland." A lady soloist filled the hall with a wordless vocalization which spiraled like a flute. The village poet, Kaspar Hefti, read a long ode to the train written in a singsong a-b-a-b rhyme and ending, "A new time moves in."

Governor Stucki spoke of the necessity for change. I looked at the rows of stern, expressionless faces and I wondered what each man was thinking. Then I heard my name and some applause and I realized the governor was calling on me.

I rose and began extemporizing about my four great-grandparents who, setting out for America, had made the journey down to Schwanden on foot, bearing their infant children; and I told how in Wisconsin they had traveled an even greater distance on foot from the Mississippi to their new home. Moved by an impulse spurred by the wine, I said that the next day I would walk down to Schwanden on the same path over which my ancestors had begun their journey. When I finished the applause rang out and Peter said, "My God, what intuition! You told them exactly what they wanted to hear." There were more songs by the women and Peter, watching the singers, said, "They have the worn faces of Gothic madonnas, all pain and anguish and denial."

When it was over Peter and I walked down to the station, where the crowds hovered about the cars waiting to return the guests to Schwanden. Like mourners at a graveside, people were unable to take their leave. Women broke flowers from the wreaths to keep as momentos and a bearded old farmer named Albrecht Elmer, wearing a gold earring in each ear, was venting his rage over the termination of the train. His words rang out like a dour prophet's, saying, "Up there in the hall men are drinking and celebrating and this is indecent for the day has no joy, only sadness, because they are putting our little train under the ground. I was a schoolboy when the train came and I have never forgotten the day. We were always so happy when it was here . . ." He began to weep and he could not continue. At that moment Kap zoomed up in his car, looking for us, and when he saw the old man he said, "He's a crazy old fool who comes down from his alp once a week to rave against progress and the sinfulness of young people and no one pays him any attention."

"They are putting our little train under the ground," the old man cried and women's voices responded with an antiphony of wails, "Farewell! Farewell!"

In the morning Kap and Peter set out with me on the walk down the mountain to Schwanden. The footpath commenced on the right side of the swollen stream and crossed at Matt to the left side. It was an area of open fields with red cows grazing in meadows of golden cowslips and here and there a few goats. I imagined that, with the exception of the railway tracks following the course of the stream, it had not been greatly different when my great-grandparents, the Elmers in 1847 and the Kublis six years later, walked down the trail, beginning the journey to America with their children. Quite certainly no one of them had ever before spent a night away from Elm. No doubt relatives and friends had walked part of the way with them. I tried to envision the excitement of the children, the tearful farewells, the turning back for a last look at the village, knowing there would be no return. I thought of their fears, of the pain and the courage, and my eyes filled.

Kap was in bounding spirits. He had a movie camera and he and Peter kept running ahead to photograph what they called my "historic journey down the Sernf." Between Matt and Engi the path crossed the river two more times and then remained on the steep, wooded south side of the canyon. Wild strawberries bloomed along the path, and columbines and primulas. I remembered that the same flowers would be blooming on the Wisconsin farm to which I would soon be returning; that the immigrants had found the same climate and seasons, the same flora in America. We passed the *Suvarovbrücke* and Kap pointed out old stone buildings where, he said, Russian bullets were imbedded in the walls.

We met a boy herding goats, passing the time whittling and whistling to music from a transistor radio. His goats fell in line behind us and followed us down the path. We tried to chase them but they refused to turn back and finally the boy had to run after us to fetch them.

Ahead of us, at the junction of the valleys, the snow-covered Glärnisch glittered. We made it to the Schwanden station two minutes before the train that Peter and I were taking to Zurich. On a station siding stood the cars of the retired *Bahnli*. The bunting and banners hung listlessly on its sides; the wreaths and sprays were wilted and the Sunday sojourners in the station were paying them no attention. They were admiring the shining new red buses which were beginning the ascent to Elm.

On my farewell visit to Elm three weeks later I was accompanied by the governor of my state, Warren Knowles of Wisconsin.

When the governor expressed a wish to visit Canton Glarus, the ancestral home of his Swiss constituents, arrangements were made for him to go with me to Elm and the people planned a celebration for the historic occasion.

Warren* is a warm-hearted gregarious man who enjoys mingling with people, a quality to which the Swiss are not accustomed in politicians. The Glarners gathered outside the hotel were at first puzzled and then enchanted by the conviviality of the handsome white-haired visitor. Warren posed for photographs, including one with my spinster cousins, Martha and Anna Ott, and the sweet old ladies almost swooned with excitement. "I bring you greetings from the good people of New Glarus," he told them and, though few understood more than "New Glarus," everyone applauded.

An hour later we set out for Elm in a caravan which included Governor Stucki and other Glarus officials. I had made it known that Governor Knowles enjoyed the company of ladies and, for the first time in my Glarus experience, two women, both English-speaking, were in the official party. They were Heidi Stucki, the felicitous wife of Governor Stucki, and Trudi Vogel, vivacious and pretty manager of the Hotel Glarnerhof.

The route up the steep valley was lined with people waiting to greet *Der Guvernoer vo Amerika.* In Engi we stopped to speak to an old lady who ran out into the road to tell the governor that she had a sister in Monticello, Wisconsin, and when I interpreted this for him, the governor wrote down the sister's name and promised to carry greetings to her.

In Elm the small square before the Hotel Elmer was filled with villagers and news photographers and television crews. American and Swiss flags flew side by side and the band, which had been rehearsing for a week, played a strained but recognizable *The Star Spangled Banner.* When it finished, Warren shook hands with everyone, stooping to hold the hand of each shy child, and the people were as awed

---

*Retired from politics, Knowles is now an investment counselor in Milwaukee.

as if a god were walking amongst them. Though he spoke no German, I had coached him in the pronunciation of *Grüezi* (Greetings), which on his unfamiliar tongue came out "Groosey." When he pumped the hand of the old widow Lisabetta Kubli, and said "Groosey!" the woman replied, "*Aber i verstoh nud Aenglisch!*"

"Groosey! Groosey!" Warren said, and the old lady, weeping with frustration and excitement, repeated, "But I don't understand English." A youth who knew a bit of English and American geography, asked the governor, "You in Madison?" and Warren replied, "No, I'm a lawyer."

The incredible reception continued with a banquet at which the young women's choir sang and Kap made a speech in English telling of Elm's pride in sharing me, "our distinguished son" with Wisconsin, and of Governor Knowles's visit being Elm's most important historic event since the two-day visit of Russian General Suvarov in 1799. When he finished, one of the girls from the choir presented the governor with an alpine staff decorated with edelweiss. The governor kissed the girl and the people of Elm gasped at his boldness and broke into applause.

In the square outside an orchestra was playing and the reserved villagers were swept into uncharacteristic merriment. I danced with Heidi Stucki and several members of the choir and the old people swayed to the music and beat time to its rhythm. Albrecht Elmer, the bearded prophet of doom, came down from the mountain and made a speech, saying, "You see how it is in America? How it will be in Switzerland with women voting? Any handsome devil who kisses women can get himself elected governor!"

31

VIABILITY FOR A RESTIVE LAND

I had not let it be known when I would arrive, and there was no one to greet me when the plane let down. I was wheeling my baggage to a taxi station when I heard a familiar voice shouting my name. Kap clattered down a staircase and embraced me. "At last you have returned," he said.

He apologized for being late. He had called Swissair to check passenger lists and had left a meeting of the Glarus Executive Council and raced sixty miles to the airport. He was *Landesstatthalter,* which is the equivalent of a lieutenant governor; the following May at the *Landsgemeinde* he would be elected *Landammann,* or governor. "We wondered if you had forgotten us," he said. "Why has it been so long?"

"I've been working," I said. "I had to finish." I tried to explain but the language which I'd hardly spoken for three years failed me. How could I tell him that during the writing of my book I could not come to Switzerland? How could I explain that to maintain some control in a very subjective work it had been necessary to keep a distance, both in geography and in time, a period for reflection and cooling of passions? How could I make Kap understand that it had been necessary, especially, to stay away from him and his persuasiveness?

"Is the book finished?" he asked.

"Not quite. I've come to check it out, to see if changes are necessary."

On the drive into town, building cranes hovered over the landscape like the predatory mandibles of giant Paleozoic insects. Kap pointed out new hotels and office buildings. High rises are not permitted in downtown Zurich and new corporate skyscrapers towering over houses and barns and grazing cows on the edge of the city formed an encircling redoubt wall.

"Wait until you see Elm," Kap said suddenly. "I wonder what you will think of it?" I understood his anxiety. He was the *Baumeister*, the Master Builder, and the renascence of the village both of us loved had become the single most important effort of his life. "Some of the changes you will like," he said. "Others you may not." During the years of planning when the renascence was a burgeoning dream I had been his frequent companion and I had not always responded with enthusiasm to his ideas. Now, with many of them accomplished, I sensed how important my approval was going to be. I did not want it to turn into a test of our friendship and I was uneasy. "When can you come?" he asked and I replied that I needed a few days in Zurich, that I would come on the weekend.

I moved into the small Hotel Helmhaus, which has become my Niederdorf home in Zurich, and for three sunny days I wandered over the familiar old streets. The city was a summer festival. Red roses spilled over gardens and walls and downtown streets transformed into pedestrian malls blazoned with armorial banners. But it did not take long to sense there was tension in the atmosphere, that the benign facade of carefree gaiety masked an undercurrent of apprehension and alarm. Behind the banners and the flowers Switzerland was reeling from the shock waves of two gigantic scandals.

The first was political and involved espionage and sex. Brigadier General Jean-Louis Jeanmaire, sixty-seven years old, one of the highest ranking officers in Switzerland's peacetime army, was found guilty in federal court of passing home-defense secrets to Russia and was given an eighteen-year prison sentence. The general's wife admitted having an affair with the Russian contact, a military attaché in the Russian Embassy in Berne.

The second scandal was the most devastating in Switzerland's banking history. The manager of the Chiasso branch of the mighty Crédit

Suisse Bank, a man named Ernest Kuhrmeier, was in jail awaiting trial for the illegal and self-serving funneling of more than $800 million into a fraudulent Liechtenstein investment firm of which Kuhrmeier himself was founder. Two other bank officers and three lawyers were under arrest.

The effect of headlines daily battering the Swiss self-image of a morally incorruptible people ranged from confusion and disbelief to panic. "Everything you have in America is now coming to us," a journalist said.

For tourists the significant changes were monetary. The dollar, which I remembered had been worth 4.25 francs on my last visit, was now reduced to 2.40 francs and would plunge even further to 1.50. A combination of currency devaluation and Swiss inflation was turning Switzerland into one of the world's most expensive countries for Americans—who were curtailing their visits. The English, for more than a century a mainstay of Switzerland's tourist industry, could no longer afford to come. West Germans, whose mark paralleled the franc in value, continued to come and Japanese were exotic newcomers. The monetary situation threatened more than tourism. A result of the franc's hegemony in the world money exchange was the pricing of Swiss export products out of the international market.

In Zurich a single change, important only as a symbol, haunted me through the summer. On Bellevue Square the venerable old Odeon, the literary cafe to which James Joyce, Thomas Mann, and Herman Hesse came to read and sometimes to write was turned into a ladies ready-to-wear boutique. In the rear a small student bar still operated but the potted rubber plants had been removed from the marble floors and most of the paneled walls were covered with ceiling-high shelves of women's garments. In its last years the Odeon had become a center for drug traffic and there was a story that a youth had been found dead of an overdose in a toilet cubicle.

On Saturday Kap met my train in Glarus and drove me up the newly widened highway toward Elm. We passed new houses being built on the roadside and great shining barns. "Elm is prosperous from the sale of water rights to a power dam and communal lands to the army," Kap said. "Farmers were able to sell land to the ski corporation and the highway department. Everyone is working. In the winter young farmers operate ski lifts. New residents are moving into the valley and the population is growing." He continued his euphoric report. The old center of the village was protected by the Elm Foundation, which Kap had organized and of which he was president. The foundation controlled building alterations and no property owners could make changes without its approval.

The highway bypassed the edge of the village and we turned from it and followed the old road through the town. Some of the old houses had been divested of stucco and siding and their original log walls were exposed and newly stained. The dark brown chalets standing against the green mountainside were strikingly beautiful. It was Kap's intent to restore all log houses from the sixteenth and seventeenth centuries to their original rusticity; twelve were already finished.

Outside the protected center of the village there were many changes. On the upper edge of the town were new ski lifts with posted maps of six trails described as either "medium" or "easy," and near the lifts was a new resort hotel named the Sardona after one of the mountains that encircle the valley. Scattered over the slopes were holiday houses built mostly for Zurichers. All around us the old ways and the new were coexisting in curious harmony. In a meadow facing the new hotel two women were spreading manure with hand forks and on ledges above the hotel men were cutting the wild hay with scythes.

The most auspicious new building was the *Gemeindehaus,* a community hall and convention center. The huge complex of wood and concrete was set in the deep valley of the Sernf River where it did not protrude into the panorama of the village. It included sleeping dormitories for student groups, bathing facilities, municipal offices, and an auditorium for six hundred persons where, on my first evening, there was a ball. The older people of Elm, dressed in traditional black, sat at tables drinking wine and watching with glistening eyes the vivacious dancing of the young.

Towering over the village like the palace of a tiny duchy was the six-story Suvarov House which was Kap's home. The restoration of the thirty-six rooms had taken six years. Now those who had called it "Rhyner's Folly" were boasting that the manor was the most elegant house in the canton. The second night I slept there, in a suite with period furniture and a sybarite's bathroom, I was awakened at 4 A.M.

by a great clatter and bawling in the street. It was the morning when cows and goats, their bells clanging, were setting out with herdsmen for the summer pastures up in the Alps.

Twilight vespers had ceased ringing in the tower when I walked around the church to a new section of the cemetery which had not been there on my last visit. Each of the recent, tightly crowded graves blazed with red begonias and was edged with green myrtle. The most impressive of the new stones was black marble and stood over the grave of my old friend Mathias Elmer, village archivist and keeper of the chronicles, who had died at the age of eighty-three.

Nearby and side by side were the graves of two Jakob Rhyners. One, whose stone was carved with ladyslippers, had been an eighty-one-year-old shoemaker. The second was the grave of a young man: "Jakob Rhyner 1941-1976." I looked at the unusual stone, at a herdsmen's hut against a background of mountain peaks incised into gray marble, and a chilling intuition passed over me. I tried to appease my suspicion by reminding myself that there were more than a score of Jakob Rhyners in Elm, most of whom I did not know. In another part of the cemetery a sexton was planting flowers on a grave and I crossed over to ask him which one of the Jakob Rhyners was buried there. The sexton verified what I now sensed to be a certainty. The one resting under the begonias was Hermes, the protector of cattle whom I'd awakened from sleep in a bower of roses on his Olympus, the Mühlibach Alp.

He was killed, said the sexton, while herding sheep and goats on the Kärpf Alp where he slipped on a ledge and plunged forty meters to immediate death. In the village, where the people had come to look on him with a kind of mystic awe as the solitary shepherd, his death had been greatly mourned. At his funeral the church was filled to hear the pastor preach on *der gute Hirt,* "the good shepherd."

I returned to the grave, which like all the others in the crowded churchyard was pitifully small, and I paced it out and found it was five feet long; and I wondered how it was possible for so lofty a spirit to rest in such strictured confinement. I gazed at the hermit's hut carved into the stone and tried to understand why the death of one I'd known only slightly should so affect me.

I could not put the good shepherd from my mind and the next day, with Karl Fassbind, a friend who came out from Zurich, I took a ski lift up the lower slopes of the mountain on which the young Jakob Rhyner died. It was a dazzlingly bright afternoon and the slopes clanged with the bells of grazing cows. On the heights we looked across the deep valley to a row of facing peaks under which the shepherd had herded his cattle in the summer of our meeting. Connecting the peaks was the crescent-shaped ledge to which I'd given the name "Hermes' Highway." The extraordinary geologic phenomenon was a rim of hard stone placed by an ancient upheaval between two layers of soft stone. We could see through *Martinsloch,* an orifice ninety-feet-high and sixty-feet-wide, a jagged passage from Glarus to Graubünden which was carved from soft stone by the wind.

We walked down the mountain, passing several perilous ledges from which the shepherd might have fallen. The descent was arduous and slippery and sometimes, carrying our shoes, we walked down in an icy stream.

The most historic change that summer in Switzerland was political. In May a fifty-four-year-old widow named Elisabeth Blunschy was elected to the most powerful government position in the land, the presidency of the *Nationalrat,* the larger of the two houses of Parliament.

To comprehend the measure of this event, some understanding of the structure of the Swiss government is necessary. Switzerland does not, like America, have a strong and powerful president. The executive power is vested in a Federal Council of seven members among whom the presidency is rotated for one-year terms. The "president" presides at Council meetings and his name is seldom remembered by the people. By contrast the president of the *Nationalrat* is the presiding officer of Parliament, the equivalent of the British Prime Minister or, in America, a combination of the Vice-President and the Speaker of the House.

Mrs. Blunschy's election, only six years after Swiss women won the right to vote, made front-page headlines across Europe and America. In Switzerland it aroused a bluster of controversy. I heard men in both Zurich and Elm express their vehement disapproval. Others gallantly assumed a wait-and-see attitude. Mrs. Blunschy's admirers spoke of her winning charm in television appearances, her forceful authority and housewifely efficiency. An anecdote was circulated about a male journalist who, after Mrs. Blunschy's first appearance before Parliament, admitted admiringly, "She presided just like a man," and a lady journalist who retorted, "You're quite wrong. She presided like a woman."

When I arrived in Switzerland I asked for an appointment with Mrs. Blunschy and to my surprise I was immediately invited to meet her in the Capitol in Berne. My appointment was for two o'clock on a Tuesday. On the train from Zurich I read through newspaper clippings and biographical material. I learned that Mrs. Blunschy was the daughter of Dr. Hans Steiner who was a member of Parliament when she was born in 1922 and later served for twenty-six years as a distinguished federal judge. Elisabeth Steiner was graduated from the law school of the University of Fribourg. She married a classmate, Dr. Alfred Blunschy, and with him set up a law firm in her hometown of Schwyz. She became known as a leader in the fight for suffrage and women's rights through two organizations, the Swiss Catholic Women's Association and the Commission for the Revision of Family Rights. In 1971 she was a candidate for the liberal Christian Democrat People's Party and became one of the first women elected to Parliament. The next year her husband died of a heart attack. She had three children, a daughter and two sons.

I arrived in Berne in time for lunch with Peter Studer, who was now political correspondent for his Zurich paper, *Tages Anzeiger*. He explained that Mrs. Blunschy's election in midterm had filled a vacancy created by the resignation of the preceding president and that her choice by a male parliament had been in part a chivalrous gesture since the office was rotated among parties and she would not be eligible to succeed herself. One of the most interesting details of Mrs. Blunschy's election was that she was not from a liberal urban area but from the small mountainous canton of Schwyz in the conservative, Catholic center of Switzerland where the opposition to women's suffrage had been especially passionate.

I had heard that Mrs. Blunschy did not speak English. Fearing that my own Swiss vocabulary might be too limited for an interview on political matters, I arranged for a French-speaking interpreter to accompany me. Shortly before two o'clock the interpreter and I arrived in the office of the secretary general of Parliament, Dr. Alois Pfister. He told us he had been a law school classmate of Mrs. Blunschy and was her close friend. "Her role of a women's liberation cover girl is completely contrary to facts," he said. "She is first of all a housewife and mother. In the law firm she ran the office and did the paper work, remaining always in the background of her husband's legal career. She has political opponents but she has no enemies. It was the men who made her president."

Dr. Pfister directed us down a long plain corridor to the office of the president. The door opened and I walked into a circle of blinding television lights and grinding cameras. With a beaming smile Mrs. Blunschy stepped forward to greet me. She apologized for the filmed reception, which she said would be over in a minute. "One doesn't meet an American professor who is also a Swiss every day," she said. Her friendly warmth and very natural poise put me immediately at ease. She was a slight and slender woman wearing a modishly simple blue summer frock. Her graying hair was smartly styled. Photographs had shown wholesome country features and kindly, twinkling eyes but they had not shown her blue-eyed, pink-cheeked luster, nor conveyed the natural radiance of a beautiful and intuitively gracious woman. She was, I remembered, fifty-five years old.

The camera crews departed. Mrs. Blunschy offered chairs at a conference table in the center of the room and took one facing me. "It is my first private office," she said. Swiss parliamentarians have no offices and operate from hotel rooms. I looked over the simply paneled, Spartan room. It was perhaps twelve-feet square. Standing at an angle in a corner was a desk on which was a neat file of papers, a portable typewriter, and two bouquets, one of roses and another of gladioli. In another corner stood a television. The only wall decorations were a calendar and a thermometer. "I have no time to watch television," Mrs. Blunschy said. "And I don't often use the typewriter. Since I've been the president I haven't had to type my own letters." Parliamentarians do not have secretaries. They use a pool of twelve secretaries directed by Dr. Pfister.

I showed Mrs. Blunschy some clippings from American newspapers describing her election to "the top-ranking position in Switzerland" and she laughed with pleasure and modesty. "Americans exaggerate," she said. "That 'most powerful' is of course theoretical. While I conduct the Parliament, I do not vote unless there is a tie to break. Of course," she added with a touch of pride, "some of the men in Parliament have not quite resolved how to react to a woman, so in the back room committees I do have some influence. But you must not forget that in our completely democratic system we have strong restraints on power. We recognize human frailties and we do not allow anyone to become too strong."

It turned out that Mrs. Blunschy, who with her husband had made a study tour of the United States in 1961, understood English, so our dialogue in English and Swiss required little help from the interpreter. I asked her why suffrage had come so late to the women of Switzerland. "There is something the world must understand," she said. "In most countries suffrage had to be approved by parliaments, the members of which are assumed to be men of political wisdom and sophistication. In our country it needed to be passed by a popular referendum of all men and this took a long time. We had to move slowly, step by step, according to our tradition. We women had first to prove that we could use the vote in a constructive way. And then of course there were the women who opposed us. They are queens who live in medieval times, who reign in their homes where their husbands are subjects. We had to fight them as well as the men. It was not until 1971 that the time was right."

For twenty years Mrs. Blunschy's public life had been directed toward gaining equal rights for women, toward liberating them from traditional male domination and control. What, I asked, were the specific reforms she supported?

"I am opposed," she said, "to a woman's loss in matrimony of her name and hereditary citizenship. I believe a choice should be made whether children take the father's or the mother's name and I do not believe a woman should be forced to give up her own. I think a woman marrying out of her canton should not have to relinquish her hereditary citizenship. My own family is one of the oldest in Schwyz and I resented having to change my citizenship because my husband was from Aargau.

"Then there is the very important matter of matrimonial property rights. Any property brought into a marriage by a wife now comes under the control of the husband. I want this law changed. I want the woman to keep control of what belongs to her."

How, I asked, did male parliamentarians react to her campaign against their historical prerogatives? "Well, of course, some are not smiling," she replied. "But even if they are startled by my ideas, they have shown their goodwill toward me personally. I think we are having an unusually friendly and happy Parliament. Quite possibly they are thinking it will all pass. They may be surprised to discover that even when I am no longer president, I and my ideas will not go away."

The Parliament meets for four three-week sessions a year and special sessions are called when necessary. Between sessions Mrs. Blunschy traveled through Switzerland for committee and political meetings. Weekends she drove seventy-five miles to her home in Schwyz. "I need to organize things for the children who are alone in the house," she said. "I see that the refrigerator and the freezer are filled for another week." The "children" were a daughter, Isabelle, twenty-four, who was a secretary for the Motor Vehicle Bureau of Schwyz, and two sons, Anthony, twenty-three, a draftsman and stonemason, and Felix, nineteen, a student. "There is also the garden. I cut the flowers and I pick the berries and make jam. But I no longer have time to pull the weeds."

On Monday mornings she returned to Berne to open her mail. "People write from all over the world to congratulate me, to ask for photos and autographs. There are always a few letters from crazy persons. But most of the mail is serious and must be answered. Because I am a woman and a mother, more people write to me about their problems than they would to a man."

Was she able to stand the pressures? Mrs. Blunschy's eyes sparkled. "For one term, yes. It is an opportunity to do so much. But for all time, perhaps not. I am by profession really a housekeeper and I think of myself as a housekeeper of the government. There is so much to be done. I never have enough sleep and I am always rushing to appointments. In an hour I must be at a meeting in Fribourg . . ."

I looked at my watch. My appointment was for an hour and I had been there almost two. I apologized. "Don't be sorry," said Mrs. Blunschy. "It has been a real pleasure for me." She flashed her most melting, disarming smile to convince me it was true, that it had been a pleasure. Being a gracious hostess she walked with me down the long corridor to the elevator and waited until it arrived. She shook my hand.

"Thank you for coming to see me," she said. "Perhaps you will visit me in Schwyz. I would like you to see my garden, and the cows grazing on the other side of the fence."

The elevator began a slow descent. Through its grill I watched the housekeeper of the government return alone to her office and I thought how that comely, graceful form embodied a revolution more sweeping and irrevocable than the men of Switzerland could possibly be aware.

Until this decade the motives and peregrinations of the Walsers, the mysterious Middle Age migrants from Germany who wandered for six centuries over the mountains of Switzerland, Italy, and Austria and settled their remote colonies in the highest, most isolated places, were matters of speculation primarily to historians. Now, suddenly, fulfilling some national longing to escape from contemporary anxieties into a rustic past, the "Vikings of the Alps" had become cultishly fashionable. A Berne historian published a popular Walser history.* Tourists sought out Walser villages. A society of Walser descendants gathered for an annual congress and it was a mark of status to be able to boast of Walser ancestors.

It was a theory of Kap's that he and I were of Walser blood, that in the late fourteenth century several Walser families, among which were Kublis and Rhyners, had climbed over the Segnes and Panixer passes and settled on land in the valley above Elm. There is another theory, supported by evidence in the Glarus archives, that the first Kublis in Switzerland were political refugees from Italy. It is possible that both theories are valid, that the first Kublis were Italians who joined and married into Walser families and settled near Elm.

One of the most reliable evidences of Walser ancestry is believed to be language. According to historians the language preserved in Walser villages is the oldest German spoken in the world today. It is similar to

---

*Paul Zinsli, *Walser Volkstum*, Berne: 1975.

Schweizerdeutsch, or Swiss-German, which is believed to have developed during a period of grammatical and vocabulary changes from the ninth to the thirteenth centuries.

Kap suggested that we visit some Walser villages and one day we drove over the Gotthard Pass into the canton of Tessin. We stayed the night on the shores of Lake Maggiore and in the morning we drove up through the winding Maggia Valley to the Walser settlement of Bosco-Gurin, the highest (4,920 feet) and only German-speaking village in the Italian-speaking canton. Though it was mid-July, the weather was cold. Many houses were abandoned; before others old people bundled in sweaters were sitting on stoops. There were tiny patches of potatoes, lettuce, onions, carrots, and spinach, the only vegetables possible in the short growing season.

We introduced ourselves to a woman operating a small souvenir kiosk and the language she spoke was our own. Her intonations and vocabulary were similar to those of upper Elm and to the dialect I spoke in Wisconsin. Bosco-Gurin, she told us, was settled in the thirteenth century and by the seventeenth century it had grown to a population of 1,200 persons. "Now we are near the end," she said with sad resignation. "Only seventy people remain and most of them are old. In the school there are eight children and when the number drops to five the school will be closed. There are thirty-five cows. Goats are not permitted because they eat the young trees and trees are necessary to control avalanches."

As we spun down the mountain, past more moribund villages, Kap launched into a familiar theme, the role of women in the deaths of old villages. "It is the women who will not stay," he said. "When they leave the young men follow and no one is left."

Perhaps. But there was more to it than that. In the death watch of Bosco-Gurin I had felt a thread of history, the passing of contentment and an advent of disquiet. For ten centuries the Walsers sought out isolation and freedom to secure their fiercely indépendent lives. Now, in the twentieth century, the world had grown too accessible, too alluring. For the new generation the old precepts were no longer viable.

"I expect the young men are as anxious to leave as the young women," I said. Kap did not reply; sometimes my disagreement made him sullen. "I could never live in Bosco-Gurin," I went on. "I felt depressed every minute we were there. Could *you* live there?"

To one as gregarious as Kap, so insatiable in his need for human stimulation, it was a rhetorical question. He laughed. "Well, not everyone is like us," he said. "Thank God for that!"

We passed some abandoned stone house. "But Elm is alive," Kap said suddenly. "Elm will never die like Bosco-Gurin."

He waited and I knew this was the opening he was providing for me to let him know what I had been thinking about the Elm renascence.

"You're right, Elm will live," I said. "It will live because you've been able to bring enough of the world into the valley so there's no reason for anyone to leave. The trick will be to know when to stop."

"Don't worry," he replied. "The village will always be preserved."

"We are talking of two different things, the village and the people."

"You're thinking the people will change."

"I know they will," I said. "I'm curious as to how they will change, and it will take some years before we know."

"There's nothing to fear. Elmers are strong. They will never give up the old values."

I hoped he was right. It was true, Elmers were strong and fiercely principled. They had proud noble natures and committed no evil voluntarily. But I was thinking how the unrelinquished old values might preclude some of the same human concepts with which Elisabeth Blunschy would change Switzerland. The people of Elm, as indeed all the Swiss, were caught in the vise of an unrelenting past and an unknown future and the present was a battlefield.

One perception was becoming clear. In a country which seemed at that moment to be changing almost before my eyes, Kap was one of the movers, a hewer and a joiner. It was through him, and other dreamers and creators like him, that Switzerland was being propelled into the twentieth century. It was absolutely unavoidable and necessary that this be so. In the course of Kap's renasance in Elm, which had gone on almost as long as I had known him, the engineer and the humanist—the antipodes of his character—had come into a harmony and the warm-hearted friend of his people was in ascendancy over the carpenter and mason. All that had been done in Elm was done for its townsmen, to enrich the qualities of their lives. No man in the village could deny it. In the very real and transcendental sense he was Elm's *Baumeister,* a Master Builder.

"You haven't told me what you think of Elm," Kap reminded me.

"It has never been so beautiful as now," I said.

"Then you like it?"

"Very much. I look on what you have done and I marvel."

He smiled and drove on.

The next day in Graubünden we turned south into the Lugnez Valley and followed the Valser Rhine up through a forested canyon. The single-lane dirt road spiraled along unguarded ledges and when two cars met both were forced to halt and one needed to reverse into a widening provided for passing.

After thirteen miles the narrow chasm opened into a wooded vale and beyond it, in a hollow, lay Vals. The large well-kept village was colonized in the thirteenth century and grew into one of the most affluent of Walser communities. Now it appeared to be deserted. On the door of the community hall we saw a notice from the village president: "Haying will be permitted on Sunday." After two weeks of rain the sun was shining in a cloudless sky and most of the 1,200 citizens were on the mountains. Cutting and raking on the high slopes of both sides, they appeared from below like colonies of scurrying insects.

We were looking for a friend, Ignaz Furger, a student at the Zurich Institute of Technology who had returned to the village earlier in the week to make the hay on land owned by his family. We found the house in which he lived but there was no one there. A lady appeared at a window in the next house and, speaking our language, pointed to a thicket of trees high on the west side of the valley where she said Ignaz would be haying.

We started up the mountain, passing families of haymakers. In one plot, no more than a half-acre in size, I counted six persons. A grandmother, mother, and two children were winnowing and raking and two men were carrying the hay down the mountain on their backs.

The incline grew steeper and we stopped twice to catch our breath. All the hayers, even the grandmothers, were wearing heavy mountain boots with cleats. I was wearing tennis sneakers and my ankles ached.

We arrived finally in the glade where Ignaz was working alone. He did not see us watching him pitch dry hay into the open door of a wooden stall. He was tall and bronzed and, stripped to the waist, stood out from the other haymakers who were fully clothed to protect themselves from the sun. Quite certainly they were accustomed to his unorthodox ways and respected them. He was pursuing a goal considered unattainable by most village youths, a higher education. To earn money he had spent his adolescent summers on the high pastures herding eighty goats, rising at 4 A.M. to milk them and then to turn the milk into cheeses. In the evening he milked the goats again, finishing at ten o'clock. During the day he read books to teach himself English, which he spoke astonishingly well. In Zurich he drove a taxi.

"*Gruezi,* Ignaz," we said. He turned and looked at us for a long silent moment.

He laughed. "I was thinking I must be hallucinating," he said. "But I have not been smoking pot so I concluded it must be a sunstroke. I cannot believe you are here!"

"We've come to give you a ride back to Zurich," said Kap. The trip on a bus and two trains was four hours long; by car it was an hour and a half.

"But I have to finish the hay," said Ignaz.

"How long will it take?" Kap asked. It was three o'clock.

"I think until nearly seven."

"How long will it take if we help?"

"I don't know," Ignaz replied uncertainly. "It depends . . ."

"On how fast we work?" said Kap. "We'll get it done by five."

Kap took up a fork and I a rake and we set to work. When the plot was cleared we moved to a lower one where we rolled the hay into huge balls on a tarpaulin that we loaded onto Ignaz's shoulders and which he carried down the slopes into a barn. On a still lower plot we loaded hay on a low-wheeled rack and, when this was finished, Kap and I climbed on top of the hay and Ignaz pulled us down into the village with a small three-cylinder tractor. Workers returning from the slopes waved as we passed. In the village word had been spread by the neighbor lady that the Lieutenant-Governor of Glarus and a writer from America had helped Ignaz Furger make his hay.

"I feel damned good," said Kap. "I can't remember the last time I made hay or when I enjoyed it more."

"I'm glad to know I can still do it," I said. Riding on the hay behind the little tractor, we were feeling boyishly, almost foolishly, happy. When we finished putting the last hay into a barn, we checked our watches. It was a quarter to five.

As we drove out of the village and down the hazardous way Ignaz, riding in the back seat, pointed to an unshielded cliff and said, "Here last week the car of two of my friends went over the edge and both were killed. At their funerals in the church so many candles were burning it was like Christmas." He continued with a chronicle of disasters, saying, "Here on Easter, 1975, a young farmer and his sixteen cows were killed in a barn by an avalanche ... here four weeks ago my father went off the road but his car was stopped by a tree and he was not hurt ... in 1951 nineteen people were killed by an avalanche ...."

"The winter of 1951 was a catastrophe for all Walser villages," Kap said. "Warm rain falling on a heavy accumulation of snow caused avalanches everywhere. In the village of Blons in the Voralberg fifty-seven persons—fifteen percent of the population—were killed."

"Such things as these which you are never allowed to forget become too heavy a burden," said Ignaz. "Sometimes I dream of disappearing into the underground of an unknown city, of changing my name and becoming another person, of freeing myself from all the inherited responsibilities and guilts. That is my impossible dream."

His words might have been spoken by any one of us. Responsibility to the past was our common Swiss burden, an anxious bond that we shared. We rode in silence and after a time Ignaz began to sing softly, some words from an American ballad, "Take it easy, but take it...."

The high slopes on which Kap maintained that Elm Walsers had settled is a cluster of farmhouses known as Steinibach, or "Stony Creek." Its population of seventy-four persons maintain their own identity as "Steinibach Elmers" and the Swiss they speak contains an archaic vocabulary which Kap and I understood and used ourselves. It was from this place that my Kubli ancestors emigrated in 1853.

In the summer a collection of twenty-four short stories, by a Steinibach writer named Walter Elmer, was published in Glarus. Its title, *Welt am Pfiischter,* "The World in the Window," referred to the window from which Elmer, a paralytic cripple, observed the life of his tiny hamlet. I secured a copy of his book and after reading it, I visited the author.

He was sitting on a bench on the shady side of the old farmhouse in which he was born and had not left for fifteen years. I told him I had been moved by his stories and he found it astonishing that I should have read them. "It was published for a readership of seventy-four persons, some of whom will not read it," he said. "You are the seventy-fifth." He was joking. The end pages of his book contained a glossary of the old vocabulary translated into modern German; this made it possible for everyone in northern Switzerland to comprehend the words. The glossary had been prepared by a local schoolteacher assisted by his pupils.

Walter Elmer was sixty-two years old. Crippled with arteriosclerosis for thirty years, he had been writing for twenty, typing with his right hand because his left was paralyzed. Some stories published in a newspaper came to the attention of a Zurich linguist who arranged for publication of the book and a subsidy for its author. "A book is something I never expected to happen," Elmer said. "I was writing for myself, making a record of how I saw things, of my feelings and thoughts." He was proud that, with the difficult dialect spelling, there were only two printing errors in the book. "The typesetter took great care; whenever there was a question, he phoned.

"If I were twenty years younger and it were possible for me to go there, I would write a novel about New Glarus," Walter Elmer said. "About a family like yours which left our village and set out for a new Canaan in an unknown wilderness to found a new Elm. I believe this to be the single most important event in our history."

We were facing a mountain called *Tierbodehorn.* Walter Elmer pointed to a high slope where a brother and his two sons and two daughters were raking and winnowing hay. How large, I asked, was the plot?

"*Ja,* how much would it be?" he replied. "Perhaps twelve *Are.*" An *Are* was a unit ten meters square, about one-fortieth of an acre. Six people were harvesting slightly over a quarter-acre of wild hay. I was thinking how in that same time on my own farm in New Glarus one man with a tractor would be harvesting one hundred acres of alfalfa.

"Land is man's responsibility to God," Walter Elmer said. "It must be tended and cherished. When land is abandoned, villages die and men's souls also die."

Pointing with his right hand, he directed my gaze above the place where the family was working to a crest of dark green forest. "There are both leaf trees and pine up there and though it is thirty years since I have been there, I know them well. This mountainside is my world and there is more here than it is possible to see in a lifetime."

Was he happy? I had no urge to ask. At that moment contentment seemed enough, contentment and a joy in the familiars of one's world. Happiness was a concept that did not greatly trouble the people of my valley. More important was the resignation out of which contentment germinated and grew. These, the resignation and the contentment, which somewhere in the duality of my origin and in the world of my time had been lost, existed still in this hamlet where it was sustained by one whose world was contained in the house in which he was born and a bench facing a mountain, a man who wrote books with words spoken by seventy-four persons and myself, whose message reached across linguistic boundaries to address the world.

I remembered that a guiding sybil in my quest, Yolande Jacobi, loved the Swiss like a mother and that she had included me. In this season of my return two persons who almost certainly will never meet, Elisabeth Blunschy and Walter Elmer, had appeared out of the hostile dominions of the past and the future and without contention were creating a viable present for a restive land.

Before I left Switzerland my son, Alex, and his wife, Tina, and their baby son visited me. On a rainy afternoon we went to the courthouse in Glarus where the genealogical archives are kept. To the company of the Kublis, to the Nicholases, Oswalds, Jacobs, and Ulrichs from the fifteenth century to the present, we added a new link, inscribing beneath my name and Alex's name the name of my grandson:

"Nicholas Alexander, born February 6, 1977."

A peace was made.